From those who have read this book:

In my 50 years in electronic marketing I have had the honor of meeting and teaching many of the most successful people in the industry, and I consider Joe Sugarman among the most talented, creative and inventive marketing people I have had the privilege of knowing. Joe presents each step of his marketing secrets in a clear, precise manner that is as exciting and interesting for the novice as it is for the most highly experienced electronic marketer.

> Alvin Eicoff, Chairman Emeritus
> A. Eicoff & Company
> A Division of Ogilvy & Mather

In addition to being one of the most knowledgeable experts in the direct marketing field, Joe Sugarman is an extraordinarily informative writer and a great teacher. His willingness to share insights and techniques that others would consider trade secrets is extraordinary. And he tells it like it is, with no punches pulled. To anyone who is interested in selling products by television—whether by infomercials, spot commercials or televised shopping channels— Television Secrets for Marketing Success *is a must-read. It's a virtual goldmine of useful information as well as a roadmap to maximizing the chances of success and minimizing the risk of failure.*

> Joe Segel
> Founder and former Chairman
> The Franklin Mint and QVC

Joe Sugarman is a true direct marketing leader and visionary. More importantly, he always gives something back. In this exciting new book Joe shows us the way to television direct marketing success making it easier in the future for all of us to follow.

> Greg Renker, President
> Guthy-Renker

Television Secrets for Marketing Success *is not a book written by a consultant. It is written by an experienced practitioner and leading expert who understands the customer, and knows what it takes to supply products, get them on air, and sell them. Joe Sugarman has experienced virtually every aspect of the televised shopping challenge, and triumphed successfully. Joe uses his insights, ideas and perspectives in this new book to clearly define what works, why it works, and how to get it to work on TV.*

> Doug Briggs, President
> QVC

There are very few competitors of mine in the industry who have the knowledge, experience and "feel" that Joe Sugarman has for TV marketing. His book gives you the real scoop on how to succeed in this difficult but very rewarding medium. I highly recommend it even though it may end up creating more competition than I care to see.

> Ron Popeil, President
> Ronco Inventions, LLC

Knowing what works and what doesn't work with television direct response before investing a dime of your own money is literally a gift. Fortunes are won and lost overnight. And while there aren't many sure things in life, I can tell you as an industry expert that carefully reading this book can save you millions of dollars in what might otherwise be hard-learned lessons. This book is written from Joe's unique perspective as a successful innovator in the direct marketing and infomercial industry. His unique understanding of what works in print offers a completely innovative viewpoint on television direct marketing.

> Steve Dworman, Editor
> *The Infomercial Marketing Report*

From the participants who attended my seminar and learned what you are about to:

I think that what you taught me in your school is beginning to work! Our 1980 Bon Ami advertising campaign won a Golden Effie award from the New York Chapter of the American Marketing Association, and Sales & Marketing Management Magazine's award for the best print advertising campaign for 1980. More important, obviously, Bon Ami sales went up 9% in a declining market!

Gordon T. Beaham, III, President
Faultless Starch/Bon Ami Company

I think you know that I came to Minocqua with very great expectations. After all, I'd been scheming to attend one of your seminars for years. Well, this is one time where the reality was not only as good as the fantasy, but many times better.

Donn Rappaport
Market Builders

I was particularly impressed with your candor and honesty. You didn't hold back. Every step was a learning experience and I picked up a thousand insights along the way. It was a real trip.

Jim Mantice
Jim Mantice Advertising

For some days I won a case at the highest court of justice in The Hague (Holland). This was a great day for me and my employees. It's strange, but I am sure that the seminar has had an important influence on my presentation (I preferred to speak without a lawyer).

> Leo Verkoelen
> Romar-Voss Chem. Fabriek
> Roggel, Holland

Of all the educational experiences I've had, nothing has equalled your seminar.

> Bern Wheeler, President
> Bern Wheeler Communications Ltd.

Television Secrets

At his exclusive marketing seminar,
Joseph Sugarman taught copywriting, marketing and
creativity to a group of mail order enthusiasts who
went on to achieve incredible success. This book
reveals many of the same television secrets that he
shared with his students, each of whom paid
thousands of dollars to attend.

Books by Joseph Sugarman

Advertising Secrets of the Written Word
Marketing Secrets of a Mail Order Maverick
Television Secrets for Marketing Success
Success Forces
Triggers

Television Secrets for Marketing Success

③

Joseph Sugarman

How to Sell Your Product on Infomercials, Home Shopping Channels and Spot TV Commercials From the Entrepreneur Who Gave You BluBlocker® Sunglasses

DELSTAR™

Printed in the United States of America

Publisher's Cataloging-in-Publication Data
(Provided by Quality Books, Inc.)

Sugarman, Joseph
    Television secrets for marketing success: how to sell your product on infomercials, home shopping channels and spot TV commercials from the entrepreneur who gave you BluBlocker® sunglasses / Joseph Sugarman.— 1st ed.
      p.   cm.
    Includes bibliographical references and index.
    ISBN: 1-891686-9-7 CL
    ISBN: 1-891686-10-0 PB
      1. Television advertising. 2. Infomercials. 3. Teleshopping.
    I. Title.
    HF6146.T42S84   1998   658.8'4
                                                QBI98-284

Attention: Schools, Ad Agencies and Corporations. DelStar books are available at quantity discounts with bulk purchases for educational or business use. For more information, please contact DelStar Books at the address below.

06 05 04 03 02 01 00 99 98 10 9 8 7 6 5 4 3 2 1

Cover design: Ron Hughes
Cartoonist: Dick Hafer

DelStar Books
3350 Palms Center Drive
Las Vegas, NV 89103
Phone: (702) 798-9000
Fax: (702) 597-2002

To Al Eicoff and Joe Segel
Thanks for starting it all.

Each problem has hidden in it an opportunity so powerful that it literally dwarfs the problem. The greatest success stories were created by people who recognized a problem and turned it into an opportunity.

—Joseph Sugarman
Success Forces, 1980

Contents

Television Secrets for Marketing Success

Foreword

"Sharing His Personal Secrets with You . . ."

By Steve Dworman, Editor, *The Infomercial Marketing Report*

In one's life, occasionally an unknown individual will spontaneously make an appearance and end up playing a pivotal role in your life over and over again.

Joe Sugarman is one of those individuals. The first time I met Joe was 20 years ago. I had developed a photographic product called "Lites-Out." I met Joe on the floor of the annual photography trade show being held in Chicago. Joe didn't know me, and at the time he had the most successful, innovative product catalog around. I had called him on the phone, told him about my product and he agreed to meet me at the convention. He didn't buy the product from me but gave me some good advice.

That's Joe. I don't know how many people around the world he has helped in one way or another. What I do know is that he's one of the few individuals I've met whom you can call with a problem and he'll stop what he's doing and give you a hand.

Several years went by and somehow we both ended up in the infomercial industry, Joe as an innovator, and myself as a consultant, analyst, and publisher of an infomercial newsletter read in over 20 countries.

In 1992 I was the first person in our industry to ask Joe to speak at our West Coast Infomercial Conference. Up until that point, Joe was very much a low-profile individual within the industry. He kept to himself and kept very quiet about his incredible success. But from the moment he got on the stage, it was gratifying to see all the fans he had in the audience—and there were hundreds! I've had him speak for me several times since then.

During the last six years, Joe and I have gotten much closer and I've had the opportunity to truly get to know the man. He is an entrepreneur in the true sense of the word—always open to new things, new experiences and new people.

He is a creative genius. Just off the top of my head I can remember six times when I picked up the phone, called Joe and told him I was stuck on an ad I was putting together. One ad in particular I had spent two days drafting with no success. Joe's response was always the same. "Let me call you back in a few minutes." Fifteen minutes later the phone would ring and Joe would read me a headline and the first three paragraphs of copy. To say they were always great is not doing his talent justice. The slant he took and the simplicity of his writing were magic.

He is one of only a few direct marketers to venture into the infomercial arena. This book is written from Joe's unique perspective as a successful innovator in the direct marketing and infomercial industry. His unique understanding of what works in print offers a completely innovative viewpoint on television direct marketing.

The style in which this book is written reveals as much about marketing as the content itself. Joe writes like he's sharing his personal secrets with you, his new best friend. Once you begin reading you can't stop. After all, Joe can be a fascinating best friend.

One of the reasons this book is so compelling is that you learn as much about Joe's failures as his successes. In fact, I've heard him say countless times that he believes his success is due to the fact that he's failed more times than most anyone else.

Knowing what works and what doesn't work with television direct response before investing a dime of your own money is literally a gift. Fortunes are won and lost overnight. And while there aren't many sure things in life, I can tell you as an industry expert that carefully reading this book can save you millions of dollars in what might otherwise be hard-learned lessons.

When people find out that I've known Joe for over 20 years, they ask me what he's really like. I tell them that he's one of the most unusual men I've had the fortune of meeting. He's a unique individual who is not easy to describe. But maybe the best way for you to truly know the man is to sit back and read this very personal book. I guarantee you'll be filled with a sense of his fun, warmth and brilliance.

So, discover for yourself the uniqueness and wonderful insights of Joe Sugarman. You're in store for a real treat.

Preface | A Book for the Novice or the Expert

By Alvin Eicoff, Chairman Emeritus
A. Eicoff & Company
A Division of Ogilvy & Mather

In my 50 years in electronic marketing I have had the honor of meeting and teaching many of the most successful people in the industry, and I consider Joe Sugarman among the most talented, creative and inventive marketing people I have had the privilege of knowing.

Joe presents each step of his marketing secrets in a clear, precise manner that is as exciting and interesting for the novice as it is for the most highly experienced electronic marketer. You'll learn how to evaluate a product's potential, the secrets of a creative presentation and the methods of testing and evaluation. You'll experience the exuberance of watching the soaring sales of a successful test and the agony of seeing your time, creative concepts and investments go down the drain in a losing cause.

Step-by-step you'll learn the secrets of success and what causes failures. You'll learn to travel the Avenues of the Harlots where the TV and cable industries were born. Most important, you'll find this to be the most interesting, revealing and spellbinding "how-to" book you've ever read. This book further confirms Joe Sugarman's genius!

Author's note: When I was nearly finished with this book I decided to submit it to Alvin Eicoff, considered one of the legends in TV direct response marketing. I had hoped that Al could read it and give me a comment or quote I could use on the back cover of this book. After all, with his 50 years' experience in the field, this was a man who witnessed the birth not only of TV direct response but of television itself. His support would be quite impressive to my potential prospect for this book.

Not only did he give me an excellent quote, Al wrote an unsolicited Preface for this book and sent me valuable historical information—some of which has never before been published. I quickly stopped production so I could include much of what he gave me as an Afterword chapter at the end of this book. Some of the information comes from the book Al wrote called *Eicoff on Broadcast Direct Marketing*, which is listed in Appendix D, and some consists of my comments on what he related to me.

I couldn't think of a more qualified person to comment on my book, its implications and the history of this exciting field of electronic direct response advertising. What Al may not have known when he supplied me with all this information was that he is one of the two pioneers to whom I've dedicated this book. Thanks, Al, for your wonderful contribution to both me and the industry.

Many people have contributed to my experience and success on TV and I would like to acknowledge them. At the top of my list is Mary Stanke, who always calmly kept things together and under control even during the roller-coaster ride that we had while on TV. Jeff Rochlis and Ed Krackhauer, who first told me I should be on cable TV. Donn Rappaport, a seminar participant who started a chain reaction by introducing me to Patricia Riley, who in turn introduced me to an infomercial producer who got me started doing infomercials. If it weren't for Donn's introduction, who knows where I'd be. Pat Riley was the motivating force that got me on TV, and she later became quite a TV success in her own right.

April has appeared on QVC selling BluBlocker sunglasses in England, Germany and the U.S.

Special thanks to April Sugarman, my daughter, who played an important role in everything from media buying to the editing of my infomercials to appearing on QVC throughout the world. She's an incredibly motivated person who will go far in this world in her new career as an actress.

To Mary Stanke's two daughters, Sheri Purdue and Teri Stanke, who run our company's administration and who are really taking care of business—just like mom. Thanks for the great job. To all our employees who have contributed so much through the years making sure we get those products packaged and shipped. There are too many to list here but you know who you are.

I wish to recognize Doug Briggs, president of QVC, whose support of my efforts and enthusiasm for my ideas kept me motivated and working more as a partner than a vendor.

A special mention to Joe Segel, one of my heroes in direct marketing and the man who launched the Franklin Mint and QVC. To Al Eicoff, the father of direct response TV, for his many contributions to both the industry and this book. To Ron Popeil for his help and suggestions and who became the "salesman of the century" through his talent on direct response TV. To Greg Renker of Guthy-Renker, who kept encouraging me to write this book. To William Hsu, our very special friend and sunglass supplier in Taiwan. To John LaFontaine, our supplier of The Pill automotive product, who represents the best of what businesspeople ought to be.

I'd like to thank all the wonderful characters and "people on the street" who have appeared in my infomercials. They made our product real and our shows interesting. Thanks to the wonderful show hosts who worked with me—Denise Gray, Kimberly Horn, Alecia Jacobs and Duke Frye.

Thanks to the hosts on QVC who have made my experience there a memorable one. Not only are you all professionals—the most talented of anybody on TV—but you've been like an extended family. The hosts in alphabetical order include Patricia Bastia, Jill Bauer, Bob Bowersox, Steve Bryant, Judy Crowell, Pat James-DeMentri, Rick Domeier, Dan Hughes, Paul Kelly, Dave King, Kathy Levine, Ron Maestri, Lisa Mason, Lisa Robertson, Mary Beth Roe, Suzanne Runyan, Jane Rudolph Treacy, Lynne Tucker, David Venable, Dan Wheeler and Leah Williams. There are now many more hosts in Canada, England and Germany—too many to list here.

Thanks to the support personnel at QVC—many are mentioned throughout this book. They include Darlene Daggett—one of the top marketing executives at QVC—Len Czabator, Roger Elvin, Tom Armstrong, Jim Breslin, Alan Massaro, P.J. Baer-McGrath, Dru Garton, Craig Adler, Lena Hoover, Tom Bottiger, Peggy Vogelmann, Rich Maurer, Maureen Kelly, Michelle Barbacane, Susan Roberts, Mark Denisewicz, Pete Willenbrock, Betty Amabile, Jack Comstock, Barbara Magner, Daphne Howard, Paula Piercy, Donna Tarantino, Paul Callaro, Elena Conte, Dennis D'Angelo, Elizabeth Buchan, Carolyn Hendrickson, Tom Merrihew, Paul Bastia, Keith Stewart, Joe Mastripolito, Chris Jascewsky, Marilyn Montross, Rich Yoegel, Chris Morley, Valarie Bruno, Ann Marie McCabe, Judy Grishaver, Debbie Gottlieb, Greg Bertoni, Karen Fonner, Rick Houseworth, Jeanine Gendrachi, Brendan McQuillan, John McGuire, Heath Cornfield, Cindy Zontek, Robb Cadigan, Jim Brooks, Carrie Colaiezzi, Mark Wennersten, Kevin Byrne, Scott Yannick, Blair Christie, Colleen Zeiznick and many more too numerous to mention.

To the wonderful personalities I have met in the Green Room at QVC including Willie Nelson—a great BluBlocker fan— George Hamilton, Susan Lucci, Joan Rivers, Naomi Judd, Lars Park Lincoln, Victoria Principal, George Foreman, John Tesch, Tim Conway, Dick Patton, Denise Austin, Tony Little, Richard Simmons and especially Tova Borgnine. And there's Mark Schneider and many of the other great vendors I have met at QVC including Susan Graver, Joy Mangano, Marvin Segel, Jennifer Kirk, Ben Levy, Eric Levine, Jan Mueller and dozens more.

Then there is the wonderful support and guidance I've been fortunate to receive from Dan Rosenfield, whose agency has been our partner during many of the infomercial years. Dan, you've always come through. To Larry Brewer, who was in charge of all our video production—a great talent whom I'm proud to have worked with. To Vikki Hunt of New Day Marketing, our media buyer, who helped guide us through the media jungles with honesty and integrity.

To the brilliant Jim Feldman, who spent his 50th birthday judging our Viper Sweepstakes, and to Fran Krasnow, who was our sweepstakes lawyer and a delight to work with.

A special thank-you to the people who played a role in the production of this book: Lyn Chaffee, Brooke Graves, Ron Hughes, Virginia Iorio and Nancy Kleban. And finally, I wish to give a special mention to Dick Hafer, whose cartoons were created specially for this book. A special thank-you also to Steve Dworman—editor of *The Infomercial Marketing Report* and one of the most knowledgeable guys in the infomercial business. Thanks for your many suggestions and your well-written Foreword.

I wish to acknowledge all my wonderful seminar participants who learned from me and went on to create or build successful businesses—all through the power of their pens and the direct marketing skills they learned. They are listed in Appendix E of this book. I learned a great deal from them. Finally, I wish to thank, with humility and gratitude, all who have exchanged their hard-earned money for this book. May you too learn and prosper.

In 1992 I was invited to speak before the National Infomercial Marketing Association (NIMA) convention in Las Vegas. When Greg Renker, one of the show organizers and president of Guthy-Renker, introduced me he made me realize something significant about this emerging industry.

"Joe Sugarman brings with him a unique perspective. He is one of the few of us who have come from a direct marketing background and he's here to share some of his insights with you."

Although I didn't say anything about Greg's introduction in my remarks, it surprised me that many of the infomercial companies were not well versed in direct marketing. Here I had thought that infomercials required all of your direct marketing skills and that without them, you couldn't survive. Yet in this room of about 400 people were entrepreneurs whose closest knowledge of direct marketing was how to process the orders they received, and the problem was they weren't doing a good job of it.

Infomercial Getting Bad Name

The infomercial as an advertising medium was starting to get a bad name. It was in its infancy and you could throw an infomercial on the air and succeed without too much direct marketing knowledge. Direct marketers know that one of the ways you build your business is by your reputation. The new wave of TV entrepreneurs were too busy finding hot-selling products to care if their products even worked.

It was at this point that I could almost predict the future of the industry. The winners in the infomercial game were going to be those companies who had the most expertise in direct marketing and cared about building a business—JS&A (at that point 15 years experience), American Telecast (10 years), Ron Popeil (most of his life) and a few other companies who were more into serving their customers than seeing what they could get away with.

And that is what eventually happened. JS&A, American Telecast, Ron Popeil—we all succeeded early in the game as well as later when the times got tougher. We all had that direct marketing experience which had taught us what worked and what didn't—and most importantly, why it worked or didn't work. And we all knew the importance of taking good care of our customers by providing a good product and good service.

Eight Successes out of Thirteen

In the seven years that I ran infomercials, I learned a great deal about the medium. I wrote, produced and directed my own shows. I had eight successful infomercials out of the 13 that I produced, which is still considered a commendable success ratio when the batting average is often one to 20 (20 shows that fail for each show that succeeds). I was also able to create some successful promotions on the TV shopping channel, QVC. One product I've presented there has sold for a long time—over six years so far with BluBlocker sunglasses. And finally, I had some successful short-form commercials—those direct response one- and two-minute spots.

But it was my print, direct mail and catalog experience that I applied to the new medium of TV that gave me a decided edge in my ability to understand what worked on TV or why it didn't work. In my seminars, upon which this book is based, I taught my students about TV direct response—sharing the really important secrets of this new medium. With their direct marketing background and understanding of direct marketing relationships, they left with a very good grasp of this powerful medium.

This book is presented in two sections. Section One will give you the flavor and history of my experiences with both infomercials and home shopping. It's really a story of my adventures with both the infomercials I produced and the home shopping promotions I launched—all with insights that you won't find in any textbook.

Section Two tells you what I learned as a result of my direct marketing background and experience on national television for over 10 years. Chapters cover, for example, what you need to know to create a winning infomercial, the importance of price, product and media costs, the "glue factor" and its importance and dozens of other helpful and relevant insights. But first a little background.

Introduced Pocket Calculator

I started a marketing company in 1971 and called it The JS&A National Sales Group and eventually shortened the name to JS&A Group, Inc. The company's first product was the pocket calculator—a brand-new product at the time.

Using my direct marketing skills to sell the pocket calculator, I built my business through mail order ads in magazines and newspapers and then eventually in a catalog called *Products That Think.*

Then in 1982 I was approached by two top executives at Mattel Corporation, Ed Krackhauer and Jeff Rochlis, who were urging me to get into cable television. They told me how it was exploding and that I would be good on TV and that I should sell my products in two-minute commercials. But I really didn't like the idea. My products required more than two minutes to explain. And, like a good salesman, if I didn't have enough time to sell my products, I did not want to make my presentation.

Then around 1986 I ran two mail order print ads that were about to change my life. One was for the BluBlocker sunglasses and the other for a new vitamin product called MDR vitamins. That's where this book starts out. You will learn how I took two successful print mail order products and translated them into two of the most successful television campaigns in the emerging infomercial industry.

The print ads for BluBlocker sunglasses and MDR vitamins, which ran in 1986, launched my TV career.

If you can produce a good infomercial, not only will you hold the goose that lays golden eggs but you will open the door to other opportunities and advantages that no other form of marketing can offer.

One opportunity is in the creation of a brand name. Most companies spend hundreds of millions of dollars to do that. Through an infomercial, however, you can actually earn a profit while you are building that brand name. Another advantage is your enhanced chance of getting on a home shopping channel. QVC, for example, loves successful infomercial products as they are already proven sellers. And finally, you build tremendous demand for your product on a mass scale thus opening up an opportunity to sell your product through retailers as well.

"This man has brought us a great product," says QVC host Bob Bowersox during his hour presentation in the Auto Shop. Home shopping brings you great opportunities to sell products after an infomercial.

There are other advantages too—the building of a customer base that you can later contact, the premium and incentive opportunities, the tie-ins with movies, the sponsorship of major sporting events, the extension of your product line and the expansion of your sales through global venues. You can, through the power of TV marketing, create literally overnight a major corporation serving the good of the public on a global scale and earn for yourself an income that will far exceed even your wildest imagination.

A successful infomercial product is like winning the lottery. Although I've never played the lottery and consequently have no idea what it is like to win, it must be a similar feeling. Think about it. You've taken a major risk to spend the dollars to create the infomercial and then you run it in a test campaign and discover your infomercial is a winner. You are now about to earn a sizable income in the coming months and years. That rush you get from the realization of having a winner is something I have had the pleasure of experiencing on several occasions. There is nothing like the exhilaration you feel and it could very easily happen to you—in fact, probably a lot more easily than winning the lottery.

Having a famous brand name gives you the opportunity to sponsor major sporting events. Here's a video shot of a car lining up at the starting line at the BluBlocker Silver State 100 Race in Nevada. The event was also taped for broadcast on the ESPN sports channel.

Understanding the Ground Rules

But first you've got to understand the product ground rules—those basic tests all products must first pass. You've got to know the nuts and bolts—the techniques you need to use to produce the infomercial. And finally, one of the valuable lessons you will learn from this book is the underlying philosophies of what works and what doesn't—the real secrets of making an infomercial.

So sit back and put down your remote control channel changer. It's storytelling time. And to get the tape rolling, let me start with the story of my early entry into infomercials.

Section One

Chapter 1   The Early JS&A TV History

The BluBlocker sunglass print ad was an immediate hit and in 1987 when we rolled out with a major ad campaign, every one of the hundreds of ads we ran paid off. At about the same time, I had tested and was running an ad for MDR vitamins. I was introduced to Patricia Riley, the owner of the vitamin company, by Donn Rappaport, one of my former seminar participants. The vitamins were a continuity product, meaning that our customers signed up for vitamins that were delivered every other month and billed to their credit card number.

Sales for both items were good, but the vitamins just barely broke even from the ad we ran. But because they were being sold as part of a continuity program, eventually they earned a profit.

I then learned of a new half-hour format that the federal government had authorized on cable TV. They were allowing commercials as long as half an hour. You could create a half-hour show to sell your product and run the program on all the cable channels and any broadcast channel that would accept your advertising.

Enough Time to Sell

The idea really appealed to me because a half hour gave me enough time to set up the proper environment to sell my products. It gave me the time to create the emotional appeal I needed to motivate and inspire. And finally, it involved direct marketing—something I was very familiar with.

I was introduced by Pat Riley to a producer in Los Angeles who agreed to produce a commercial with me for a fee. I would write it, pay for the production and he would videotape the commercial. If the test was successful, he would purchase the media and make a commission on everything he bought.

The infomercial format sounded really exciting to me. So I sat down and came up with a format to present my two initial products—the BluBlocker sunglasses and the MDR vitamins.

The show's format was a consumer evaluation show called *Consumer Challenge.* And within the format of our *Consumer Challenge,* we sent out "investigative reporters" who handed our sunglasses to people on the street and had them try them on. We talked to doctors and experts and reached the conclusion that our sunglasses were a pretty good product.

To make it balanced, we even included negative comments by some of the people we interviewed. All the facts we stated were accurate and correct. We announced—both at the beginning of the show and at the end—that the infomercial was a paid commercial from JS&A Group, Inc., the sponsors of the show.

We even included negative comments.

We kept the infomercial balanced to show objectivity.

In the vitamin commercial, we talked to flight attendants, people on the street, students, doctors, nutritionists and the vitamin manufacturer. In both shows I appeared briefly as the president of JS&A—the company selling the product.

We launched both shows at almost the same time, and the results were so impressive I found them almost hard to believe. When I was advertising in print it took me six months to sell 100,000 pairs of sunglasses, but it took only one month on TV to equal the total we sold in print. This was incredible—almost too good to believe. The vitamin commercial also did well and we even made money before taking into account the profits which were to be earned in the future from the continuity program that was already in place.

The media cost for each BluBlocker order started out at a low $3. In other words, for every sale we made, the cost of advertising to make that sale was $3. Subtract that and the few dollars that the product cost us, and that left us with our gross profit. Our product retail during our initial show was $39.95. And we couldn't get enough product. "Wow," I thought. "This new infomercial format is a direct marketer's dream. It is the ultimate form of direct marketing."

And we couldn't do anything wrong. The sales started in

The **Consumer Challenge** *set with our investigative reporters talking about their experiences with BluBlocker sunglasses. The FTC didn't like our show format.*

July of 1987 and continued throughout the winter right into the next spring. And for over a year and a half, that same commercial ran and produced a nice profit.

Soon, however, both the BluBlocker and MDR vitamin commercials started to fade. And I had received a complaint from the Federal Trade Commission (FTC) that they did not like the *Consumer Challenge* format. It seemed too close to regular programming—which was my intent. In print, I've always tried to get as close as possible to the typical editorial look and content of the magazine in which I advertised, and on TV I wanted to look as close to a typical program as I could get. Even though we announced the fact that it was a commercial both at the beginning and the end of our show, the FTC requested that we place in the middle of the show a statement to the effect that the commercial was indeed a commercial.

I had no problem with their request and in fact went beyond what they requested. (I'll explain how later.) Nevertheless, I felt I was on a roll. I had two products I had tested in print that worked as half-hour TV commercials. I had other products that might work too.

One of them was a pet food supplement called Prozyme— an enzyme-based product that was both a preventative and a

The two ads did OK in my catalog, but when I ran the products on TV in an infomercial they bombed. I soon figured out why.

cure. It cured many ailments that typically affected dogs, cats and horses and was also a preventative in that it prevented many of the same diseases it helped cure. I gave it to my dog, Gadget, who stayed pretty healthy, and I decided to try it on TV. The second product was an electronic game called the Perceptron, which helped improve your psychic ability. It was presented by Uri Geller, the spoon-bending psychic from England and a personal friend. He acted as my celebrity spokesperson.

Both ads were shot in the fall of 1987, soon after I had experienced the first flush of success with the first two commercials. Prior to editing them into full shows, I experienced quite a shock. My sister was giving a birthday party for her two dogs and invited my wife and me. While driving to visit my sister's home in suburban Chicago on October 24, 1987, a drunk driver swerved out in front of my car and the head-on collision at a combined 90 miles per hour (I was going 30 and the drunk driver was going 60) put my wife and me in the hospital—my wife for one day with minor injuries and me for two weeks with pretty serious stuff. I had everything wrong from broken ribs, ankles and shoulders to a collapsed lung.

I almost lost my life. And ironically, one minute before the accident, I had turned to my wife and asked her if she was wearing her seat belt. She asked, "Why?"

"Because I have this funny feeling about having an accident," I replied. And one minute later I was unexpectedly hit. About six weeks later, in a full leg cast and still very weak from the accident, I was a guest on the *Oprah Winfrey* show. She was doing a program on ordinary people who had had psychic experiences and I certainly qualified.

While I was recovering, the two shows that I had shot weren't getting done and were just sitting in the can. Finally, when I was able to complete them and test them, I discovered that neither of them worked. In analyzing why they didn't work after the shows

Looking weak and exhausted six weeks after my accident, I was featured on the **Oprah** *show as having psychic powers. I wish I could have predicted the results of my infomercial.*

were scrapped, I remembered the old mail order axiom that you could easily sell a cure but that a preventative was something to be avoided. And I soon discovered that there just weren't enough sick dogs to create a mass market to support the show.

The electronic game was not a mass-appeal kind of game. And even with a celebrity guest, a product of average or low appeal just will not work regardless of who is pushing it. In addition, my margins were quite poor. The product cost me $16 and sold for $39. On TV your margins have to be much greater, which we'll discuss later in this book.

There was one other clue that could have told me that these products wouldn't work. First, I had tested Prozyme in print and it was a marginal product at best. So was the Perceptron. BluBlocker sunglasses and the MDR vitamins, on the other hand, were quite profitable in print. It was then that I realized that if a product didn't sell in print, there was a good probability it might not do too well on TV in an infomercial either.

Market Getting Crowded

The infomercial market was starting to get crowded. We had two successes out of four, and the two winners more than covered my losses in the two unsuccessful commercials. I had also decided to produce my own shows in the future. And after the FTC matter, I wanted to come up with a format that could still display our products in a good light without leaving any doubt that ours was a commercial and not an actual program. I renamed the show *The Making of a Commercial* and ran many disclaimers throughout the infomercial. The FTC had to be quite pleased and there was no doubt that our show was a commercial and not a program.

I also got a letter from a decathlon champion practicing for the Olympics who wore BluBlockers when he competed. He claimed that when he wore our sunglasses, it made him feel stronger. We interviewed him and he appeared in our commercial. We even sponsored him for a while until he got himself a manager who demanded too much money from us. We dropped him. The athlete's name was Dave Johnson and he later went on to become one of the stars of the 1992 Olympics.

In the first two commercials I produced, I appeared as the president and chief executive officer representing my company. I was reluctant to do this but did not see any way out. The part called for somebody of authority from the company to add credibility to the product and I felt that I needed to be the one.

I received a number of comments from people who insisted that I added just the right credibility the commercial needed and even suggested that I be the show host for the next commercial. Pat Riley, owner of the vitamin company, told me, "Joe, you are really believable and you'd make a good show host yourself." She said this enough times to me to finally convince me to give it a try.

I Became the Co-Host

In the next BluBlocker commercial we ran, in 1989, I co-hosted along with Denise Gray, an actress from Kansas City. We worked together hosting the next few BluBlocker shows.

We were still running the MDR vitamin commercial, but sales were starting to fade. Our margins were 50%—far too small to make it in the long run. And the continuity customers only lasted an average of about three shipments before canceling—shorter than the average of five to six months we received from our print customers. Of course, there were some customers who

"I feel great!" Chuck Connors appeared in our MDR
vitamin show, which did very well for two years. The
low margins, however, didn't allow us to run the show
for a longer time.

stayed on for many years, but it is the average that you have to consider when evaluating your results.

Pat Riley sold us the vitamins and did the data processing for our orders. And she did the mailing of the vitamins for us as well as taking care of customer service. It therefore was a relatively easy product for us to handle, but the slim margins of 50% for TV did not allow us to run the program much longer than the few years we did. I turned the program over to Pat and suggested that she do it herself for her company. The infomercial I handed her would work for her as she was making a much bigger margin. She could then continually update the show and keep it running for many more years. She did just that and ran the show with Pat Boone as her spokesperson.

JS&A kept the profits generated from our customers each month until 1995 and then she took over, acquiring our customers and the associated profits. That was our deal. Many of our customers were with us for eight years, and during that time, even though we ran no advertising in the previous six years, we were earning enough money to almost cover the cost of our overhead. Continuity programs are a great concept.

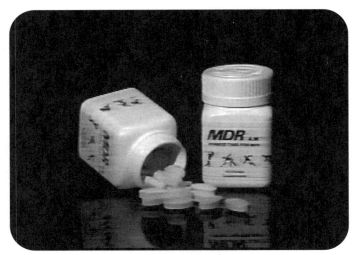

The MDR vitamins were well received by consumers and provided solid sales for over eight years.

Chapter 2 | The Other Sunglass Product

While I was visiting the Far East during one of my many trips there to procure sunglasses, I created a product called Rear Vision sunglasses.

The idea came to me from Uri Geller, who gave me a pair of sunglasses with miniature rotating mirrors on the sides. The sunglasses he gave me were actually used by private detectives and spies and sold for a lot of money through underground organizations. I tried to create my own version of the unique style for a lot less money in the Far East, but they were still very expensive to make because of the mirrors that needed to be located on the sides of the frame and therefore were too expensive for the mass market, the area I specialized in.

Then while I was in Taiwan I picked up a pair of sunglasses with flat lenses and saw a reflection behind me. I then requested that the manufacturer add a slight mirror coating to the farther edges of the inside of the lenses, and presto—I had the sunglasses

A young woman trying out our Rear Vision sunglasses. The show was shot at Venice Beach in a few hours and created quite a stir at retail.

that Uri Geller had been trying to get me to develop but with a much simpler design, a pair that could be mass-produced for a very reasonable price.

The Rear Vision sunglasses consisted of a frame with flat lenses and a slight mirror coating on just the far inside part of the lens—the part facing the user. When you looked to the side of the lens, the inside mirror coating reflected the light so you were actually able to see behind you. It was a fun novelty and it really worked.

I flew back from Taiwan. I was passing through Los Angeles where I had previously made arrangements with a production company to shoot some footage on Venice Beach for my next BluBlocker commercial. On a hunch, I brought a few pairs of my Rear Vision sunglasses with me to experiment with and see what kind of reaction I would get when I handed somebody a pair and asked for their comments.

Entire Show in a Few Hours

Some of the reactions were hysterical. People laughed and joked about it and we ended up shooting some of the most incredible footage I've ever shot. In fact, within that same day, we ended up shooting an entire new show for Rear Vision sunglasses and we also shot some good footage for the BluBlocker show as well.

I flew back to Chicago and realized what a great coup I had made. First I had produced a fairly complete and interesting show for the new Rear Vision style in just three hours. This was certainly a record for me. All I needed was two show hosts and we could complete the infomercial. So I picked the segments that I wanted to use from my time-coded tapes and had my new ad agency, Rosenfield & Lane in Kansas City, put together all the segments of the show in what is called a rough cut. A rough cut means simply taking the footage you want to use and putting it together in a loose format, knowing that you will need to edit it again to make a final show. Then I worked with Dan Rosenfield, president of the agency, to put a studio scene together and have a host and hostess introduce the segments.

The shoot went well and we ended up with a great show to test. I was going to sell the product for $19.95—fairly low for an infomercial product, but I was focusing on the retail market and really only wanted to use the infomercial to develop the retail business.

Having a few thousand of the sunglasses ready to ship, I tested the Rear Vision show and it did very well. Now was my opportunity. I could now run the Rear Vision sunglass infomercial nationally and at the same time ship the product to drug chains to offer as a retail item. The infomercial would drive the sales at retail and we would have our first retail success.

"The Making of a National Commercial" was the name of my Rear Vision sunglass TV show. I hired Denise Gray and another host, shown here on the set of the show, which was shot in Kansas City under the direction of my new ad agency.

So I really prepared. I developed an expensive vacuum-formed display for the drug chains and simultaneously sold Rear Vision sunglasses on our infomercial. I also ran 90-second direct response spots. The strategy worked great. We were selling hundreds of thousands of them on our infomercial. Although we were not making much money through our infomercial, we started to get some pretty good orders from the drug chains. And that was our goal.

Sales from our Rear Vision infomercial started to slow, but we expected that. After all, people were now able to get the product at retail and the infomercial was supposed to support its sales. But we soon discovered that all the sunglass knockoff artists and importers were selling copies of our sunglasses to the drug chains. The chains were then putting them into *our displays* and selling them thanks to *our advertising*. This was really a dirty trick on the part of the stores. Their lack of integrity amazed me.

To add insult to injury, the stores were returning our sunglasses claiming that they didn't sell—all the while filling the displays with cheap imitations. And then they even returned some of the knockoff pairs, attempting to get credit for them.

We sold our pairs to the drug chains for slightly more than the importers did. But the importers didn't have to pay the advertising costs nor provide any displays nor support any drug chain advertising as we did. Manufacturers in Taiwan were working overtime to produce these knockoff glasses and all of the money we were spending for advertising was now going to waste. I was now losing my shirt on this product.

So I stopped advertising. And the sales came to a sudden halt not only for our company but for all the drug chains and for all the importers as well. Since they depended on our advertising, the stores were stuck with their product and the importers were stuck with theirs. I had the last laugh as I had managed to reduce our inventory to a reasonable level before I pulled the plug on the advertising. In the long run, we didn't make much money from the promotion. But it taught me some very valuable lessons.

The Lessons It Taught

It taught me that if you have a product that can easily be copied, knockoff artists will copy it. It further taught me that if they can copy it, there will be somebody undercutting your price, and in order to offset this, you need to come up with two types of products—the higher-priced, better-quality version and the cheap one to compete with the knockoff artists. And finally, I learned about the morality of some of the drug chains which really disappointed and surprised me.

But fortunately I had my long-running BluBlocker show which continued to do well. And as soon as I pulled the Rear Vision show off the air, I had my BluBlocker show ready to take its place. JS&A was doing just great and we were continuing to grow.

Chapter 3 | Back to the Future

I completely directed and produced my second BluBlocker commercial. I supervised all the shooting, did the rough cut and also did the final editing. For the first time, we used a number of celebrities. We interviewed Roy Clark, the famous country singer who was also a BluBlocker fan. We also featured Andre Dawson of the Chicago Cubs baseball team and Keith Hernandez of the New York Mets. The response to the show was very good and we ended up with our second successful BluBlocker production.

Roy Clark, shown in our second BluBlocker commercial, wearing a pair of BluBlockers. Clark was one of our earlier BluBlocker supporters. We also sponsored a few of his worthwhile causes.

This was great news. It was nice to have a second BluBlocker show under my belt, but here I had a show that featured me as the show host along with Denise Gray, my co-host from Kansas City. By this time, in 1989, I had been actively working with my new advertising agency in Kansas City, Rosenfield & Lane, and its president, Dan Rosenfield. Dan helped me not only with my second commercial but with every one since then.

While my infomercial was running and earning a nice income, I got a call from Dan. "Joe, there's a new sequel to that very successful movie *Back to the Future* called *Back to the Future II*. Steven Spielberg's Amblin Entertainment is producing the show and I found out they have a segment that takes place in the future and they could use some innovative futuristic sunglasses for the movie. If we can develop the styles for the movie, they could give us what is called 'signage' in the movie so the BluBlocker brand name will appear in connection with the futuristic sunglasses."

This sounded like a great idea. I had never had an opportunity like this before. The exposure would certainly help our brand name, which was starting to become well known. I then flew to Taiwan and visited our sunglass designers and had them design a series of sunglasses. I also searched the Far East for unusual futuristic styles. I found many. I also had some prototypes made of some of the styles that were designed in Taiwan. We presented them to Amblin and they accepted a number of them for the movie.

Dan also noticed from the list of companies who were getting signage that Pizza Hut was appearing in the same future scene as our sunglasses. Dan suggested that we approach the people at Pizza Hut who were located in Wichita and see if we could have them distribute our futuristic sunglasses in their restaurants in a national premium program. The idea that was proposed was to have Pizza Hut sell these sunglasses for $2 each, promoting them as the sunglasses that appeared in the movie *Back to the Future II*.

Dan and I worked out a deal with Pizza Hut to provide four different styles of sunglasses to their stores to be sold as a premium when customers bought a certain size pizza. Pizza Hut tested the concept and it met with favorable reaction, and Amblin agreed to show the sunglass styles in the movie. Pizza Hut polled their stores and regional managers and ended up ordering 10 million pairs from us in the biggest single sunglass order in history. We had 10 factories producing around the clock to make them and an entire logistics team stationed in Taiwan organizing the

NO KID... IT REALLY **IS**... SEE... HERE...

It was all on the film editor's floor.

production. In fact, I ended up living there for six months myself in order to prepare for production and coordinate this diverse network of sunglass makers.

The logistics of producing and shipping 10 million pairs during a production cycle of less than six weeks was quite a challenge. But we did it thanks to our organization back home and Mary Stanke, the company's general manager, and our team in Taiwan. The sunglasses were produced at budget and delivered on time. We also made shipments to Pizza Hut restaurants in England, Australia, New Zealand and Canada, all of which were participating.

After the last shipment was made, I treated all of the Taiwan factory heads to an all-expense-paid trip to Los Angeles to see the world premiere of the movie. That was one of my incentives to them for finishing on time. We all had a wonderful dinner and I awarded each one of them with a plaque for the historic occasion of being involved in the single largest sunglass order in the history of the sunglass business. We then went to see the movie only to discover that the sunglasses that were supposed to be in the movie were not. Instead, the sunglasses were on film that was on the cutting-room floor. Our manufacturers were puzzled, I was embarrassed and Pizza Hut was furious as all of their point-of-purchase signs and materials carried the phrase "As seen in *Back to the Future II*."

Nevertheless, the promotion was launched and Pizza Hut experienced a success with an increase in the sale of their products and a lot of happy customers. The lessons learned from the movie industry and this promotion are still talked about at Pizza Hut even today.

Chapter 4

The Use of Talent

Meanwhile, BluBlocker sunglasses continued to sell from our second infomercial, which featured a number of celebrities who all added to the interest in the show. I was the host for the infomercial and it proved successful. And it ran for one and a half years—the same as our previous BluBlocker show—until I replaced it with a third show in early '90. And the third show worked, but this time without a single celebrity.

Having our third show work without using a single celebrity seemed a major accomplishment to me. It meant that the show itself, along with the product, had to carry the entire program, keep it interesting and add credibility. The product was king and that was fine with me. No expensive celebrity contracts, no having to deal with anybody but the people on the street and my own ad agency. And this third show worked for one and a half years as well.

A String of Successes

By now I was getting quite confident. One Rear Vision show, three BluBlocker shows and one MDR vitamin show—five major hits over four and a half years and only two losing shows. Millions of sunglasses were sold and our last show was the best one of them all—no celebrity and no star host, yet we had the best response of all of our previous shows. We were building momentum and although there were now plenty of knockoffs at retail, I was quite pleased with my results and I didn't have to compete at retail with the knockoffs. My memories were still fresh from my experience at retail with the Rear Vision sunglasses and how the drug chains had used my display and advertising to sell other knockoff products. In fact, I was kind of glad I wasn't selling BluBlocker sunglasses at these stores.

Then in early '91 I had an idea. Why not produce three shows at once? Why not go to New Orleans where we had previously shot some really good testimonials, go to San Francisco where we had a cable car operator we could interview who raved about the pair and then go to Maui, Hawaii, where I had some great customer service testimonials and beach scenes? I would do a show at each location and then rotate them on the air. And that's exactly what I did. I then went to each city, got some great interviews and produced the three shows in succession. This was great. If they worked, I might be able to create a series like the commercial broadcasts.

An Italian film star we interviewed at a famous windsurfing beach in Maui where I shot our show. We ended up with a winner, but not what I expected.

I then tested the three shows and discovered to my surprise that they were not that good. The Maui show did just OK, the San Francisco show broke even, and the New Orleans show lost money. The idea I had didn't work. Although the Maui show would have been considered a winner by infomercial standards, I was spoiled from the successes of my other more powerful shows.

It was about this time that I learned a valuable lesson—namely, that an infomercial is really a three-act play with the titles of each act being "Entertainment," "Selling" and "Closing." Later, in Chapter 19, I'll explain this concept in detail.

I combined the material from the three shows with about 12 minutes that I shot later in Chicago and Venice Beach, California, and ended up with some very powerful segments that when seen together were really dynamic.

I then wrote the copy that was to go between each of the segments—copy for both my show hostess, Denise Gray, and me. But Dan Rosenfield, the president of my ad agency, suggested a new show hostess—a beautiful girl from Los Angeles who appeared in a number of his photo sessions. "She's such an incredible knockout gal that we should give her a shot. We might even discover an incredible talent and she'll stop the viewers and really hold them," remarked Dan.

A Meeting Arranged

I arranged to meet the girl in Las Vegas to make sure she could do the job. She flew to Las Vegas from Los Angeles and I picked her up at the airport. Not only was she beautiful, but she looked wholesome—just like the gal next door or the home-coming queen at your local high school. I was blown away by her looks.

We then went out to dinner and talked about her aspirations of not only being a top model but getting into television and how doing the commercial would be a wonderful stepping-stone. She seemed very knowledgeable, very articulate and intelligent. I had no qualms about hiring her at the end of the evening. "I've heard enough. You're the one we'll use as my hostess in the infomercial," I announced to her at the end of dinner. Thrilled, she caught the next flight back to Los Angeles and we arranged to film the show in Las Vegas the following week.

Dan and two other crew members set up the scene, which was outdoors right in the middle of a hot Las Vegas 100 degree June day. We started to shoot. There were only 10 lines she had to read, so I expected the shoot to only take a half hour. But it didn't take long for me to realize that as pretty as she was, as articulate and intelligent as she seemed, when it came to reading lines she was horrible. We tried and strained through two hours of prompting and reshoots as I slowly turned the color of a freshly cooked lobster. In fact, you can see the progression on tape—from an enthusiastic and fair-skinned host to a limp piece of roasted salami. It was a horrible experience that I certainly wouldn't want to go through again.

Dan left with the crew. He knew that whatever we shot was not worth saving. I left with one of the worst sunburns I can remember. I was almost delirious. And I reflected on what had happened. This was ridiculous. Why not get Denise Gray, the previous hostess with whom I worked several shows before. She was a known quantity. I knew she could do the job and I had to get the show on the air quickly. We were about to miss the sunglass season if I delayed any longer, and messing around with unknown talent was not very smart at this late date. So I gave Denise an emergency call and she was able to fly to Las Vegas where I organized another shoot.

But when Denise arrived, she didn't look well. And just prior to the shoot she threw up all over the inside of my brand-new Mercedes 500SL as we were driving to the shooting location. During the shoot, she wasn't herself, the camera angles were bad

Denise Gray and myself doing a BluBlocker show in Florida. I thought she would be perfect for my new show until she threw up in my brand-new car.

and it seemed as if all flights leaving McCarran International Airport in Las Vegas were purposely flying over our set. It was another bad experience and the shoot was finally scrapped. I was still without the thread that was to bind the fabulous segments we had edited for the commercial.

This was frustrating. I finally had the segments and the show

I wanted. I had the script for the show. And I also had the pressure of having to come up with an infomercial pretty soon and yet things just weren't flowing smoothly. When I see that events aren't flowing smoothly I usually take a deep breath, relax and take a different course of action—something that would be totally out of context with the situation. So I simply hopped on a plane and flew to Maui, script in hand, with no idea of what I was going to do.

I brought the script with me just in case something serendipitous happened during my stay. I'm always open and prepared to accept coincidences.

I arrived in the late afternoon, went to my hotel and relaxed. My first meeting the next day was going to be for breakfast with a friend, David Brenner.

No, not David Brenner the famous comedian, but rather a financial advisor who had given me advice from time to time. The next morning was no exception. He had a lot of advice and I politely listened. Then, knowing that I was involved with shooting a lot of video, he asked me if I was planning on shooting any commercials in Maui. It seemed that a friend of his owned a video camera and wanted to shoot some of our stuff.

David gave me the videographer's card and I called him right after breakfast. "David Brenner said that you have broadcast-quality video equipment and are looking for some work. But do you know of any talented girl who could act as a show host for my infomercial?"

He said he did. "I've got a gal, Kimberly Horn, who's terrific. She's in a play right now but I can give you her number, and if she's OK just let me know and I can arrange to bring her with me and do a shoot with you."

He gave me her number and I called. This time, I wasn't going to take any chances. I asked her if she could read some lines for me and go through an audition. She agreed and met me at the Intercontinental Hotel where I was staying. I had her read me the lines. She was perfect. She had the right inflection, the right sound, the right spirit—the perfect combination I was looking for. And she was pretty good-looking too.

I got permission from the Intercontinental to shoot on their grounds right by the ocean and organized everybody to be there

Sometimes the "energy" just isn't right.

around 11 AM when the sun was high enough and the ocean calm. We all arrived and we started to shoot. Just as we started, a stunt plane started flying overhead. Then smoke started to billow up over the trees from the mountain side of the island. Fire trucks, with their sirens blaring, were rushing to the scene to put out a major fire that was raging through the area. The wonderful quiet atmosphere at the Intercontinental Hotel turned almost magically into one of the noisiest you could imagine, not to mention the problems caused by the smoke blocking out half the sky.

I was determined to shoot the remaining part of the commercial. There were gaps in the sirens and the airplane finally flew away. And the smoke made a nice filter for the bright sunlight. I explained to Kimberly how to read her lines to tie in the various segments even though she hadn't seen any of them herself.

Finally, between the sirens, airplanes, smoke and fire, we finished shooting. Kimberly wasn't quite sure of the significance of what she had just done but was happy to help out. I took the tapes and express-mailed them to Dan in Kansas City. I called my daughter April, who was working during the summer at my office and I asked her to fly down to Kansas City to help Dan and his videographer, Larry Brewer, turn all the tape we shot into a final infomercial.

April is one of those gifted advertising people with the "feel" of knowing how to best bring out the emotion in a selling message. She had worked with me in the media department, in the customer service area and had been with me on a number of shoots as an assistant. Dan and Larry were great at video editing and with April there too, I knew I had a good team to finish the show while I spent the last few days relaxing in Maui.

April worked with Dan and Larry through the night and by the following afternoon, barely able to keep their eyes open, they advised me that the commercial was finally finished.

I had them rush me a copy and Mary Stanke shipped a few of the tapes to some of our test stations. When I finally got the chance to view the tapes, I found them to be fine except for a few things I wanted to change—mostly minor stuff. When it comes to one of my creative products, I always strive for perfection.

I arranged to have the changes made, but first we ran our test exposure for the infomercial. What happened next took me totally by surprise. The response was so strong that the profit generated from the test exposures paid for the entire cost of the previous

Dr. Geek was the surprise hit of our show when he performed an impromptu rap as we rolled the cameras. He later became famous, appearing on several TV shows and being recognized wherever he went.

three infomercials we shot in New Orleans, San Francisco and Maui plus the final show we edited to finish the project. I didn't even wait to make those minor changes.

A scene from my last BluBlocker infomercial. I eventually did the show with Kimberly Horn, who did an outstanding job without even knowing what the show was about.

The new show was far surpassing the infomercial that we were currently running, and by such a margin that my only goal was to get new tapes to every TV station running my old infomercial regardless of the cost. Tapes, or dubs as they are called, cost about $100 each. We had to send hundreds of dubs to the stations broadcasting our show. Even though I knew that eventually I would want to replace each tape I sent out, I still mailed those costly dubs to each station. And eventually I did replace them with my revised version.

By this time, in July of 1991, I was back in Northbrook, Illinois—a suburb north of Chicago and the corporate headquarters of JS&A. I was in my offices organizing the distribution of tapes to all the TV stations. The commercial was a huge success and I was well on my way to another successful year and a half of sales. But it still wasn't all that easy.

Lens Supplier Quits

Our sunglass lens supplier had just informed us that they were converting their plant and would be making optical prescription lenses. They no longer had the capacity for our sunglass lens production. We had the hottest BluBlocker commercial in our string of several and we couldn't make sunglasses because we couldn't get lenses.

In a series of quick moves, we were able to locate a new supplier, improve the quality of our lenses and meet the deadlines of going on the air, but it was a close call. Our commercial not only ran for the next few years, but it played throughout the world. It was the catalyst for major sales in New Zealand, Australia, Singapore, Taiwan, and countries in Europe. And it was also the catalyst for my start on QVC as a guest presenter of BluBlocker sunglasses. This relationship has lasted more than six years and continues as I write this.

It was also the last BluBlocker infomercial I intended to produce. I saw the problems the infomercial business was about to face before most of the other industry participants and decided to bow out. In fact, shortly after I finished this last infomercial, I gave a speech at an infomercial conference and announced that I felt the entire business was in serious jeopardy. What were my reasons? What did I see that nobody else saw?

First, I saw media rates starting to rise. Prices were doubling—even tripling. As many of the broadcast stations were getting fat from a growing and prosperous economy, they didn't need the revenue from the infomercial marketers. And later in Chapter 30 you'll learn the importance of media rates for the survival of our business.

Big Companies Get into the Act

I also saw the Fortune 500 corporations starting to make infomercials. But unlike the smaller mail order companies, their agenda was different. They didn't care about response rates, product margins and return on advertising investment. They just wanted the exposure, rating points and the cheaper advertising rates common in this new format. They dealt through ad agencies who bought media the same way they bought all their other

A four-camera time-coded rough cut of the "Sudden Fame" show that was a complete disaster. My desk looked huge, the participants froze and the energy was even worse.

media, which was a big mistake. Rates went up. Infomercial time is really bought differently, as you will soon learn.

After the success of this last infomercial, I still produced two more. One of them did not make a profit and we quickly dropped it. The other was a moderate success. The moderate success was for a food supplement called Miracell and the loser was a BluBlocker reunion video called "Sudden Fame" in which I took many of our previous infomercial interviewees and brought them back in a *Today Show* format to ask them how they were affected by the sudden fame from their appearance in the BluBlocker sunglass commercial. It was an interesting show but didn't move product.

What I learned from the "Sudden Fame" experience was that the spontaneity of the BluBlocker commercial was missing when people were interviewed in a studio audience setting. The participants were nervous, they didn't sound as interesting and the show just didn't have many of the elements of our previous shows. I chalked it up to a learning experience and we all had a good time doing it.

By this time I learned that there is often an energy present during a shoot which seems to affect the entire production. When the energy is right you can end up with a complete show in three hours, as we did when I filmed my Rear Vision commercial. And then there are times when the energy isn't quite right, like the time my co-host threw up all over my new car. It either flows right or it doesn't, and the key is to recognize that you'll have days when the energy is not right. Don't be frustrated or discouraged. If you're patient and persistent, you'll overcome any obstacle and you'll be surrounded by the right energy.

Denise Gray appeared as the hostess of several of our most successful shows.

The Lessons Learned

You can do 10 infomercials and bomb on each one of them until you hit a winner, and then within a few weeks you can make up for all the losers. The same goes for the shooting process. You can have some bad shoots, but then a good shoot will more than make up for all the bad ones.

Before I took my leave of absence from the infomercial industry I did one last show that was one of the most difficult and most expensive ones I've ever done. The following is the story of Miracell—a product in which I invested more than a million dollars, more money than I'd ever invested in any product before.

Chapter 5

The Wrinkle Pill Infomercial

In almost every form of direct response, you can test relatively inexpensively to determine if you have a winner or loser. Not so with infomercials.

There is often a tremendous amount of work, effort and expense in making an infomercial before you can test it and determine its success.

Typically, an infomercial could cost anywhere from $50,000 to $300,000 just in production costs and that's not including some of the other costs involved such as product development and inventory to support the infomercial. Of course, you can do a simple interview-style infomercial for $10,000, but very few of those shows really work. But it still costs $10,000 in production costs and more in TV time before you know the results.

Print Is an Easy Way to Test

I have found that print is one way to test a product before making a major investment in an infomercial. When I did my first two infomercials—for BluBlocker sunglasses and MDR vitamins—I already knew I had a success in print and had the confidence that it would work on TV if presented properly. The way I presented both products on TV differed totally from the way I sold them in print, but it was print that gave me the assurance that I had a winning product. Not so with my next product, however.

I had over $1 million invested in the most expensive infomercial I've ever produced as well as in inventory to support the infomercial—and all before I even ran it. Ironically, I did not want to test it in print because I was limited by Food and Drug Administration (FDA) regulations as to what I could or couldn't say about it. I therefore had to resort to a major gamble on TV where I had much more freedom to express the benefits of the product.

This story is about my experience with Miracell—a food supplement in the form of a pill that reduces wrinkles while providing a whole series of other benefits.

A Caller from the Past

Hokan Cederberg was a man I had known for a number of years but with whom I had not done business. He was in the health food industry and sold a number of products that never quite passed my criteria—primarily because I specialized in selling electronic products during most of the time I knew him.

One day in 1992 he called me and said rather excitedly, "Watch the *Jenny Jones* show this coming Tuesday and you'll see our new product. It's creating tremendous interest and we can hardly supply enough of it."

"What is the product?" I inquired. "What does it do?"

"It's a pill that smoothes out wrinkles," was the reply.

I continued to ask questions and found out that the pill Hokan was referring to was made in Sweden and was in such demand overseas that they couldn't produce the product fast enough. You simply took this pill every day and in about two to three months, you started to notice a dramatic difference in the skin all over your body. Wrinkles would dramatically lessen.

The skin of a 50-year-old person after taking Miracell looked like the skin of a 20-year-old when viewed under a microscope. Wrinkles were reduced, the skin was better hydrated, had more elastin and tightened and firmed.

It truly sounded like a miracle product. And when I watched the *Jenny Jones* show, the audience responded very enthusiastically. In fact, I was so impressed, I decided to start taking the pill myself. If I could see a difference within a few months, then I assured Hokan that I would consider selling the product.

Unusual Dosage Recommended

The dosage was rather unusual. You took two pills a day each day for three months and then you dropped down to one pill a day after three months. By taking two pills a day for the first three months, you supposedly sped up the effect of this product so that you could see results rather quickly. Then it was down to one pill a day to maintain and continue the program.

Within a few weeks of taking the wrinkle pill, I noticed some incredible results. Unlike taking vitamins where you think you are feeling better, I was actually experiencing the results. The effect on me was so noticeable that others were seeing a difference too. That alone was enough to cause me to take a very serious look at this product, but I experienced more.

I started seeing other effects rather quickly, and some of the results were unexpected. My nails started to get stronger, my hair was getting thicker and healthier looking and then I started noticing differences in my skin. The thin skin under my eyes was getting thicker, the skin around my neck was getting tighter and I seemed to have a lot more energy.

I Was Totally Enthusiastic

I was getting very curious about this product as you can imagine. It was the type of product that I could throw my entire enthusiasm behind because of my own personal experience. And it did more for me than any other vitamin or food supplement I had previously tried.

I called Hokan and told him about my experience. I agreed to do whatever it took to put a commercial together and advertise the product, which I decided to call Miracell—a name my daughter April had coined. Little did I know how big a commitment I had made.

The first thing I discovered was the necessity to hire an attorney experienced in FDA matters. The product would be regulated by the FDA (as our sunglasses are), so I had to make sure I had the proper guidance to avoid any conflict with their rules. Then I discovered that I needed two double-blind studies to prove many of the wrinkle claims that I was planning to make in my commercial. And I had to learn as much as I could about the rules and regulations regarding the sale of food or dietary supplements so that I could effectively craft my infomercial and stay within the guidelines of the FDA.

I set up two double-blind studies—one with a lab in New York and another with a famous skin specialist, Dr. Peter Pugliese, in Pennsylvania. Neither knew that the other was doing a similar study. And when I approached them and presented a pill that was supposed to reduce wrinkles, both laughed at the premise but agreed to do the test despite their skepticism.

The studies were expensive. Each one cost around $100,000 and involved three months of testing. In one study, biopsies of

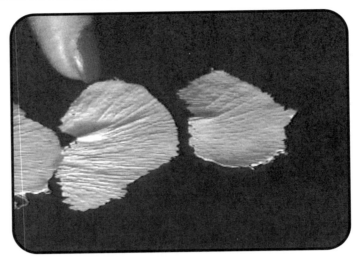

The plaster casts demonstrated a dramatic improvement around the corners of participants' eyes and was one of the few scenes we could use from our six hours of shooting. Note how much smoother the skin casting on the right was.

the participants were taken before and after the study, plaster molds of the skin around the eyes were taken periodically to provide objective visual comparisons and photographs were taken on a regular basis. The elasticity of the skin was tested with a special device made for the study and there were several other tests to determine the health of the skin. Ages of the participants ranged from 35 to 60 and the results were compared to the skin of a 20-year-old to see how effective the pill really was at improving the skin.

I needed the studies not only for FDA purposes but for the Federal Trade Commission (FTC) as well. The FTC regulates advertising, and their rules covering infomercials and advertising claims required us to do studies regardless of what the FDA demanded. And then there was my curiosity. I knew the stuff worked on me, but would it work on others? I really didn't know, although it was selling very nicely in Europe.

After waiting three months for the tests to be completed, the results came in and the very same researchers who were laughing at me when I brought them Miracell were now taking Miracell themselves. The results were indeed dramatic. And although we focused on the skin, some of the participants in the study were reporting many improvements in their hair and nails. Miracell was truly an incredible product.

I then decided to hire a camera crew and fly them down to Pennsylvania, where the testing was conducted, to interview some of the participants. I interviewed Dr. Peter Pugliese—one of the top skin researchers in the nation—as well as the participants and even the lab technician who supervised the independent tests. Everybody was enthusiastic—so much so that I took over six hours of some of the most incredible footage you could imagine.

We knew how to identify and reach our potential customers.

On my return home to Chicago, I reviewed all the tapes and put together a powerful 12-minute segment that would have convinced even the most skeptical person of the power of Miracell. It was 12 minutes that literally sold every person I showed it to. I also sent it to my FDA lawyer in Washington for review to determine if it was within the guidelines of the FDA rules.

The lawyer called me back with disappointing news. "You probably could use only about 90 seconds of what I have just seen," was his reply. It seems that although the footage accurately portrayed the double-blind study, the resulting video would imply that the product was actually a drug and not a natural food supplement.

It meant that of the six hours of tape I had taken and reduced to 12 minutes, I ended up with only 90 seconds to use in the final show. When you factor in the cost of the studies and all the video expense those 90 seconds cost me, I was paying over $2,200 a second. At this rate, a full 28-1/2 minute infomercial would have cost me nearly $4 million. Obviously any future shooting was going to have to cost a lot less.

Unusual Experience at Hotel

In the meantime, I prepared a few other segments for the infomercial. I was with Dr. Pugliese and his wife at the Great Valley Desmond Hotel in Malvern, Pennsylvania. Dr. Pugliese's wife was 60 years old but looked like she was only in her early 40s. She looked amazingly young for her age. As we were standing in the lobby a man nearby happened to look over at her. Seeing this, I blurted out to him, "How old do you think this young lady is?"

Rather startled, he looked at her and said, "I'd guess somewhere in her late 30s."

I then took the liberty of saying she was actually 60, and this man's face dropped in surprise as he responded, "Really? I'd like to be takin' the same stuff she's been takin'!"

His comment triggered a big idea. Many people might be skeptical about the possibility of someone looking 20 years younger than their actual age. What if I could show that indeed it was possible and that there were many people, such as Mrs. Pugliese, who did look younger. I would use these examples at the beginning of the show and create a very attention-getting introduction.

So I ran an ad in the *Los Angeles Times* asking for women to respond who looked 20 years younger than their actual age and who would be interested in appearing in our commercial. I got approximately 400 replies complete with pictures and written stories. Some of the women indeed looked 20 years younger than their age. I then arranged to hold an audition in which I would meet with the top 40 respondents and videotape and interview them and ask them to state their age on camera.

Many Things In Common

I then did the interviews with the 40 women and picked out about six for the commercial's introduction. In the process I discovered that these women had something in common. Each drank a lot of water, had a good sense of humor and did not smoke, drink or expose their skin to the sun. It was something I mentioned in the commercial.

I then arranged to interview a plastic surgeon to learn what it would cost to do plastic surgery and what the results might look like, so I could make a comparison with the advantages of Miracell. After flying to Los Angeles, hiring a camera crew and driving an hour and a half to visit the plastic surgeon in Orange

County who had previously agreed to do the interview, I discovered that he had changed his mind. Why couldn't he have called me and told me beforehand? The plastic surgeon had cost me $2,000 and a lot of my time and it was totally wasted.

I then arranged to interview a young lady in Las Vegas who worked in the Excalibur Hotel carnival. Her job was to guess the ages of people who would step into her booth. If she was off by over two years, then she would give a prize to the person whose age she guessed wrong. But she was incredibly accurate. I wanted to find out how she was able to guess a person's age simply by looking at them.

After the Excalibur Hotel refused to allow us access, we had to set up a different location and re-create the same scene as at the carnival. She told the audience how she accurately guessed somebody's age by observing their wrinkles.

She told me that she determined age by looking at a person's wrinkles and the tightness of their skin. This would be both interesting and informative for my audience and I wanted to get this on tape. But the Excalibur Hotel wouldn't give me permission to film in the hotel. So I simply went up to her, asked her if she was willing to appear in our commercial and then I set up a similar carnival scene at a studio and interviewed her there to get my footage.

I then went to many of the actual users of the Miracell product who had originally bought it from Hokan. They were located in New York, Chicago and Los Angeles, and despite all the travel, I got great interviews. I also ran an ad in the New York newspapers asking people who had plastic surgery with good results to contact me. I wanted to get their opinions on plastic surgery—something my Orange County plastic surgeon had refused to provide for me. The interviews all worked out well with great footage.

By this time, I was becoming an expert on what I could and couldn't say on TV according to what the FDA would accept. When I would interview Miracell users and others in the infomercial, I was careful to make sure I asked the right questions. I also knew what I had to cut out, how to edit it and what to avoid. The main thrust of what I could say was that the product was a food supplement providing the same benefits as eating carrots, apples or any naturally grown food. What I couldn't say was a little more complex: anything that would give the viewer the impression that the product cured a disease or substantially altered the structure or function of the body. By the way, the FDA considers sun-damaged skin a disease.

Talent Chosen for Show

I named the show "How Young Can You Be?" and hired my ad agency in Kansas City to create the set and supply the two show hosts, Alecia Jacobs, a beauty pageant winner from Las Vegas, and Duke Frye, a local sportscaster from Kansas City. We shot the hosts and created two different sales pitches. The first one offered the product describing its suggested usage—two pills per day for three months and then one pill per day after three months. This meant that you paid $50 per month for the first three months and then $25 per month thereafter. I also added information on our "automatic shipping club," which was my name for a continuity program. If you ordered from the show, we would automatically ship you a box of Miracell each month and charge your credit card. But the offer was confusing, and for three reasons.

First of all, it was too complicated. There were too many numbers to remember and I felt I had to explain the routine twice to make sure it was understood. The second problem involved pricing. During the first three months you had to pay twice as much for the product as in the future when you reduced your daily dosage. This also was against the marketing principles I had learned. You always wanted the lower price in the beginning to "hook" your prospect and then later you could raise the price similar to the technique used by many video clubs.

Finally, I told viewers about the continuity program up front and on the air. Typically, this is something you don't sell on the air but rather as a supplemental offer on the telephone when your prospect calls to order the product.

Although I knew instinctively that by making the offer complicated I was violating many of the rules I had taught at my seminar, I still wanted to take a chance and use the complicated offer. I felt the product was so strong that people would do anything to get it and would accept the complicated offer and the continuity program without pause. But I also shot backup footage which didn't discuss the complicated dosage and pricing schedule but rather offered the product at a flat $25 price each month. In short, there was only one low price per month. In essence, I was giving away a box for each of the first three months and investing in my belief that this continuity program would be successful for a long time.

This 70-year-old woman could easily have passed as being in her 40s. Many of our guests looked incredibly young for their age.

I decided to run a test with the more complicated version first. If it did well, then I was home free and had a real winner. The continuity program meant that I could ship the product every month for an unspecified period of time to a list of satisfied customers and then bill them each month for the shipment. This would further assure the success of the program. I also knew that if my first show didn't work, I had my backup show already edited and ready to substitute.

The commercial was finished. I had crafted it personally from beginning to end. It reflected months of planning, hundreds of thousands of dollars first in research and testing and then in shooting and editing. It required ads in the *New York Times* and *Los Angeles Times* to procure testimonials and subjects, and layered on top of all this expense and time was one factor that was both costly and unexpected, and which I have not mentioned.

Three Months in Advance

One of the things I had to do from the very beginning was to commit to the production of Miracell three months in advance since it was made in Sweden. Not knowing how the product would do, I had to guess how much of the product to order to fill my pipeline when I started running the commercial. Back when I gave this estimate, it was based on a monthly allocation for just a few months. But considering the time required for the double-blind studies and the shooting as well as final production, I was running into a 10-month time schedule. Inventory was piling up in my warehouse. Part of our agreement was for the manufacturer in Sweden to provide a continuous supply each month, but I was now 10 months into the program and I had yet to sell the first pill. In fact, I had over $700,000 worth of product, and my total investment in this project including the cost of the infomercial was approaching $1 million.

When you have this much time, effort and money riding on an infomercial, you pray a lot. And when the show was run, it bombed—there were not enough orders to cover a fraction of the advertising cost. Even with the continuity factored in, it was still a losing proposition.

Simpler Backup Show

But remember, I had a backup show that had a much simpler albeit less profitable offer. One box and a $25 price per month—

period. Nothing mentioned that I was going to ship them two boxes per month and then reduce it to one box after three months. Nothing about the fact that they were getting a free box on us. It was just plain simple.

The new version ran and fortunately it was successful. Despite how strongly I personally felt about the product, the public remained a little skeptical and had to be sold a simple and inexpensive way for them to at least give it a try.

The offer that worked was a simple offer. It cost us more, but in the long run, the simpler offer worked the best.

After the test, I developed plans to advertise the product nationally. As a precaution, I sent a copy of the show to my attorney for his final approval before making any major advertising commitment. I had the marketing test results, knew I had a winner and needed only his final nod to make sure we were following all the FDA rules. He quickly reviewed the tape and called me.

"Joe, I reviewed the commercial and I must commend you on an excellent job of producing a perfectly legal rule-following presentation while still getting the full impact of the product to your audience. You've done a splendid job."

It Came as a Shock

I smiled as I listened proudly to him on the phone. Yes, I had learned well from my attorney and followed his guidelines to the letter. And I put a show together that followed all the rules he conveyed to me and yet was almost conservative compared to what was typically done with product claims. No wild claims, no puffery—just plain facts and images to create the impact I needed to sell the product.

"And Joe, one further thing," commented my attorney. "I will be proud to defend you when the FDA investigates you."

"What?" I responded. "What do you mean?"

"As clean and as well done as your commercial is, the FDA won't like a food supplement doing what your product can indeed do, and they will more than likely conduct a thorough investigation to check out your claims. But like I say, I'll be proud to represent you, as I know there won't be a problem."

I was shocked. I knew how the FDA worked and how many other federal agencies such as the FTC operated. I knew that these agencies had the power to harass legitimate companies. I thanked my attorney for his advice, hung up the phone and thought about what he had said.

Many Questions Raised

I thought about the tremendous investment I had in product and the amount of time and energy I had put in this project only to be discouraged by what a federal agency might or might not do. And I realized that what I was doing was responsible and correct. Despite the odds of a potential investigation from the government, I decided to proceed anyway. I had fought a lot to reach this point, I was right in what I was doing, I was helping a lot of people and I was confident that I was doing what needed to be done in an honest and correct way.

Then one day in February of 1993, about a few months into the program, I read a full-page ad in one of the big national newspapers about a wrinkle pill being offered by another company making claims that I knew were flagrant violations of the FDA rules. I also felt that the product probably had no scientific double-blind studies to back it up, might have been a bogus product anyway, and that if the FDA were to go after them, they might go after me at the same time and make it sound like we were as crooked as the other company. And it was my guess that the other company was trying to hook onto our advertising coattails.

Even Dr. Peter Pugliese, a medical doctor who conducted the study, took Miracell. It was an excellent product that convinced him from his tests to become a believer.

Time to Phase Out Product

BluBlocker sunglasses were so successful by now that I was wondering about whether it really paid to keep running the Miracell infomercial and risk any negative publicity. Media rates were starting to escalate and I had established enough momentum through the sale of Miracell to keep selling the product on a continuity program for many years. Why continue to risk any more than I already had?

And then, faced with potential problems with our government and the potential damage that could be caused by this fly-by-night company that was offering what could have been a bogus wrinkle pill, I decided to stop running the Miracell infomercial. But I may have made the wrong move.

I've never had any problems from the government about Miracell or from anybody using the product. If anything, I have such a loyal group of customers that I might still be selling this product for several more years just from our continuity program.

The lessons I learned were many. The price I paid in effort was high. And although I further crafted my skill as an infomercial producer through this experience, I wasn't quite sure it was really worth all the time and expense. But in retrospect I might have been wrong by prematurely taking the product off the air.

I still personally take Miracell. People think I look at least 10 years younger than my age. And all the benefits I experienced from using the product throughout the years have certainly had a positive payoff.

Indeed, even Dr. Pugliese, who has been using Miracell for the past five years, claims that he is looking and feeling better than he did before he started taking the product. And I'm considering putting Miracell on the air once more by running the same infomercial and featuring the product on QVC.

The promotion taught me the importance of a simple offer even for the most exciting of products. It taught me to be very careful when committing to inventory in advance. It taught me that anything can go wrong and will.

The Miracell infomercial was my last infomercial as I write this book. I do have a few more infomercials left in me and may be doing some after this book is published. But the lessons learned and the observations I have made can be very helpful if you are getting into this exciting field.

In the following chapter, I talk about some more of my infomercial observations. I had spent almost seven years of fun and excitement in this field and I was able to reap many rewards. But before you jump in, read the next chapter for some of the valuable insights I've realized through all of these experiences.

I will be back on the air with an infomercial. I don't know when, but I do know that I will be using the medium differently than I have in the past. What worked so wonderfully back when I started doing infomercials was based on low media costs and a consumer who had little experience in what to expect from the purveyors of infomercial products.

Since then, the media rates have gone up and the public has had much more experience with buying from infomercials. Unfortunately, it has not often been a good experience. Delays in shipments, poor customer service and shoddy products with high return rates have negatively influenced the public toward the industry.

To order BluBlocker Sunglasses call
1-800-233-2700

It was the characters we interviewed who made our shows interesting. This scene at the Chicago lakefront was one of our most interesting.

JS&A ran its company like it expected to stay in business for years. It was the only way I knew to run a business and it was part of my core belief system in direct marketing. But I also saw how these new infomercial companies, interested only in the bottom line with total disregard for the consumer, were going to affect the entire industry.

Legitimate Companies Survive

The predictions I made when I first started out in the industry seem to have come true. Many of the legitimate companies, knowledgeable about direct marketing and running their businesses well, were tainted by the fly-by-nights. Nevertheless, the legitimate companies outlasted the fly-by-nights and eventually prospered.

There are still vast opportunities for marketing products in half-hour commercials, and like print advertising, the infomercial will go through its cycles as well. It will return even stronger than it is today.

During all the years I ran our commercials, I kept as low a profile as possible. Few people knew of our success. Many of the other public companies and aspiring-to-go-public companies who were constantly bragging about their successes were doing so to attract media publicity. Some even hired media consultants and PR firms. I hired none of those.

JS&A quietly and unobtrusively marched to our own tune for seven years selling over 9 million pairs of BluBlocker sunglasses to the public and 10 million more sunglasses to Pizza Hut. It was only the telemarketing companies taking our telephone orders who really knew which were the successful companies and which were not. But the order-taking companies also kept this information confidential.

And true to my predictions in the introduction to this book, the companies that lasted and did very well were the ones with a direct response background—those who knew how to conduct a direct marketing business with all its implications and responsibilities.

Providing an Important Service

My greatest compliment and a truly gratifying reward for all my years of marketing BluBlocker sunglasses came from one of the heads of research at Johns Hopkins University, Dr. John Gottsch. For several years, BluBlocker Corporation sponsored research at the university. Dr. Gottsch was a medical professional—an ophthalmologist who saw patients at the university hospital and directed a great deal of the eye research at the university.

He once pulled me aside as we were walking through the research labs. "Joe," he said, "I can help, if I'm lucky, maybe 25 patients a day with all sorts of eye diseases. But do you realize that you are protecting millions of people from ever having to see me in the first place? You should be really proud of yourself." And put in these terms, I was indeed very proud.

And I think there is also a good message in Dr. Gottsch's comment for infomercials as a medium of communication. The power of an infomercial can be used to provide a great deal of good to society—educating the public to dangers and providing products that protect against these dangers as in the case of BluBlocker sunglasses. Or infomercials can simply provide a platform for presenting products that need explanations and demonstrations for which TV is ideally suited. Infomercials have

Infomercials can serve a valuable service in consumer education. BluBlocker Corporation was the first company to expose the dangers of UV radiation and present a product that provided outstanding protection against the sun's dangerous rays. This serious scene, highlighting safety, was taken from a very successful BluBlocker infomercial taped in San Francisco.

already been used in political campaigns, new car introductions, money-saving products and several health-related supplements and exercise devices. If we are just a bit smarter and just a bit safer from having watched an infomercial and purchased a product, then the medium has served the public well, and can continue to serve them well for many years to come.

This fun couple made a great interview for our BluBlocker infomercial. The spontaneity in all our interviews made for a lively show.

In the next chapter I talk about my experiences with the home shopping revolution. It was a fun and exciting part of my TV experience and something that you'll find very interesting as well.

Chapter 7 | The Early Home Shopping Experience

My experience with the home shopping revolution started in 1979 during the very early stages of that industry. I was in Tampa, Florida, giving a speech before the Florida Direct Marketing Association at the invitation of a former seminar participant and friend of mine, Keith Halford.

After my speech, Keith invited me to visit his new place of employment—a home shopping club in Clearwater, Florida. I didn't know what a home shopping club was or what to expect, but Keith explained that I was in store for an eye-opening experience. Keith formerly worked for the Franklin Mint and left there to pursue this new position with a company he claimed was "going to be the future of direct marketing."

Keith and I drove up to a large structure. We stepped out of the car and walked into what seemed like a side entrance. The guard acknowledged Keith and we both walked into a large well-lit room. At the head of the room on a raised platform was a brightly colored set. There was obviously a television performance taking place as somebody was talking to a large video camera. But instead of an audience, there were hundreds of telephone operators all busy taking orders. You could hear the hum of the operators in the background.

The Start of TV Home Shopping

"What you're seeing here is incredible," Keith explained. "In all my years of direct marketing I've never seen such potential."

Keith then described the early months of TV home shopping. A Tampa radio station owned by Roy Speer was owed a few thousand dollars by an advertiser. The advertiser said that he was short of cash but could give the station can openers in exchange for the debt. Bud Paxson, the general manager of the station at the time, accepted the deal and offered the can openers on the air at a special price to his local audience in an effort to liquidate the product and consequently the debt. The can openers "blew out the doors," enthused Keith, "and the home shopping revolution was born."

Paxson wondered if he were to offer other products on the air, would they do well too? He tried it and indeed he experienced similar results.

It didn't take long before Speer and Paxson realized that a cable TV show where viewers could see the products being offered would be a viable concept. This also worked, and soon they expanded it into a 24-hour shopping experience. But it was quite different than it is today.

You Had to Pick Up Your Package

First, it was strictly a local show. Only the viewers in the Tampa area were receiving the show. Second, in order to get your purchase, you had to go to a local warehouse and actually pick it up yourself. I visited one of the warehouse locations and I couldn't believe the huge inventory and the size of the warehouse. Here in one small city, they were generating more sales than any other retailer in that city. The place was packed as TV buyers were waiting in line just to pick up their purchases.

I returned to the station to meet with Bud Paxson and get a closer look at the TV setup. The show consisted of a host presenting products and giving away prizes occasionally to entice viewership. I commented to Keith, "This is a direct marketing program with a game show element. It's entertainment, showmanship and salesmanship all wrapped up in one show. But why don't you take this national? And why aren't you shipping the products instead of forcing your customers to pick them up?"

"That's coming," Keith replied. "Within a short period of time, we'll be expanding this into other cities and that's when you'll really see this thing unfold."

I then met with Bud Paxson. I was by then quite well known in the direct marketing industry and Bud had a pretty good understanding of what I did. "If you have any closeout products you want to get rid of, please give me a call and we'll work out a deal," Paxson offered. "One of our biggest problems now is getting enough good products at exceptional prices. We're mostly interested in closeouts—really bargain-type stuff for our audience."

I Wanted a Piece of It

I made one comment to Paxson that I still remember. I said, "I have never copied anybody nor have I ever been interested in obtaining a franchise from anybody, but if there is ever an opportunity to get a piece of this and run it, please let me know. There is no question in my mind that this is the future of direct marketing."

Paxson smiled and nodded his head. "Yes, we think the same thing and we'll certainly keep in touch."

I left after getting a few more insights into what appeared to be an incredible company. Keith drove me to the airport where I caught my plane to Chicago. I couldn't help but think that I had just witnessed a revolution in the making.

Paxson called me afterwards and we worked out a sale for some old products that were just lying around in our inventory. We sold them for cash. Paxson got a great deal and we moved a lot of our excess inventory.

The following year his Home Shopping Network went national and it exploded as I had thought it would into a billion-dollar corporation reaching 50 million TV homes and becoming one of the hottest stocks on Wall Street.

I Watched It Grow and Grow

I never did much more with Paxson as I didn't have large amounts of closeout merchandise but it was fun watching the Home Shopping Network grow and develop into what was to become an industry unto itself.

I have predicted many things in my career. This prediction wasn't something that was difficult to see. It was obvious from the very beginning and it didn't take long to materialize. But I was soon to get involved with it in ways I did not expect when I first visited Paxson and his company back in 1979.

Chapter 8 | Home Shopping Really Arrives

I kept in touch with my friend Keith Halford while he worked for the Home Shopping Network. Keith would call me and discuss some of the problems he was experiencing with the growth of the company and ask my advice.

One day in the early '80s he called and told me that he was totally disillusioned with what he was going through. He told me that he was unhappy working for the Home Shopping Network and would be going to a new company shortly. Joe Segel, Keith's former employer when he was at the Franklin Mint, was opening a home shopping network in Pennsylvania called QVC, which stands for "Quality, Value and Convenience," and Keith was going to be joining QVC as one of its founders. "You should call Joe Segel and talk about the opportunities there and give him some of your thoughts," Keith suggested.

He Was One of My Heroes

Joe Segel was the entrepreneur who started the Franklin Mint. I remembered his name because I was a fan of the Franklin Mint and an admirer of the job that he had personally done there. In fact, coincidentally, I had clipped a front-page article from *The Wall Street Journal* in the '60s on Joe's concept of selling coins to service stations as premiums and I followed his career from that early beginning to his fabulous success with the Mint. Joe was one of my heroes, and for many reasons. His work ethic and marketing skills were already legendary. And he became even more of a personal hero later when he started QVC.

I called Joe and we had quite a long discussion. I told him I felt that he was right in his assumption that there was room for competition or a second home shopping club.

Joe explained how his show was going to be more upscale— not the flea-market style of the Home Shopping Network (HSN). And he explained how he wasn't going to offer discounted close-out products but rather good value. I disagreed. I told him that one of the driving engines of HSN was the exceptional value that caused that TV impulse purchase.

Spent Time Talking About Concept

We must have spent a good half hour on the phone discussing this one subject. He was saying that you didn't have to discount and I was saying that it was extremely important in the context of the concept to discount. In retrospect, we were both right. He eventually offered products lower than you could get at retail, which thus represented good value, but they were not of the close-out variety you would find on HSN. QVC raised the image of the home shopping business.

Joe suggested that I purchase stock in the company and I told him that I would consider it. Unfortunately, at the time I was still reeling from the effects of a long protracted fight with the government and was still getting back on my feet, but it was obviously a great investment opportunity that I missed. QVC stock made millionaires out of its early investors.

My next contact with QVC was in the late '80s when I received a call from Keith Halford telling me that QVC was up and running and on 24 hours a day. "We're growing like crazy and I'd like you to come to Philadelphia and see the operation."

I Visit QVC for the First Time

"I'll come over," I replied, "if I can present my sunglasses to your buyers. I think they'd make a great QVC product."

Keith agreed to set up a meeting with the buyer and me. When I arrived at QVC, Keith introduced me to Joe Segel, who up to this point I had not yet personally met. I also met many of the other founders of QVC. I toured the facility. It was huge. And the winding corridors going off into all kinds of directions had me totally confused. But Keith had them all figured out.

He showed me the fulfillment department, the order-taking room where the studio with its robotic cameras was located, introduced me to a number of the QVC personnel and eventually we met the buyer. I made my presentation and I was given a courteous response and told to leave my samples.

Instead of calling back the buyer, who was becoming deluged with companies approaching her, I kept in touch with Keith, who eventually told me that QVC was selling somebody else's brand of sunglasses even though the brand was a knockoff of my product. He couldn't do anything more than go along with their decision not to accept BluBlocker sunglasses as one of their products. "Otherwise I'd have to do her job," Keith remarked, referring to the buyer in the department responsible for sunglasses.

Keith Leaves QVC

I understood and kept running my infomercial. Our infomercials were now in their fifth year, and we were doing exceptionally well. Keith would call me from QVC and ask for advice on certain projects and I would give it to him. After all, he was a former seminar participant and I was always available to help my former students when they contacted me for advice.

Then one day in 1991 Keith informed me that he was no longer going to stay at QVC and that he had a new challenge: a new company called Via TV—a satellite home shopping channel out of Knoxville, Tennessee.

Ironically, around the time Keith left, I was contacted by one of the big infomercial producers who offered me the opportunity to appear on either HSN or QVC with my BluBlocker sunglasses. Apparently, the two home shopping clubs suddenly realized the power that infomercial products had when featured on the home shopping channels and decided that they wanted to get as many of those products as possible.

I Was to Appear on the Air

The infomercial producer would represent us, receive a small commission and place the product on QVC. I wanted QVC to do very well with our product. I gave the producer my lowest price to convey to QVC and he then was to sell the BluBlockers to QVC. As part of the representation, I would be given the opportunity to appear on the air. I would be accompanied to QVC by a representative from the producer's company and they would take care of all my arrangements, treating me like some media star.

I was supposed to sign a contract agreeing to all the terms, but delayed signing it for a few days on a hunch. When the big order finally came over the fax machine from the producer, I discovered that this company had not been telling me the truth. (I'm being nice.) It turned out that the fax was sent to me by mistake.

It was the fax that was supposed to go to QVC and I saw that these people were actually taking an enormous commission and pocketing all the profit that I had allocated for QVC's benefit. Remember, I wanted QVC to make a nice profit on my product but most of it was being skimmed off the top by my representative.

I was upset and could have taken the product away from the representative and gone directly to QVC, but instead I gave a fair commission to the producer and passed on the better price to QVC. I felt a loyalty to both QVC and the producer and this resolution worked for everybody.

QVC was scheduled to order 40,000 pairs of BluBlocker sunglasses for their first show. I was scheduled to appear about five times in 12-minute segments. My product in my infomercial was selling for $50, but we included another pair free of charge. In short, they were $25 a pair when you averaged in the free pair. Since I wanted to give QVC a terrific value and a big edge even over JS&A and their current infomercial, I suggested that QVC drop the price to $24.95 per pair.

I Get a Call from Doug Briggs

Doug Briggs, then the vice president of marketing at QVC, called me on the phone to confirm the decision. "Are you sure you want to go out at this low a price? Won't it interfere with your infomercial?"

"It might," I answered. "But it will give QVC an incredible opportunity and it's my way of making sure you succeed."

To my surprise, QVC only ordered 20,000 pairs or $500,000 worth of product at retail. They explained that they wanted to test the concept first.

I arrived at the station and waited in the Green Room to go on the air. Going on TV was obviously not a new experience for me. After giving hundreds of speeches and appearing in many of my infomercials as well as on TV talk shows, it was something for which I had no trepidation. I was first and foremost a salesman and secondly a direct marketer and I knew how to handle the cameras. The only difference here was that I would be on live TV.

My first appearance, in November 1991, was with Dan Wheeler, one of the most inspiring of the QVC hosts. You always remember the first of anything. I remember practically everybody who attended my very first seminar, but ask me who attended my second or my last and I couldn't tell you. I remember that first experience with Dan as if it were yesterday.

A Complete Sellout

I got on the air and in a matter of a few minutes we had sold out practically our entire inventory. There was no need for me to go on again. When I got off stage, unclipped my microphone and walked into the Green Room, Doug Briggs was there along with several of the top executives at QVC. "You've got a huge winner, Joe. We're looking for this product to do some 10 million dollars this year."

I was pumped. I had done it. The product was a real winner and I had a future with QVC. I found out that in the days ahead, a few of the top executives who hadn't seen my show asked to see a tape of it to find out if I had said anything illegal. They couldn't believe that I sold that many sunglasses without saying something that might get them in trouble. Of course, I didn't. I just got up and told the audience what a value the product represented and the product features and that was all. Dan Wheeler and I worked well together and we moved a lot of product.

My schedule was now set. From now on, I would appear on the air a number of times each month. QVC then brought in 50,000 pairs or over $1.2 million at retail and I was slated to go on the air several times to move all that product.

I went on and sales were fantastic. In each appearance, not only did I do exceptionally well, but the number of new customers who ordered from QVC was even more impressive. New customers are the lifeblood of QVC and so my appearances became even more important.

I Needed to Sell 7,000 Pairs

I was on my last show and I needed to sell another 7,000 pairs to reach the 50,000 mark and leave the QVC studio with a complete sellout. The QVC host was Steve Colantuno, a happy-go-lucky guy who had a great sense of humor and was pretty easy to work with. I asked Steve before we went on the air if, at the end of the presentation, he would allow me to speak directly to the audience for about 45 seconds. "Please make room for me to deliver a final message," were my exact words.

Steve did. Sales were going well but I could see from the order count that I needed that one extra push to sell all 50,000 pairs. Back then, you could glance down at a monitor and see how well or how poorly you were doing. Unfortunately, you can't do that today. That's why I wanted and needed that 45 seconds to appeal to the audience one last time.

I looked straight into the camera and said, "If everybody in America were to go to their washrooms at the same time and flush their toilets, we'd have a tremendous and sudden water shortage. This is my last time on the air and I'd like every one of the viewers to go to your telephone, pick up the receiver and call QVC's toll-free number and bury this network with orders for BluBlocker sunglasses. Thank you."

I stepped off the set as Steve continued to wrap up the hour. I unhooked my microphone and walked into the Green Room to monitor the station and see the count on the computer terminal that was located in the well-equipped room. One of the nice features about selling on QVC is that you can see your sales on the computer monitor in the Green Room, and often that is where I would go after appearing on the air.

Here I am with tall David Venable, a QVC show host. I always wore loud ties to make sure those channel surfers would stop for a moment and hear my voice. And once they saw me, I always asked for the order.

The phone lines were literally jammed. Thousands of calls were clogging the lines. My urging had paid off. I could see we were approaching the 50,000 mark and there was a good chance we would make it. I was noticing the tally and watching Steve present some of the other products when a phone call came in to Steve while he was on the air. QVC takes live phone calls as a matter of course and you never quite know what you're going to hear.

"Steve," said the woman caller, "I just wanted you to know I purchased a pair of BluBlocker sunglasses. And by the way, I went into my washroom and flushed the toilet too." I swear that is what she said.

The next day, I was told that QVC didn't appreciate my comments at the end of the show and asked that I not make them again. But we did sell all 50,000 pairs and it was an incredibly successful series of appearances.

For over a year I appeared selling the exact same two products—my BluBlocker aviator-style sunglasses and a pair of clip-ons for prescription wearers. In fact, BluBlocker sunglasses were among the top-selling single products on QVC that first year and although we weren't getting much recognition for it, QVC was giving us ample opportunity to sell our product.

Plenty of Support and Help

In the meantime, I was making very good friends at QVC. Len Czabator, a coordinating producer, would support my requests prior to going on the air. He would give me words of advice on what management really liked and didn't like. The other QVC hosts were all very supportive and became like family. In fact, West Chester, Pennsylvania, where QVC is located, was becoming almost like a second home and the QVC family an extension of my own family.

As I looked back at the end of that first year, I realized a few things. First, I had mastered and succeeded in practically every form of direct marketing—from print to catalogs, from infomercials to home shopping. I had a full palette of experience.

The second thing I realized was that I needed something to follow up my success of the past year. I couldn't just expect a single style to continue to succeed on QVC. I needed something entirely different—I had to reinvent myself. That's when I approached Doug Briggs, the vice president of marketing.

We featured a variety of styles, hoping to discover a popular "QVC style".

At a meeting with Doug Briggs in the fall of 1992 following my successful first year on QVC, I suggested to him that something be done the following year to give BluBlocker sunglasses a new life. "I suggest a one-hour show in which we feature a variety of new styles. Maybe from the new styles we'll discover a very popular new one and really exploit the style during the year." I also showed him the several new styles that I felt might make an interesting one-hour show.

He agreed. Why not give me a chance to prove what I could do for the second year? I went on the air with my first one-hour BluBlocker show and we did quite well. We would introduce new styles for practically each show and in the process I soon discovered what worked and what didn't.

One of the things I mentioned to Doug in our meeting was our need to take our product into the retail environment. Our first foray was to be with the Walgreens drug chain in December of '92. They were going to offer our sunglasses for $19.95, not the $24.95 they had been selling for during the past year on QVC. Doug was a little concerned and decided to take the pair off the air for four months and allow enough time so QVC wouldn't be too embarrassed by the price drop at retail. He would then run the product again on QVC but at the lower price point. He understood my position and appreciated the advance notice so he could prepare to suspend the sale of our two most popular styles.

Whenever the QVC customers responded positively to a new pair of sunglasses, we kept it in our QVC line. Some of the styles sold from $39 up to $69. And since we were about to go retail with the basic $25 BluBlockers, we wanted to differentiate QVC product from what we were offering at retail. Retailers wanted to hit the magic price point of $19.95 even though they were paying more for the product than QVC, but that was OK because there was already a pent-up demand for BluBlocker sunglasses at retail. It was now a matter of tapping into that demand while still keeping QVC happy.

Sales Kept Pace

The new lower price point, the new styles and the various other high-end styles did quite well for QVC that second year. I had a continuous stream of one-hour shows and although our sales did not do as well as they had the previous year, they were very close. We sold about as many units and the average sale price stayed pretty much the same because the more expensive pairs offset the lower-priced standard model. With similar volume, we generated many new customers who ordered for the first time from QVC—again, an important contribution to the company. QVC was still not ready to throw me a party. But it didn't matter. Sales were good, QVC was happy and we attracted many new customers for them.

It might be appropriate at this point to explain how we were working with QVC. After it became apparent in the late '80s that we had a very hot product, I decided to spin off the BluBlocker brand name, which had been sold under JS&A, into a separate company called "BluBlocker Corporation." The new company was to become a wholesaler eventually selling to retailers and to QVC. At first, BluBlocker only sold to JS&A (my company) and a few smaller accounts in the mail order business such as catalogs and syndicators. I estimated that sales to JS&A represented 95% of the BluBlocker business. After we went retail and started selling to QVC and we stopped running our infomercials, 95% of our sales were then primarily to companies other than JS&A. In short, we used our marketing company, JS&A, to establish brand-name recognition which built up the demand and consequently made the sale of the sunglasses an attractive opportunity to offer other retailers.

The Advantages of a Brand Name

Those old days when we were marketing Rear Vision sunglasses through the drug chains were long gone and forgotten. And the excitement of home shopping was starting to grow.

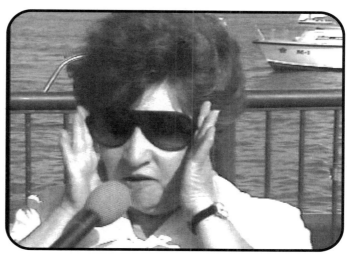

Another character who tried on our BluBlocker sunglasses in our infomercial. We always played clips from our infomercials on QVC to strengthen our sales message.

QVC was a customer just like any other retailer except that instead of relying totally on our advertising to drive sales, QVC invested millions into advertising our product on TV. Consequently, this was taken into consideration in price negotiations for the product. Other than the above exception, the only difference between selling to a retailer and selling to QVC was that I had to personally appear before QVC's cameras and assist them in selling our product. I was the expert. I was the founder of the company and the person who was the driving force behind the company. I was certainly experienced in front of a camera and in selling this product. So I worked with QVC as one of their guest hosts pitching BluBlocker sunglasses to their responsive audience each month. But selling sunglasses required more than just appearing before cameras.

I wanted to do something on the air that was different. I always wore colorful ties to stop the channel surfers but my anniversary show was coming up in October 1993 and I wanted to do something special for the event. After all, this was the first time QVC was doing something really special in recognition of our two consecutive years of continued success. So I had made, at my expense, a very bright red silk formal jacket. I then bought

Here I am in my bright red formal outfit appearing with QVC show host Dan Wheeler. Viewers stopped when they saw me wearing that "silly outfit," but somebody from "above" was obviously not happy.

a cumberbund, bow tie and fancy white shirt. I was finally being honored so I was going to dress up for the occasion. If this wouldn't stop the channel surfers, nothing would.

And indeed it did. I was on with Dan Wheeler—the host I first went on the air with in 1991. Dan was dressed in blue jeans and a sports shirt and I was dressed like the head waiter at the Ritz-Carlton. The show was terrific and generated big sales, especially given the afternoon hour of my appearance. And the "new-name generation" was very strong too. When measuring results of how well a product does on the air, QVC always looks at how many new customers a specific product attracts. The more new names, the more they can expect future sales from those new customers. My concept of stopping viewers by wearing bright-colored clothes seemed to have worked well and was attracting a very large percentage of new customers.

Then I got a call at my hotel from Len Czabator, a coordinating producer, as I was dressing in that same outfit for my next show. "Joe, I just got word from above that they don't want to see you on the air anymore with that silly outfit you wore."

I tried to find out who this mystery person from above was, but Len wouldn't tell me. So when I went on again with my typical business suit, instead of doing big numbers as we did in our previous show, the response was considerably less. Some person at QVC—maybe one of the lower-echelon executives—didn't like seeing me in my formal attire. Consequently sales volume was reduced. Len couldn't even give me the reason. Believe me, it wasn't a matter of image or being out of character. It was simply that I was not to wear it again. No explanation given.

The Decision Cost QVC Sales

I'm the type of person who isn't afraid to challenge authority or even race up to Doug Briggs' office to file a complaint. Doug always welcomed suggestions and appreciated my involvement with his company. He also knew that when I was upset, it was for a good reason that affected more than just me. But this seemed so petty that I overlooked it. I shouldn't have. Eventually, I realized that this simple arbitrary decision cost QVC sales and also inhibited me from wearing anything too creative in the future.

I now had to reinvent myself and come up with a powerful new concept to keep my product alive and exciting on QVC. This is the background behind my third year on QVC.

Chapter 10 | The Third Year on QVC

For my third year on QVC I wanted to reinvent myself on QVC. I wanted to do something more powerful and exciting than anything we had done before. I knew it had to be different. None of the new styles were smash hits even though sales were still pretty substantial.

Retail was doing quite well for us. We were selling only our two styles at retail, so QVC basically had an exclusive on many of the new styles we were offering their customers. I sat down one day and thought to myself, "OK. If I were to do something totally different, what could I do that would be different but acceptable to QVC and their conservative approach to promotions?"

I noticed that QVC was running a sweepstakes in connection with a tie they were selling and giving away a used Mercedes-Benz sports car as the prize—probably donated by the owner of the tie company as a way to write off the full value of the car.

It Made More Sense for BluBlocker

I thought about BluBlocker sunglasses and realized that they were something you indeed wore a lot more in a car than a tie. In short, a sweepstakes with a car as the grand prize made more sense for the BluBlocker sunglasses than for a tie, and since QVC already had a sweepstakes with a car as the grand prize, they might be more inclined to accept a similar promotion instead of some radical idea.

So I presented a concept to QVC that would be considerably more exciting than a used Mercedes-Benz. My concept was to give away a brand-new Dodge Viper—one of the most sought-after cars in America. I already owned the name Viper for sunglasses—a name that I coincidentally reserved a long time before the car became famous. So I decided to use the name on a new and exciting pair of sunglasses.

I had a pair designed that indeed looked like a pair you would wear if you drove a Viper. I then took a major risk. I ordered 50,000 pairs of them for the opening day of the promotion and procured a series of other travel prizes including trips to Hawaii and cruises to add to the thousands of other minor prizes we organized. It truly was a well-thought-out promotion.

It was about a year earlier that show business executive Barry Diller became interested in QVC. As a result of the success of Diane Von Furstenberg and her appearances on QVC, Diller, a friend of Von Furstenberg, had taken an interest in buying and running the company. Joe Segel, the current chairman, was ready to retire and Diller wanted to bring new life into the network and later use QVC to acquire other broadcast properties.

Presence Felt Almost Instantly

Diller's presence was felt almost instantly. The quality of the QVC fashion models improved. Both on-air and behind-the-scene changes were becoming evident and Diller opened a branch in England. There was also a reshuffling of several jobs, and in general, QVC became the focus of an enormous amount of national publicity. It was as if QVC had been discovered not just by the financial community but more by the public. My appearances on QVC now felt more significant. I was appearing on Barry Diller's QVC and to my friends who saw me on the air, it was as if just being at QVC meant that I knew Barry Diller. I didn't, and didn't have any reason to know him. I had my own job to do and had no reason to meet him. But it was clear that his involvement with QVC brought a very high level of awareness to the home shopping format. But anyway, back to the QVC promotion.

The opening day of the sweepstakes was around the middle of March 1994 and I was very excited and a little nervous. Since the Dodge Viper was in such demand, I managed to acquire one at a premium price and had it shipped to West Chester, Pennsylvania where QVC is located. On the day of the promotion, we had the car on the set, the sunglasses were in stock in great abundance—in short, we had a small fortune riding on the success of the promotion. It was, in retrospect, a very big gamble.

Would the Viper BluBlocker sunglasses be a popular style with the QVC audience? If it wasn't, I'd have a big inventory problem. And then there was the matter of my reputation. I was being viewed by QVC as a winner—somebody who rarely failed them—and I had to be successful to keep that reputation alive. Once you had a few bad shows, you weren't given many more opportunities, and here I found myself out on a really big limb. For if the sweepstakes didn't work, chances were that my days at QVC would be numbered.

The Loudest Tie I Could Find

I dressed for the day in my loudest tie and left for the studio. I had discovered that the louder the tie, the more it stopped those channel surfers watching television. So I always wore and continue to wear unusually loud ties or ties that are different.

Bob Bowersox was the QVC show host for the introduction. He appreciated cars and the Viper was one of his personal favorites. On his own, Bob created a script for one of the most exciting introductions I've heard for any product and he did it so well that the phone lines started to jam up. The excitement he generated that very first hour was spectacular. Anybody who called up and bought any pair of sunglasses would be automatically entered in our sweepstakes and the calls were coming in so fast that the counter on the screen could hardly keep up.

After that first exciting hour, there was no question that the sweepstakes was a huge success and that we would sell out of all 50,000 pairs of Vipers. Even more importantly, we discovered a hot new style that soon became one of the most popular styles in our young history.

The Viper promotion turned out to be one of the biggest promotions in QVC history up to that point, and the Viper sunglasses became a standard model for both QVC and the retail market in which we were now firmly entrenched. Everybody was excited with the results at QVC and I was receiving congratulations from everybody who had worked on it. P.J. Baer-McGrath and Holly Rutkowski—both QVC staffers who had faith in the concept and made sure it passed all of the approvals—came up and congratulated me. Producers and show hosts shook their heads in disbelief at the strong results.

What's Next?

After that first show when it became evident that we had an extremely successful promotion, my mind wasn't so much on the success and how we were going to gear up production to meet the sales potential, but rather on how I was going to follow the promotion. I thought, "What will I do next year?"

Maybe a flight on the space shuttle, was Steve Bryant's suggestion. Steve was also one of the hosts for the show and we often brainstormed on ways to sell BluBlockers. I took his idea seriously and contacted NASA, but without success.

We not only sold out all 50,000 Viper sunglasses by the end of the day, but we sold thousands in other styles that we presented as well. That gave us a total of approximately $1.4 million in retail sales. On that crazy day in March, I walked up to Doug Briggs' office and asked his secretary Lena Hoover if I could see him for a moment.

"He's busy right now and he's got an investment banking meeting going on in the conference room next door and he's got to be in there in just a few minutes," said Lena. "But let me mention that you're out here."

As I was waiting, I looked out Doug's office window which I could see from Lena's desk and saw a small March blizzard blowing snow everywhere. A late snowstorm was blanketing the area in what is called a whiteout. You couldn't see 10 feet in front of you and it was mid-afternoon.

Doug waved me into his office. "Joe, I can't really talk to you now. I've got a meeting with some investment bankers, but what is it?"

"Just two things, really quick," I snapped. "The first is our promotion. The Viper promotion was a huge success."

Doug walked over to his computer and looked up the results. "Wow. You did do pretty good. Congratulations. Thanks for telling me. What else?"

The Perfect Sunglass Weather

"When you go into that investment meeting with all those straight financial types, tell them to look out the window at the snow. Then tell them that we only sold 350,000 dollars worth of these sunglasses the last hour and see if that cracks them up." I handed Doug the sunglasses and he walked into the conference room. A few moments later I heard loud laughter.

The promotion lasted for three months and it generated thousands of new customers and over 350,000 sweepstakes

QVC show host Daliza Crane demonstrating the BluBlocker Viper sunglasses during our Viper Sweepstakes. The entire promotion was a coordinated effort featuring a Viper sports car and over 1,500 other prizes—all centered around a beautiful sunglass style called the Viper.

responses. The response was so great that when it came time to choose the winner on Father's Day, QVC couldn't use their standard sweepstakes barrel. They had to bring in a large portable swimming pool to hold all the entries. They used models in bathing suits to churn up the entries for the big selection process.

We hired James Feldman—an independent, experienced sweepstakes judge—to make sure the selection process was done in accordance with the rules of the sweepstakes. Jim's oversight was needed for legal reasons.

That third year was a big success. We had discovered a hot new item—the Viper sunglasses—and we conducted one of the most memorable and successful sweepstakes in QVC's history. The Viper continues to sell to this day along with the standard aviator style and the popular clip-on style BluBlockers. The sunglass season for QVC ended in October and QVC decided to throw a few anniversary shows for me to celebrate three full years on their network and two full years featuring our one-hour shows.

In one of the shows, a cake was presented to me in the shape of a head wearing BluBlocker sunglasses. It was an incredible masterpiece and so well done that I was afraid to even cut it. But we cut it on the air and it really felt nice to be recognized this way. It was a total surprise.

The success of the Viper promotion put together from scratch and a great year in general was reward enough. But the recognition from QVC sure felt good. I was still one of the top producers at QVC.

Chapter 11 | A Hummer of a Sweepstakes

As I was entering my fourth year at QVC I was getting a little disillusioned. The incident with the formal attire was minor compared to what was happening in my interaction with the buying department. I couldn't get answers when I requested them. I couldn't get purchase orders issued to me to make sure we had product in time for our shows, and we were often running out of the products that were our best sellers only because there was such poor planning on the part of the buyer.

I once submitted a request for a style that many of our customers had repeatedly asked for, but because we couldn't get a purchase order, we couldn't ship the product for over six months. Ours was the most important product in that department and despite this, we were being treated quite poorly. I would estimate that the buying department was responsible for a 20% loss in sales simply because of the mistakes they were making and the inattention they were giving us.

Trouble from the Buying Department

I found out that I wasn't the only one who was getting treated poorly. One of my good friends, Mark Schneider, had a product called Cool Dana. He too was complaining to me about the buying department.

It didn't take too long before word got out to the buyer's boss. I was called into his office and asked if I had any complaints. He suspected that things were not being run properly. "Be very frank with me. If you are, we can straighten out a lot of problems and it's going to make your life a lot better, and mine as well."

I looked at him and said that I didn't think it was appropriate for me to complain about somebody who had been working with me for the past three years. "But if you suspect something," I said, "you won't have to go very far. Just ask her for all of our correspondence. Meanwhile, I'll send you a copy of the letters I've sent and you'll see that all the issues are well documented. Then draw your own conclusions."

I sent copies of letters. Apparently I was one of several people who had experienced difficulties with the buyer and she was soon fired. In her place they put Maureen Kelly, a bright, articulate and follow-through type of person—a sharp contrast to the gal I had been working with before. I was once again enthused. And I went out of my way to point out my satisfaction with the change not only to her department boss but to Doug Briggs, who had been promoted and was now the new president of QVC.

The Hummer Promotion

In our fourth year, I suggested a new promotion. NASA said no to sending a QVC viewer into outer space, so I had to come up with something else as outrageously successful as the previous year's promotion, or even better. That's when I dreamed up my new idea—the QVC BluBlocker Go Anywhere Sweepstakes. As a grand prize we offered the Hummer—the same all-terrain vehicle used in the Gulf War. The Hummer, like the Viper, was an unusual vehicle. And it tied nicely into the "go anywhere" nature of the promotion.

We also introduced a very hip sunglass style which we called our "Go Anywhere" Lights. It was a very lightweight contemporary style, but I sensed it would not be as strong a seller as the Viper was the year before. The Hummer was the ultimate four-wheel-drive vehicle and fit the concept of the "go anywhere" theme of our promotion. Kathy Levine, one of the top QVC show hosts, didn't know what a Hummer was. "My dad used to see some babe with big breasts and would call them 'hummers,' but I'm not familiar with the car," said Kathy.

In addition, we offered two United Airlines tickets to anywhere in the world United flew and a few other similar go-anywhere prizes along with thousands of other minor gifts.

Steve Bryant, one of the top QVC show hosts, introduced the promotion with a well-planned pitch just like Bob Bowersox had done the year before. Steve introduced the Hummer and described its many unique features such as its ability to climb a 14-inch curb and easily drive in two feet of water. We showed the Hummer backstage and I was sitting in the vehicle with Steve as he was giving his presentation. The vehicle was huge and they could hardly get it into the studio. By this time in my career, I had sold over 1.2 million pairs of sunglasses on QVC—a tremendous amount of product from a single company with a single product concept. And the Hummer promotion was off to a good start.

WHEN YOU SAID "HUMMERS", I
THOUGHT YOU MEANT... PST...PST...

Kathy had a different image of what a Hummer was.

Sales of the Lights were not as great as the previous year's sales of the Viper model. I figured that would be the case. The QVC viewer is a little more conservative than the mass market. But during the promotion, we also introduced a new model called the StarShield—a very hot-selling item that more than made up for the slower sales of the Go Anywhere Lights model. The StarShield was a wraparound pair that you wore over prescription glasses—perfect for the QVC audience.

But the QVC staff saw that the Lights weren't pulling as much as the Viper and, ignoring the huge success of the StarShield, elected to cut down our airtime considerably. I pleaded with them, pointing out that our total sales were on a par with the previous year, but to no avail. They were focused on the sale of the Lights and ignored the overall success of the promotion.

Ironically the total sales were practically the same as in the previous year despite the fewer shows with the Lights, as the StarShield combined with the Lights equaled the sales of the previous year's Viper. And our entire product line moved evenly and smoothly and in substantial volume.

Winner Confused About Car

The winner of the Hummer was called and congratulated, but he was confused. He had bought his pair of sunglasses not because he expected to be entered into the sweepstakes but because he needed a pair of sunglasses. He didn't want the publicity that the winning of the Hummer would require according

This BluBlocker commercial that was played nationally to promote BluBlocker sunglasses at retail was also played quite often on QVC. This scene, featuring the country duo of Darryl and Don, was filmed live.

to the rules. He didn't even want the vehicle and, like Kathy Levine, didn't even know what a Hummer was. We ended up having to give him a cash payout in lieu of the vehicle and I later sold the vehicle to a car dealer in Pennsylvania.

Our sales for the fourth year were quite strong. Our product line had expanded and the styles that were hugely successful on QVC were eventually sold at retail. QVC proved to be not only a good sales vehicle for us, but a good test vehicle as well. And of course QVC also had the advantage of offering a nationally recognized brand name along with many of our new styles before they were available at any retail store. We also kept our retail distribution rather limited to make sure that QVC indeed had a good strong sunglass franchise. And finally, we supported QVC with what became some of their most successful promotions and we paid dearly for the privilege. After all, we had to pay for all the prizes, risk supplying the inventory and then pay for all the sweepstakes expenses.

QVC was once again fun. We now had a solid two-year history of successful promotions and we were ready for our next big promotion and our fifth big year. We were stoked and eager to suggest a major promotion in plenty of time for 1996.

Chapter 12 | A Star Is Born and Then Quickly Fades

In 1995, nearing my fourth-year QVC anniversary, I was given the opportunity to suggest my next big promotion—a sweepstakes without a car as a prize and unlike any other done before in the history of QVC promotions—one that had Hollywood written all over it. In fact, it was unlike any other promotion in history that I'm aware of, and only QVC could have pulled this one off. Let me explain.

QVC was growing quite rapidly and it was becoming difficult to get airtime. Rather than fight for the airtime, I simply pushed for the hours during the peak sunglass selling season and then skipped entirely the off-season period from August through September. In October, people buy sunglasses for the holiday season and this was a good time to start up again. Finally, in January and February, I stayed away and prepared for the next big promotion called "Reach for Your Star."

I was told that QVC was very interested in tying into Hollywood movies and in particular famous movie stars. They were also interested in lots of publicity as it was this publicity that gave the company recognition and caused people to tune in to the show and eventually become customers.

Something Really Different Wanted

I was also told that to do another car promotion was not that exciting to QVC. They wanted something really different. They wanted to do something that would really reach out and capture customers who would never think of watching QVC.

This was a tall order. I almost felt that I was being discouraged from even doing a sweepstakes because of all the logistics that had to be organized now by many of the QVC staff. So I decided to come up with a promotion that fitted each and every one of the parameters that I felt QVC would agree to accept.

There were no cars to give away, no round-the-world trips to award—just the opportunity to pick your favorite star and spend an evening at dinner with him or her. Dinner with what star? With any star—from sports to TV to movies, even to business—whoever you chose if you won the grand prize. The second prize was dinner with the QVC host of your choice and the third prize was a bit part in a major motion picture or a national TV show.

Imagine having dinner with your absolutely favorite star: Michael Jordan, Madonna or even Harrison Ford. You could pick Microsoft's Bill Gates or Jay Leno, or news broadcaster Tom Brokaw or even a famous country star like Garth Brooks. Whichever star you wanted would be your prize.

Having Dinner with Madonna

Now you might wonder how I was going to pull this off. To some, flying on the space shuttle might be an easier prize to procure than having dinner with Madonna. But I had a plan that would be unique to QVC and would be unlike any other promotion ever done.

To understand the promotion, you first have to understand the way QVC works. A host presents a product on the air and if it is a product that has been presented before, the host will often ask viewers to call the station and talk on the air and describe their experience with the product.

Because the QVC show is done live, the callers are first screened to determine if they might have a tendency to blurt out obscenities. After all, this is live television. In short, every caller has to pass through a person who screens the callers before they go on the air.

Even with this process, it is common to have somebody slip through the cracks and say some pretty awful stuff right on the air, but this rarely happens. And because it is live, QVC cannot censor what is being said once the caller is on the air.

We Couldn't Just Pick a Star

If, as a sponsor of a promotion, we selected a specific star such as Harrison Ford to be the person with whom the grand prize winner would have dinner, we would have two problems. First, the mass audience may not feel that Harrison Ford is the person they would most like to have dinner with. And finally, the grand prize winner might not want to have dinner with Harrison Ford. We would have to spend a small fortune to get the services of Harrison Ford and he might not even appeal to the mass audience as their top pick. In fact, even the country's most popular star would not appeal to everybody. No problem. I solved this dilemma with a very simple concept.

By simply having the caller select the star of his or her choice on the air, the person is selecting exactly who he or she wants. The other viewers watching the show can fantasize over who they would choose if they won the sweepstakes. In short, by having a "fill in the blank" name for a star and having the callers blurt out the name of who they would select opens the entire promotion up to every star and appeals to QVC's entire audience.

Now you may have a few questions. "OK, Sugarman, what if the star doesn't want to participate in this scheme? What if the star is selected and doesn't want to have dinner with the winner—refuses to even consider it unless they would be paid some outrageous sum?"

What Star Would Refuse?

Simple. We allocate $100,000 for the winning star. If, for example, Harrison Ford was selected, we would call his agent and offer Ford $50,000 as his share to simply have dinner with our winner plus $50,000 to give to the charity of his choice. What star would want to refuse helping a charity and getting the positive publicity of being picked out of all the other stars in the universe? Not too many.

But what if one really decided not to participate? What if Madonna was picked and she didn't want any part of it? The backup plan was that the winner would then have the wonderful opportunity of picking the charity of his or her choice and would pocket the $50,000 that was earmarked for the star. This would all be explained in the sweepstakes rules and on TV. Everybody wins in this promotion.

I checked this out with QVC's legal counsel and she approved it after careful scrutiny. I checked this out with my sweepstakes attorney, Fran Krasnow, and she approved it as well.

For the publicity department at QVC this was a dream promotion. First, the nature of the promotion could generate many stories as people speculated whether or not the star selected would even participate and who the star might be. Then the QVC audience would be quite curious as to who would win and who that winner would choose. And finally there was the follow-up publicity. QVC could sell the rights to a news magazine to cover the private dinner and subsequently interview the winner.

The Follow-up Would Be Big

Then there would be the follow-up stories in newspapers and magazines. And if the star refused, there would be a big story about that and the effort expended to convince the star. Or there might be a story about the disappointment of the winners or the joy when the winners received a prize anyway. And then there was the charity that would be the recipient of the contribution. That story might create some good publicity as well.

I had put together one of the most perfectly suited promotions I could ever come up with for QVC. It was approved legally and passed all criteria for audience appeal. I had submitted it early enough so that it had ample time to go through all the channels that a promotion had to go through to be approved. And I had a track record with two of the most successful promotions in the history of QVC.

In the meantime, I named a new sunglass style "Star" to tie in with the name of the sweepstakes, which I called "Reach for Your Star." You could reach for your Star BluBlocker sunglasses or reach for your favorite movie, TV, recording artist or business star. You had the choice.

I had submitted the proposal in mid-1995. By the time it went through all the channels it was already late January of 1996, and to implement the program, I needed approval quickly. Finally, in early February word came down that the committee chose not to have the "Reach for Your Star" sweepstakes as they were now sponsoring a NASCAR racing car and were going to run a sweepstakes for that. Consequently they would not have the resources to conduct another sweepstakes.

Protecting Their Investment

This was devastating news. Not only was the promotion important for our continued success, but it would have done a lot better and been a more appealing promotion to QVC's primary audience than a NASCAR promotion, even though NASCAR was very popular with QVC viewers. But there was an important difference between my sweepstakes and QVC's NASCAR promotion. QVC had invested millions of dollars to sponsor their race car. They had a major commitment and they needed to support it with all their resources.

With BluBlocker there was no major commitment. We had already had a few successful promotions and it was time to try something new and different. I have no idea how well or how poorly the NASCAR promotion went. I suspect not as well as our promotion could have done. But without our planned "Star" promotion, we were left without an exciting program for the year. We were not in a position to launch a new promotion as it was already February and too late to do anything major for our March product introduction of summer styles. Sales suffered as a consequence and our fifth year started out far below our previous years on QVC. To top it off, there was another change in QVC buyers and it was like starting over again as the new buyer, Betty Amabile, had to get acquainted with our line and our support personnel.

But during the year a few nice things started to happen. My older daughter, April, decided that she wanted to pursue an acting career. She had done a really good job with me in our offices and I suggested that if she was going into acting, she should become familiar with the entire line of BluBlocker sunglasses and appear on QVC with me or in place of me. She did and the audience loved her. I have never received fan mail for my appearances on QVC but she has already received several letters commenting on what a good presentation she made. I then suggested that she appear on the air in England and Canada where our sunglasses are also sold. She agreed and has been appearing on QVC in the USA, on HSN in Canada, and on QVC in England and more recently in Germany.

This would be a good time to review what is happening to the home shopping revolution throughout the world from my perspective and my experiences. On April 9, 1997, I achieved one of my dreams. I appeared on the QVC home shopping show in Dusseldorf, Germany, and speaking in German, I sold out all my inventory of BluBlocker sunglasses.

During my 20s I was in military intelligence with the U.S. Army and stationed at Fort Holabird, Maryland—a training school for spies. It was 1962 and the East Germans had erected the Berlin Wall. American troops were needed in Germany and the military also needed intelligence personnel. I was chosen to go to Germany and the Army consequently sent me to a language school.

I apparently had a knack for languages as I learned fluent German in six months while training at two different schools—one in Oberammergau in southern Germany and one in Wiesbaden near Frankfurt. Between the intensity of the courses and a few German girlfriends, I learned to speak German well enough that you couldn't tell I was an American. I spoke with hardly any accent and my vocabulary was quite extensive.

Selling on German TV

For the 35 years since my German experience, I had always wanted to use my German in business but never had much of an opportunity. Occasionally I'd meet a German businessman, but most German businessmen speak fluent English and would rather practice their English language skills on me. Nevertheless, I kept in touch with many of my acquaintances in Germany, and I practiced using German whenever I could so I wouldn't lose my speaking ability.

My most important goal, however, was to someday use the skills the Army taught me and sell a product on German television. I had some recognition in Germany as a result of my

BluBlocker infomercial which appeared throughout the country. The voice had been dubbed by the group that was syndicating the show, so it wasn't really me. A live appearance on a German TV station—ahh, that was what I wanted to achieve. Live and in person and selling products in German to Germans. And that was what I achieved on April 9, 1997.

Here I am without my beard in August 1997 appearing with one of the German show hosts on QVC in Germany. It was lots of fun and the fulfillment of one of my dreams.

My experience with selling on TV in other countries actually goes back much further. I was invited about three years earlier to appear on the new QVC home shopping station in London, England. I was in Doug Briggs' office and we were talking about various promotions around the time that Barry Diller was at the helm. He mentioned to me that as a result of Diller's advice, QVC was now operating in England and if I wanted to help QVC, he would appreciate it if I could fly to London and sell my sunglasses on British television.

"You won't sell much and the money you make may not

even cover your hotel bill, but it would really help me to get some American companies over there presenting their products," Doug urged.

"Hey, why not," I thought. QVC had been very good to me and I knew they would appreciate this support. I then flew to London, stayed at a small hotel near the Chelsea Bridge where QVC was located and appeared on British television. Doug was right. Sales didn't even cover my hotel bill, but that was OK. It was the help I was providing that was the important thing.

In the next years, I continued to appear on QVC's London station, and after that first year I noticed that the appearances were starting to turn profitable. First, I covered all my expenses and then I started to actually make a profit on my sales. England soon became quite profitable and a good venue for our products. I sent my daughter April to London and she did well on the air there too.

Meanwhile Canada was another venue that was presented to me. We had been selling our BluBlocker sunglasses from our infomercial in Canada. Our representative there was Richard Stacey, who owned a company that bought our product and then shipped it in response to our commercial. He also had good relations with the new Canadian Home Shopping Network (CHSN).

He wondered if I could appear on CHSN and sell my sunglasses as I was doing on QVC. Since QVC did not have an affiliate in Canada, I was free to do so. But I was really surprised with what I encountered.

First, sales were very poor. When I got off the air and found out I had sold only 12 pairs of one of my styles, I was shocked. But the host was excited. "That's terrific," she said. "We've got a hit."

A Very Small Audience

It was hardly worth the effort to sell the sunglasses on Canadian television as the audience was so small. But there was one other major factor that you might find hard to believe. The Canadian government did not allow full TV motion. In short, all CHSN could do is show slides of the product and of the hosts presenting the products.

If you think that is stupid, you should have seen the results. You would be filmed with a TV camera that would sequence a shot to create a slide every six or seven seconds, so you saw freeze-frames of yourself with your mouth wide open or making some gesture that looked ridiculous in freeze action.

The idea behind this limitation was rather bizarre. If the Canadian government allowed full motion, the audience might be so mesmerized by the shopping club broadcast that they would buy more than they needed, and therefore full motion was taking unfair advantage of the viewer. Really. That was the reason for the limitation.

But something interesting resulted from this activity. The hosts were among the most vocally animated I had ever heard. They had to be in order to hold the attention of viewers who were just seeing slides. So the slide approach was creating a group of highly polished presenters who could hold an audience's attention even with the restriction of slides.

Soon CHSN switched from sequenced shots to posed slides so the mouths of the presenters and guests didn't look so ridiculous when they were caught wide open during a freeze-frame. This made very little difference to sales because it was still boring but it was an improvement.

Full Motion Finally Allowed

Then finally, in 1995, the Canadian government passed a law which permitted full-motion TV and sales did much better. Did citizens all over Canada become mesmerized and buy with wild abandon products they didn't need? Actually sales did increase and the presenters were among the best in the business—entertaining and very knowledgeable about the selling process and finally able to really use their finely tuned skills. Sales continued to increase year after year and it is my guess that unless there is another home shopping club in Canada to compete with them, CHSN will continue to grow and flourish.

Despite the increase in sales, it still was very marginal running BluBlocker sunglasses on Canadian television, but again, we were doing it as a favor for our Canadian partner, Richard Stacey, and it didn't matter as long as he was happy.

Stacey also ran our infomercials after midnight. Why after midnight? It was another strange quirk of the Canadian government. They didn't allow any infomercial to be broadcast before midnight. You see, gullibility ended around midnight and the government needed to protect the poor souls who saw an infomercial at 11:30 PM and might feel compelled to buy a product they didn't want to buy, but if you were up after midnight, then it was your tough luck. You should be in bed and not watching TV anyway. Sorry, I'm getting carried away, but the rule was just as silly and ridiculous as the slide shows they required on CHSN. As far as I know, these laws are still in effect.

German home shopping will take a while to develop too. First a customer base must be built and then the network must expand to reach the potential 80 million German homes. When that happens, watch out. Germany can be one of the most successful of the home shopping venues. In the meantime, QVC's potential audience in Germany currently is only 3 million. But it will grow.

They are opening up a home shopping show in Japan and Australia. But these shows are very small in terms of their reach and their audience due to government restrictions and other local factors.

The implications for developing a successful infomercial and consequently a brand name extend potentially throughout the world.

Chapter 14 | My Other QVC Products

...SO EACH TIME YOU FILL YOUR GAS TANK, YOU JUST DROP IN ONE OF THESE PILLS...

At first they laughed at us.

During my second year with BluBlockers on QVC, I was searching for a way to expand my success. I was also looking for another product to present on QVC in the event BluBlockers stopped selling and I needed another product to stay on the air.

"The Pill" Fuel Conditioner

I presented an automotive product—a fuel additive in the form of a pill that you put in your gas tank whenever you filled up. The product—called simply "The Pill"—gives better gas mileage, cleans out the engine and improves performance. In fact, it was one of those miracle products that worked so well, most people could not believe it. Not even the buyers at QVC.

When I presented the product at QVC, they laughed at me. "*Me* put that pill in *my* car? You've got to be kidding," said Paul Jones, formerly the head of QVC's Quality Assurance Department. He made that statement as I was sitting in a meeting with John LaFontaine, a representative of the company that developed the product, Doug Briggs (then the VP of marketing at QVC), Karen Fonner, the automotive buyer, and of course, Paul Jones.

During the meeting, John LaFontaine, who seemed to have an answer for all their objections, made them realize that The Pill was indeed a special product and they should at least give it a personal test in their own vehicles. And that was all it took. About 50 boxes, or 500 treatments, were passed out to anybody at QVC willing to try The Pill in their car. Many of those who tried it noticed an increase in power, better gas mileage and the absence of many of the problems they had been having with their cars before they started using The Pill. After the test, Karen Fonner agreed to put the product on the air and ordered 5,000 boxes.

It was a $19.95 item that we priced at an introductory value of $17.52 and it sold out very quickly. In fact, it was a big success—so big that it became a steady item on the network with an incredibly low 3% return rate. A return rate is simply the percentage of products that are returned by customers for a refund, for any number of reasons. In short, when The Pill was sold, it stayed sold and QVC was very pleased. Typically QVC gets anywhere from 15 to 30% returns on many of its products.

Interesting Pitch for The Pill

The way I pitched The Pill on QVC was also interesting. Instead of promoting it as an automotive product, I pitched it as the perfect car care product for women. From some of the calls I got while I was on the air and in some informal field testing I did, I found that the biggest fear women had about their cars was not what you'd think. It wasn't getting stuck on a lonely highway or running out of gas in a bad neighborhood, but rather pulling into a car repair place and being overcharged for service.

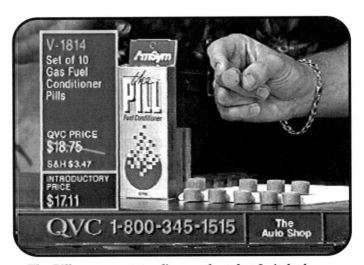

The Pill was an outstanding product that I pitched on QVC primarily to women. But the male viewers were attracted to the product as well.

The Pill was perfect for women. Regular use of this product would prevent many of the service visits women would have to make to get their cars repaired. It would eliminate ping, give their cars more power and each time they pulled into a service station, they could easily plop a pill into their tank. It was simple, it solved a lot of their concerns and since QVC's audience was mostly women, my approach to selling it would have broad appeal. My strategy was that by pitching this to women I could also count on the men to realize that this was a good product for them too.

The strategy worked. We got many calls from women who told us about being overcharged by various car repair shops. Some women experienced dramatic increases in mileage. One even told a tale of having to go to two different service stations to get her car repaired and could not resolve her problem until she used The Pill.

After these on-air phone calls, sales would jump. We also noticed that almost a third of the orders were for more than one box. The Pill was also selling even when I wasn't on the air. In short, people were reordering The Pill when they ran out, or on an average of every two months.

The Pill Introduced in Europe

I also introduced The Pill at QVC in London and sales did quite well there too. My approach in England was to point out two things about English drivers that I discovered from my visits there. The first was that, in general, the English loved their cars and took very good care of them, more so than most Americans. The second thing I discovered was that the English were quite skeptical—again, much more than Americans. I then proceeded to ask the audience to suspend their skepticism just long enough to test The Pill in their petrol tanks. And guess what? Many did and we had excellent sales. Again, I positioned the product to fit the nature of my audience. In the U.S. my audience was primarily female, and in England my audience was primarily skeptical—both male and female.

Then in 1996, after successfully running this product for two and a half years, I was approached by the new automotive buyer, Rich Yoegel, who wanted to increase sales of The Pill. By this time, the product had been selling well in England and was selling well on QVC in the U.S. Rich suggested that we try a continuity program for The Pill in which we would offer a one-year program. You could order The Pill and QVC would ship it to you bimonthly and bill the shipment to your credit card. This way, there would be no need to reorder each time you ran out. We also gave a special gift of a car plug-in flashlight to customers who enrolled in the continuity program and ordered one year's supply.

The results were amazing. Over one-third of all purchasers chose the continuity program. It was a huge success. Often you are lucky to get a 10% continuity from the sale of vitamins, but we had reached 35% of total sales. Now, along with the low return rate and the continuity program, we had one of those ideal products for QVC—something I felt could last on the air for a long time. But I was in store for a big surprise.

Then Came the Shock

Exactly three weeks later, Rich Yoegel called me on the phone to tell me the news. "We're taking The Pill off the air."

I couldn't believe it. "Am I hearing this right?" I asked him.

"I know," he said. "This wasn't my choice and I don't even know why. It's not for me to even question." And so I accepted Rich's decision even though The Pill was a successful continuity product on QVC and was still selling in England.

If there's a very important point about this new medium, it is simply this: A success on QVC is not simply a matter of appearing on the air, selling lots of product and shipping it out. Few realize the risks that even a successful vendor has on any one of the home shopping networks. You could end up with a heavy inventory problem if you're cut off suddenly as I was. You could wear the wrong suit and upset one of the executives with some power. They could offer your product at too high a price and kill the sales potential forever on the station. (They rarely drop prices on QVC.) They could buy too much product and then return it all. They could order the wrong product mix, and you end up holding the bag for it. I've experienced all of these problems and if we were not a substantial company able to handle the financial risks associated with these issues, we would not have lasted as long as we did. But with all the headaches, the opportunities far outweigh the risks.

"Laser Blades" Wiper Blades

An inventor came to me and presented a set of windshield wipers that I personally tried and loved. I named them "Laser

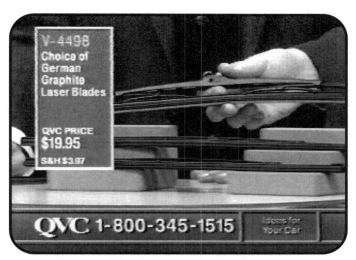

The Laser Blades were an excellent product and sold
very well on QVC. But I was being overexposed and was
replaced by the inventor of the product.

Blades." (They were cut with a laser instead of the traditional
method of manufacture and therefore the blades were extremely
straight.) I sent them to the QVC automotive buyer, Karen Fonner,
and suggested that I give the product a try on the air, which she
arranged for me to do. It too was a huge success. Once more the
response choked the QVC lines and it sold out the very first day.

Despite my success with all these products, QVC management started to feel that I was being overexposed. They thought
I would cause confusion with the viewers who saw me for one
hour with BluBlockers and the next with another product. They
asked that I reduce the number of products I represented on the
air. "Find somebody else who can go on instead of you for the
Laser Blades."

I wasn't too pleased with my involvement with the wiper
blades anyway. I had made a mistake and created a three-way
partnership with the inventor in which he and an outside
investor each owned a third. I not only represented the product
on the air but handled all warehousing, shipping and financing
for the shipments from the Far East. It wasn't what I had envi-
sioned for my involvement with the product, and when the profits were divided into thirds, it didn't seem worth it. I suggested
that the inventor form his own company and sell directly to QVC

and appear as a guest presenter himself as I had been doing. He did and the product ran just a year before it was taken off the air.

"Card Wear" Greeting Cards

I also had a big failure on QVC. I had heard that QVC was looking for a greeting card line to offer on-air. But you can get greeting cards at any store and I thought that if they wanted to offer something really different, why not offer a greeting card with a matching silk-screened T-shirt. In short, the giver would give both the card and the T-shirt as a gift—both with the same image.

I presented the idea to Doug Briggs and he thought it was a good one. He selected one of his best merchandise people at the time, Nancy O'Hara, to oversee the project and we developed a line of three love-themed T-shirts and matching greeting cards. The artist, Dick Hafer (who drew the cartoons for this book), did a very good design job and the T-shirts were gift-packaged in a beautiful metallic container. It was a very nice presentation just in time for Valentine's Day.

When it went on the air, I was a little surprised to see the price at $22. I had expected it to be sold for $19.95 as this price point made it more of an impulse item. Mary Beth Roe did a very good job of presenting it, but unfortunately it didn't sell. It was tried again with Jeff Hewson—one of QVC's superstars at the time—and he really gave it a big push—but again it didn't sell. It was taken off the air and relegated to the trash heap of great ideas that for some reason never executed well on TV. I really don't think it was the price point either. That's how bad it was. But at least I was given a chance to try out my concept even though it failed.

"Car Care for Women"

I also made another suggestion to QVC. "Why not have an hour entitled 'Car Care for Women'?" This was the same concept I used to sell The Pill successfully. Why wouldn't it work for an entire hour? I would present The Pill and the producers could slate other automotive products that would appeal primarily to women.

I had to sell the suggestion to the staff and I used all my persuasive ability to do so. I really believed in the idea. To their credit, QVC gave it a try. The show was successful but not successful enough to justify segregating all their future shows into

On the air with The Pill and QVC host Dan Hughes.
Note the counter in the lower right-hand portion of
the screen. This device created a sense of urgency to
respond to an offer, which I explain further on page 160.

two automotive categories—one for men and one for women.
But I respected their willingness to at least test the idea.

"BluBlocker" Sunscreen

One of the product extensions we developed for the
BluBlocker brand name was BluBlocker sunscreen. The brand
extension made sense. We protected people's eyes from the dangerous rays of the sun, why not protect their skin as well?

Formulated with some of the finest and most expensive ingre-
dients, this 24-hour waterproof and moisturizing sunscreen was
something I could really be proud of. It was developed by a pharmaceutical company who we licensed. One of the arrangements we
had with them was the right to present the product on QVC.

George Hamilton already had a sunscreen on QVC but
because of the strong BluBlocker brand identification we had
with them, we were given the chance to present the product on
the air. It didn't sell too well. It may have been the price point (it
sold for $19.95, which was expensive for a sunscreen) or it could
have been the time of year (it was late in the summer). Whatever
the reason, it just didn't fly off the shelves.

Often brand extensions are very difficult to make work. When

One of the side benefits of appearing on QVC was this appearance on the Joan Rivers show, **Can We Shop.** *In this scene, I'm explaining the advantages of my new BluBlocker sunscreen, which we were packaging with a pair of BluBlocker sunglasses. The complete package sold well on her show.*

Xerox came out with word processing typewriters in the late '70s, they had a hard time convincing people that their typewriters were as good as their copiers. There are hundreds of examples of brand extensions that haven't worked. I thought ours just might. It didn't.

Ironically, when I took the product on the Joan Rivers show, *Can We Shop,* and added a pair of sunglasses to the sunscreen package, the product sold well.

Later the pharmaceutical company, with little experience at retail, didn't do too well either and the product died.

Many companies try hard to get their products on QVC or another home shopping club. It's obviously a lot easier if you are already on QVC and have a track record. Later, in Chapter 17, I will give you six ways to get your product on QVC if you don't have the advantage of already being one of their vendors.

I really enjoy working in the exciting environment of QVC in the trenches with the buyers and the show hosts. It's fun, rewarding and you have some very interesting moments as you'll soon discover in the next chapter.

Chapter 15 | QVC Hosts, Producers, Buyers and Insights

The topic of this chapter is why BluBlockers have lasted so long as a successful product on QVC—something that might provide some good insights for you. It is also a little about the people both behind the scene and in front of the cameras at this unique selling machine.

Typically a hot product on QVC will be hot in the beginning, stay hot for a while, fade and then disappear. This could happen within a few months, but it usually happens within a year. BluBlocker sunglasses have managed to stay at a fairly high and consistent sales rate since their introduction over six years ago. You've already read how this was accomplished through new styles, exciting promotions and the effort to reinvent the line year after year.

It also comes from the limited distribution of many of the styles at retail. In short, QVC has a franchise. Of the millions of people in the U.S. who own and want to buy more BluBlockers, the only place to purchase a really unique style would be on QVC.

How Some People Buy

When I was in Hawaii taking my first golf lesson last year (I've learned that you can master copywriting a lot quicker than you can master golf), the golf teacher was an avid BluBlocker fan. "I love the pair and it is the only pair I can wear because of my sensitive eyes. But the only place I buy them is on QVC. I check their program schedule, find out when you're going to be on and then I tune in, select the style I want and place an order."

Another reason for the BluBlocker longevity is something that I didn't expect. People are now collecting them. From the many calls I get, people now own several pairs—one to keep in their car, one at home and one for their other car. It is not surprising to find customers who own several pairs just to match their outfits or their mood of the day. And finally, many give them as gifts. They are inexpensive and packaged very nicely so they make good gifts for any occasion. And I do push all of the reasons to buy BluBlockers when I'm up there presenting the product.

When I present the BluBlocker sunglasses on QVC, I do so passionately because I really believe in them. I have studied the optical science supporting their use and the protection they provide, I have researched the benefits—both the visual and health—and I speak with some authority as a result of this knowledge. It is this authority combined with credibility and passion that comes through during my TV appearances. You can't fool the marketplace. They instinctively know if you are genuine and they respond accordingly.

Live Phone Calls on the Air

When the phone calls are taken live while I'm on the air, I never know what I'm going to hear. I always have to be prepared. And even the way I handle calls becomes part of how I build that credibility. For example, let us say I'm on the air and Julie, a QVC and BluBlocker customer, calls in and says, "I love your sunglasses but they broke the other day after I sat on them." My immediate reaction is to take this negative and turn it around into a positive. I would usually say the following:

"This is a great call. You know why? Because given the proper circumstances, anything will break. But it's what we do with a customer who breaks a pair that really makes us stand out. Julie, simply send your pair to our customer service department and for a small postage and handling charge, our policy is to replace your pair with a brand-new one at no further charge to you even if it is your fault. This is for the life of that pair of BluBlockers. And we replace it within 48 hours after we receive it at our service center. Thank you, Julie, for helping me point that out."

I sometimes get calls asking me questions about eye diseases from people who think that I'm an eye doctor. I clearly state that I'm not a medical doctor or an eye-care professional, but often I can recognize symptoms of eye diseases and explain the role BluBlocker sunglasses can play in helping that person.

I've been on the air enough over six years that I can often anticipate questions and work very closely with the hosts.

Unlike some products that are more category specific such as cooking, electronics or automotive, BluBlockers can be presented by practically any host—male or female. A cooking product is best presented by one of the hosts who is an expert on cooking. Bob Bowersox is a great cook and a regular hour show on QVC is named "In the Kitchen with Bob." In fact, Bob wrote a book, *In the Kitchen with Bob*, and sold 150,000 copies on QVC in one day. Because my product is both scientific, style-oriented and general in nature, I've had the fun and enjoyment of working with practically every one of the hosts over this six-year period.

The Experiences I Remember Most

During this time, I've had some funny and sometimes frightening experiences. Two incidents come to mind.

I was doing a BluBlocker show with Kathy Levine, one of the top show hosts on QVC since its inception. We were standing doing a presentation of BluBlocker sunglasses and on stage was a very attractive model who was wearing the various sunglass styles as we would present them. I was just talking about how light BluBlocker sunglasses were and how the light weight meant that you could wear them all day long without even knowing that they were on your face. I even related a story about Kathy and the time she was looking all over her house for her pair of BluBlockers and couldn't find them until she looked in the mirror and realized she was wearing them. "That's *really* light for you," remarked Kathy.

Then one of the backstage assistants who are supposed to hand you the product to present (usually off-camera) hands a pair of our extremely lightweight sunglasses to the model, who was sitting on a wooden chair. At the moment the sunglasses were handed to her, the chair collapsed sending the model sprawling onto the floor and throwing Kathy into a laughing fit that she couldn't control. The weight of the lightest pair of sunglasses we sold caused the model to collapse in her chair. It really was a funny scene. Fortunately, the model was not hurt and the shot viewers were seeing at the time was a close-up of the sunglasses and not of the scene that was taking place in the studio.

I Couldn't Laugh

Meanwhile the producer, seeing all this commotion, continues to show a tight shot of the sunglasses while I carry on the conversation. Remember, Kathy is in no condition to continue. She is now doubled-up laughing and cannot stop.

I calmly carried on, "That loud bang you just heard was a little problem we've just had here in the studio." There was a short pause, and seeing Kathy continuing to roll in laughter, I knew that I was the only one left who was capable of talking. So I continued to present the product, tell its features, talk some more and then finally the producer cut to a taped promotion. It seemed like the whole scene lasted for about three minutes.

By the time they cut to the promotional spot, Kathy was able to regain her composure and the model was able to stand up and get the chair replaced. Afterwards, the producer walked up to me and said, "Joe, that was amazing. You didn't crack so much as a smile. You just kept going as if nothing happened."

"Believe me, it wasn't that hard," I responded. "I was scared stiff when I realized that I was the only one left who could talk."

The second incident was actually very frightening. I like to stand up during my presentations. The producer arranges for a table in front of me and the product is placed waist high. I stand and refer to the products on the table during my explanations. The co-host then stands next to me and we talk about the various styles I'm presenting.

The Experience Was Not Very Pleasant

I like to stand. I've given hundreds of speeches and I never stand behind a podium because I like to stand right in front of the audience. I really feel it allows me to do a more effective job of communicating, selling or conveying my emotional message. The other option used by many of the other hosts is to sit on a couch or in a living-room setting, but that has never seemed comfortable to me and QVC has been very accommodating with my requests to stand behind a tall table.

One day my co-host was Donna Harfinest. Donna was one of those hosts I was on with several times prior to this time and we always had fun. After my first show in which we both appeared, I got a nice note from her telling me that she really enjoyed being on the air with me and wished me success in the future. She was always thoughtful and considerate in that way. On the day when I was appearing with her, she was about three or four months pregnant, but she said that standing for an hour would be no problem.

About twenty minutes into the show, Donna suddenly stopped talking. I sensed something was strange, but without missing a beat I picked up the conversation. The camera cut to a tight shot of the sunglasses and suddenly Donna walked off the set. As she neared the end of the stage, she knelt over and some of the support personnel rushed to help her. Something was horribly wrong.

I continued talking as if nothing had happened, but all the time I was really worried if Donna was going to be OK. I talked about the features of BluBlocker sunglasses with one eye on the camera and another on Donna. I kept talking and quite frankly I don't even remember what I said. Meanwhile, an emergency call was made to Dan Wheeler, the host who was going to follow Donna on the air. Dan was in the host lounge and it was up to him to run down and prepare to go on the air if Donna couldn't recover.

High Drama and No Viewer Knew

Dan then appeared in front of the stage at the producer's booth but just stood there while I kept talking alone on the show. For what seemed like several minutes I managed to find enough to say about BluBlocker sunglasses to make the show interesting. I filled the time until the producer managed to run a series of promotional spots—enough to restore order to the set and allow Donna sufficient time to catch her breath.

Thank goodness, Donna was OK. She was simply experiencing a slight fainting spell due to her pregnancy. Fortunately she was able to go back on the air and sat on a tall stool to finish the show. And Donna was able to finish not only my show but the following show as well.

As I stepped off the set, the first person I saw was Dan Wheeler. "Joe," he said, "I told the producer not to worry while you were up there alone. I knew you could handle it by yourself." Once again, I was thrown into a situation where the viewers had no idea of what was going on while high drama was taking place right on live television.

Those times were challenging and gave me the confidence that I could handle most any unexpected event. When you go on the air, the producer or assistant producer attaches a microphone to your tie or suit and puts what is called an IFB in one of your ears. The IFB (internal foldback) is the device by which the producer passes messages to the show host and the guest host. Through the IFB the show host gets instructions on what to mention on the air, when to move to the next product and when a phone caller is waiting on line. The guest host, the role I play, only hears the phone callers. We used to hear the phone calls only on loudspeakers but now it is either through the IFB or the loudspeakers—the choice being ours.

Callers Are Very Spontaneous

Phone calls are a way of life on QVC and a very valuable part of the marketing presentation. Because QVC is live (no 10-second delay or any delay for that matter), the callers are very spontaneous.

The callers often tip the scales for any undecided buyers watching the show and therefore they are a very vital part of the sales success of any show. In a print ad or an infomercial, it is the testimonial that adds tremendous credibility to the product. But pre-recorded testimonials in an infomercial or written testimonials in a print ad are not as effective as those real-time, on-the-air comments by a satisfied viewer.

And often viewers can say things that I can't say. For example, when I was selling my automotive fuel-conditioning pill, I would mention that a user can get "up to 8 miles more per gallon of gas."

But when a viewer calls and says that she got 18 miles more per gallon of gas, it is the customer stating the fact, not me. I then point out that we only promise 8 miles per gallon savings but there are circumstances where more than 8 miles per gallon can be achieved. The audience really pays more attention to the lady on the phone line than they do to my comments, and sales really start to fly.

I know for a fact that under certain circumstances a user could get 18 miles more per gallon. But since any claim that I make could be challenged if everybody didn't get the same mileage, the caller's testimonial makes me look conservative and gives the other viewers just the right encouragement to dig into their pockets and exchange their hard-earned money for my product.

Major Difference with Strong Testimonials

In fact, whenever I went on the air with The Pill, sales may have been good without any testimonials, but with a few great testimonials sales could be absolutely fantastic, especially for a product that seemed too good to be true (my biggest problem with The Pill). The same holds true with BluBlocker sunglasses. We always talk about our wonderful warranty, but when a customer calls and tells us how wonderful our warranty is and how quickly we replaced their broken pair, it adds a tremendous amount of credibility to the success of our presentation.

Part of my routine is to go up to the producer and remind him or her how important a testimonial is. The producer will then remind the host through the IFB to ask for testimonials at the beginning of the show. Or sometimes I will personally remind the audience if the producer or the host forgets.

One day I was sitting in my hotel room after appearing on QVC and I was watching one of my friends, Mark Schneider, selling one of his Cool Dana products. The product is a bandanna that you first put in a freezer and then when you take it out an hour later, its frozen gel keeps you cool when you wear it around your neck. It really works great and I wanted to order one. So I called QVC, gave them my QVC number and then the operator wanted to know if I wouldn't mind talking on the air. I actually got nervous and after thinking about it I said, "Thanks, but not this time."

Ironically when I got home and saw my wife the next day, she told me that she saw me on QVC and that she also saw this Cool Dana product and without knowing Mark was a friend ordered it too. "But it was the strangest thing," she said. "They wanted to put me on the air and I refused."

The Unsung Heroes of QVC

Among the unsung heroes at QVC are the producers who sit behind the desk and literally organize everything you see on the screen. If something goes wrong, it is these guys and gals who are blamed. Producers are also the ones who get the brunt of the criticism from guest hosts when the hosts step off the set and realize that their sales were not what they thought they should be.

*On the air with The Pill. I was given more time than
I deserved.*

I remember one day giving a presentation on The Pill when
I was given about 15 minutes instead of the 12 minutes I was
allotted. We had been doing very well with the sale of the product and often the producers have the option of extending the on-
air time a little. When my presentation ended, I stepped off the
stage and walked to the producer's desk to hand him my IFB and
microphone. As I handed them over I made the comment, "Boy,
that was more time than I deserved."

Both the producer and the assistant producer started to laugh
at what I had just said. I asked them what was so funny.

The producer looked at me and said, "You're the first person
who has ever said that to us. Typically it's more like, 'Why didn't
you give me more time?' What you said I've never heard before."

Producers are just as sensitive as anybody else, and often
these comments are taken personally by the producers, who start
to feel a little guilty for the products that don't sell. One producer
told me, "It really makes us feel bad to see a product do poorly
and when we hear it from a guest host, they often make us feel
like it was our fault."

What I Didn't Do

Producers really appreciated something that I didn't do.
I didn't hang around the producer's desk waiting to see the

returns come in like after an election. In the Green Room, QVC installed a computer monitor tied in to the mainframe that displays real-time results for all the products. Too often, guest hosts step off the set and go behind the producer's desk and insist on staying there to get the results, bothering both the assistant producer and the producer. The producers can't soothe a disappointed guest host and supply information while trying to run their next important show. But often the guest hosts don't know or appreciate this fact.

In the new QVC studio that opened in October 1997 a few miles from the original studio, the producers are now separated from the guest hosts so there are no longer the interruptions and problems producers used to encounter. It is one of the advantages of the newer and bigger studio. The producers are now left to do their job and not be responsible for soothing the egos of a few disgruntled guest hosts.

A Very Dedicated Group

I am writing this while I am still selling BluBlockers on QVC. And you might think that I will only say nice things about QVC and some of its people that I normally might not say if I were off the air and no longer had any ties with them. You know the typical story—"The Uncensored Truth About QVC" type garbage. This is not the case. What you are reading here is the truth. If there was somebody or something I didn't like, I wouldn't mention names but I would tell you. Conversely, if there was something that I particularly appreciated, I would mention that as well.

There is a large group of QVC people whom I particularly want to single out and you may even know them. These are the QVC hosts themselves. Not that they are unsung or not recognized by others. They are. But it is the dedication that they have to their craft that makes them so unique. As I mentioned before, I have worked with practically all of them.

First and foremost, they are professionals. They know how to relate to their audience and bring out the excitement in the products they are selling. Think about it. You're on TV for three straight hours. You have to keep your energy level up and your mind focused not only on your job but on the instructions that come pouring out of the IFB from the producers. You're often guiding guest hosts, taking phone calls, coordinating the product, and prior to all of this, you've got to study and educate yourself on the products you're presenting. You've got to be good. Sure, it might appear to be a glamorous occupation, but it's indeed a very difficult challenge and only the best make it.

But what sets the hosts apart from anybody else is not what they do but who they are. These are some of the most down-to-earth compassionate people you will ever want to meet. They are all, without exception, real people—the type of people you would want to come into your living room day after day. And therein lies the secret of their success on QVC.

The Pride They Take

By bringing together not a group of celebrities but a group of real people—people who have related so well to their audience—QVC has managed to build a loyalty that extends beyond anything that exists today with any retailer. Hosts conceivably could get standoffish and act like the celebrities they have become. But that is not their style. And it all comes through—hour after hour, day after day, year after year.

Two QVC models demonstrating BluBlocker sunglasses. QVC would traditionally supply models to demonstrate the different styles while the show host and I would describe them.

Dan Wheeler, a QVC show host, doing a backflip and handspring to demonstrate how BluBlocker sunglasses remain on your face. He almost broke his back doing it.

When it came to a point in our BluBlocker hour when I was trying to convince the audience of how BluBlocker sunglasses stayed on your head and did not come off, Dan Wheeler put on a pair and did a handspring flipping 360 degrees and landed on his feet. The pair remained on his face. Dan has always tried very hard to sell every product he offers. He takes great pride in his shows and their success.

I was fortunate enough in having Bob Bowersox and Steve Bryant introduce my two major sweepstakes. Each wrote his own script—something neither was paid to do. Steve is an accomplished magician, author and electronics guru and Bob is a top culinary expert in his own right.

I could write an entire book on Kathy Levine. But she has already done that herself. And it is a good book if you want to find out what it's like being a host on QVC. I've had the pleasure of working with her many times.

It is always a pleasure to be on the air with Judy Crowell. She unfortunately became quite a celebrity when the handsome show host she married, Jeff Hewson, decided to make a circus out of their relationship and subsequent separation. Judy took the high ground and, despite unfair and false public criticism

QVC show host Dan Wheeler with my daughter April Sugarman, selling the Go Anywhere Lights—a very lightweight BluBlocker style. April does about half of my shows on QVC and most of them in Europe. The hosts love to work with her.

generated by her estranged husband, never commented about the incident. Jeff Hewson eventually was fired from QVC and Judy remains today. She is one of my favorite people there.

There are other great hosts—many of whom I mention in my Acknowledgments at the front of this book. In fact, there are many more stories I can relate, but the above will give you a pretty good sampling.

Chapter 16 | Missing the Beat at QVC

In my sixth year at QVC I was now down to only one product—BluBlocker sunglasses. We had run for five consecutive years and now in 1997 we were into our sixth year. Sales were down the previous year because of the canceling of our "Reach for Your Star" promotion by QVC as I explained in Chapter 12 and we were on the station long enough that by now most of the regular QVC customers already had several pairs. And they were not losing them fast enough. Something new had to be presented or we would lose our long-standing franchise and be taken off the air. In short, I felt my presence on QVC needed an infusion.

I always realized that the day might come when I would no longer be presenting BluBlocker sunglasses. After all, I knew I was only as good as my last couple of appearances and maybe, because we had a long-standing track record, my last three appearances. If I strung three bad ones in a row, look out. It might be over rather quickly.

I met with my buyer, Betty Amabile, her boss, Keith Stewart, and his boss, Lance Graves, in January of 1997. We had to come up with a plan to bring life back into the BluBlocker franchise. Instead of presenting several new styles, I came up with what I felt was my last and only chance to hold on to what I had spent over five years in developing—namely, a loyal following.

Reinventing the Product Line

I suggested selling only polarized BluBlocker products. Prior to this, our polarized product sold for over $50. The lenses cost five times the standard lens and when all the other expenses were factored in, the retail price ended up in the $50 range.

The QVC customer appreciated the variety of options we offered and many serious sunglass buyers were happy with our wide selection and higher-priced models.

My new proposal offered the BluBlocker polarized sunglasses for $24.95. I was able to do this for two reasons: First, we were able to obtain the lenses at a much more attractive price now that the dollar was a lot stronger against the yen. Second, we had a large supply of polarized lenses in inventory and wanted to liquidate many of them at our cost and replace them with the lower-priced product.

I was presented with the opportunity of selling a BluBlocker metal-framed aviator-style sunglass for $19.95 on what is called a TSV or Today's Special Value. QVC would buy $1.2 million worth of my product (at retail) and would sell it making much less profit than usual. Viewers could buy the product at a very attractive price. I would then appear on the air several times during the day and pitch the product and the value.

In the meantime, I would prepare to offer several new styles using our polarized lens which would be manufactured exclusively for QVC. Since we didn't offer a polarized pair to our retail customers (only to our JS&A mail order customers), QVC would have a major advantage with this exclusive opportunity.

Surprise Discovery Leads to Revelation

The buying group loved my suggestion and I left with great hopes that we would have another successful year. We had a new lease on life, a new product extension (polarization) and we were ready to continue our string of successes with QVC.

The first step for me was to get the TSV into production immediately. When I got back to my office I discovered that we didn't have 60,000 pairs of polarized lenses in inventory as I had thought. We only had 40,000.

Sitting in our warehouse, however, was a collection of various tinted lenses that we had acquired when we bought out a lens company that had gone bankrupt in Japan. We would sell these lenses to other sunglass companies for use in their product as we could only use BluBlocker lenses in our frames.

Among this collection in inventory were approximately 60,000 pairs of gray lenses. When we submitted them to our testing lab previously, we discovered that they blocked a majority of the blue light and therefore could be called a blue-blocking type of lens. But they had one advantage over the BluBlocker lens. BluBlocker lenses blocked all of the blue light, but in the process you looked through a yellowish lens that enhanced some colors and distorted others. Many people liked the effect; some didn't. The gray lenses, on the other hand, did not distort the colors at all. Colors appeared true.

A few years earlier I had registered the name "BluBalance" and decided that if I didn't sell my inventory of different tinted lenses, I would at least be able to develop a new product using the gray lens and call it BluBalance—a product that provided a better light balance to give you true colors while still blocking most of the blue light.

I decided to launch the BluBalance lens out of necessity. I called Betty Amabile at QVC and requested that she accept in QVC's order 20,000 pairs with a gray lens to give customers a choice and I told her about our BluBalance concept. She liked the idea and we then went into full production.

The Shock of a Lawsuit

Then something totally unexpected happened. I was in England appearing on QVC in April when I got word that our company was being sued along with all of our retail outlet customers and several other companies for using the BluBlocker lens. It seems that an envious competitor filed a lawsuit against us claiming we were violating their patent.

All of our customers were sued: Wal-Mart, Walgreens, American Drug Company, The Sharper Image and the list went on. April was the critical start of the sunglass season and we were faced with the prospect of having all our customers return our product.

We considered the lawsuit a frivolous one and I am being kind with that description. Not only were we not infringing on their patent, but in the judgment of experts, the patent wasn't even valid.

I also discovered that the lawyers hired by the company suing us were hired on a contingency basis and that the company filing the lawsuit had nothing to lose simply by going after us. In fact, I found out later that litigation against us was an important part of their business strategy. We had millions of dollars in inventory at risk and the possibility loomed that we would not be able to sell it.

I can remember my thoughts at the time. I had spent over

ten years working very hard and building my company, and somebody with a flawed patent could sue me and overnight practically put me out of business.

Glitch Caused Loss of Sales

After we spoke to many of our retailers, they all agreed to support us and accept and sell our product. We also managed to get our retailers out of the lawsuit. But QVC was the only company that halted our sales right at the critical time we were to be on the air.

We also had most of the TSV product completed and ready for the show—60,000 pairs were ready for shipment. Fortunately we did get clearance from QVC and shipped the product, but we had already canceled all the new product we were producing for our new concept. This left us with nothing much more than the product we were supplying for the TSV and a small amount of product we had to support our new concept.

Incidentally, almost one year later on Friday, February 13, 1998 in United States District Court in Alexandria, Virginia, Judge Leonie M. Brinkema granted BluBlocker Corporation summary judgment in the patent lawsuit. We weren't violating the patent and we had won. But the victory was shallow. We had spent close to one million dollars defending ourselves, lost sales to QVC and finally were embarrassed in the eyes of many of our suppliers—a few of whom stopped doing business with us. The damage was extensive.

The Benchmark Was Surpassed

When you have a TSV, you go on the air at midnight (eastern time) and you first present your product. The last time I had a TSV product on QVC was a few years earlier when I sold a total of 135,000 sunglasses in one day. Not bad for a day's work.

What I had learned was that if you sell 15% of your total inventory at the midnight hour, you had a sellout by the end of the following day or 24-hour period. That's what happened when I sold 135,000 pairs. We sold over 15% in that hour and from then on it was all downhill.

When I went on the air for my new TSV, I was holding my breath. The ideal scenario would be for us to sell two pairs of sunglasses with the BluBlocker lens and one pair with the gray lens. In this way we would move all our inventory by the end of the day. But I wondered if we would sell many of the gray lenses. Why? Because our focus had always been on BluBlocker and total blue-blocking lenses. That's how we developed our reputation—not only with the public but with the QVC viewer as well.

So I really expected to have many of the gray lenses coming back to us and selling out of the BluBlocker lens product rather quickly.

I went on the air and did my presentation and the lines lit up. Phone calls were pouring in and I spoke to many people on the phone who were ordering various pairs. One lady mentioned she was ordering a pair of BluBlocker lenses for herself and a pair of gray lenses for her husband. A few calls came in for the BluBlocker product and some for the BluBalance product. I couldn't make any sense from the phone calls if we were selling enough gray lenses, but I would soon know when I stepped off the stage.

I'm Congratulated for Success

After I finished, I walked up to the producer's desk and he said, "Congratulations. You sold over 10,000 pairs, which means you'll definitely sell out by this time tomorrow."

We needed to sell 9,000 pairs to hit 15%—exactly what I needed to reach a sellout. But I had sold even more than that and I was thrilled—that is, until I walked into the Green Room and looked at the count on the QVC computer. We had sold 10,000 pairs all right, but for every pair of BluBlocker sunglasses, we had sold four pairs of the gray BluBalance sunglasses. Although we were ahead of projections, we would not sell out because our inventory was totally backwards.

Sure enough, when I went on again, I sold as high as five to one (gray lenses over BluBlocker lenses). This was a total shock, not because we wouldn't sell out but because of the high percentage of people who were buying our gray lens. This was not the franchise I thought we had. Then another realization crossed my mind.

We created a new display for our retailers and decided to load the display with some product that was outdated. One of the sunglasses was a style called ColorVision. It had an expensive lens that enhanced the three color receptors we have in our eyes—green, blue and red. When you put on a pair, it really brightened what you saw because it accentuated the primary colors—those basic colors by which we see.

The Shocking Surprise Discovery

The first to sell out on our displays were the ColorVision sunglasses. But we couldn't replenish them as we had discontinued producing them.

I then tied in our success at retail with the test we had just run at QVC and I realized that BluBlocker was more a brand name than the name of a specific type of lens. In short, both tests told me that we could dramatically expand our market by offering gray as well as other color lenses as long as they blocked most of the blue light. Our market could double and triple with this valuable piece of news.

QVC immediately ordered more gray lens sunglasses. As this is being written, plans are being prepared for our programs for 1998. QVC should be a good marketing vehicle for at least a few more years with this important breakthrough revelation that flew in the face of marketing wisdom. We thought we had a franchise with our BluBlocker lens when all along our franchise was more our brand name rather than any particular lens as long as the lens blocked most of the blue light.

But it was again a series of serendipitous events that changed the course of our company. Had it not been for the fact that we were out of our standard BluBlocker lens and had to substitute gray, had it not been for the amazing success of another color lens at retail, and had it not been for our test on QVC which made us realize that our brand name is what our real franchise is, we would not have been ready to expand our line and continue our strong position in home shopping and other retail venues.

One of the things I'm asked an awful lot is how to get a product onto QVC or into an infomercial without having to mortgage a home. It can be done and it is being done all the time. In the following chapter I am going to show you what to do to accomplish what many people want to do—namely, get on TV with the lowest possible investment.

Chapter 17 | Getting Your Product on TV

Let us say you have a great product, little experience in direct marketing, no company to run a direct marketing campaign let alone an infomercial and you want to exploit a product that you own. Great! This chapter will help you present your product to both QVC and many of the infomercial companies. And then in Chapter 18 I'll take you through the steps you'll need to go through once your product is accepted by the home shopping networks.

If you're already on the air or are a major infomercial producer, you might also find some pretty good tips in the next few chapters.

The home shopping venue and the infomercial each require their own margins to be successful. Later, in Chapter 26, I discuss the ways you can determine if your product is suitable for TV. I discuss the margins required for an infomercial and those for home shopping. The home shopping networks can afford to pay more for your product because they already have a customer base for their products. The people who have previously bought from a home shopping club constitute their customer base. These people have been culled from the mass market and have indicated a desire and preference to order their products via the home shopping format.

The Culling Process

In an infomercial, you do not have a customer base of people who have bought from you before and are therefore comfortable in responding to your offer. You are simply culling from the mass market those people who are willing to exchange their hard-earned money for your product.

The culling process is a lot more expensive than having a customer base ready and prepared to buy again. And so infomercial companies need a lot more margin than home shopping shows. Typically in a home shopping show, your margins can be as high as 50% of the retail price depending on the category. In some categories there is less margin. In general, however, there are better margins for you if you sell a product to the home shopping shows.

Once you get your product on a home shopping show you have a tremendous advantage if it sells. You have your foot in the door and you will find it easier to locate a buyer interested in your next product. Success breeds success and everybody is willing to take a chance if they see you've had other winners.

But this chapter is for somebody who does not yet have his or her foot in the door. In that case there are six ways you can get your product on QVC or HSN.

Method One. Be related to Doug Briggs, Jim Held or Barry Diller. These are the guys who run the bulk of home shopping in the U.S. and they represent about $3 billion in sales. Doug Briggs is the president of QVC, Jim Held is the president of HSN and Barry Diller owns HSN. On the other hand, I've known these guys to be very tough on relatives too so maybe this isn't such a good idea. But I will try to make one point here. In my experience, if Doug Briggs likes a product, the word will quickly filter through QVC. Your success is assured up to the time you present your product on QVC, and then it is the audience who decides if you're going to stay. The problem, of course, is to get to Doug because he's a busy guy. And besides, he's got an entire organization behind him to review products. I am assuming this also

There are shortcuts to getting your product on QVC.

holds true for Jim Held and Barry Diller. So forget you ever read this entire paragraph as it's not going to help you anyway. In fact, let me revise the list and let's say there are five realistic ways to get your product on QVC.

Method One Revised. Write or contact the Vendor Relations Department. Don't send your product, however. Just send a description of it, how it works, pictures, and maybe a brochure if you have one. List the suggested retail price and the price you'll be able to sell it to QVC for. If QVC is interested, they will funnel the presentation to the right buyer and the buyer will review it and report back to the Vendor Relations Department. They will then call you for a sample of your product. This will start an entire process which I will discuss later in Chapter 18. But if they request your product, there is a pretty good chance that you're moving in the right direction. I have included a question and answer sheet that covers the most commonly asked QVC questions in Appendix A.

Method Two. Contact a manufacturer's representative who already deals with QVC. A few independent reps know how to evaluate a product and determine if it is suitable for QVC. They also know what buyer to present it to. Reps are important assets of QVC as they provide a filter for many of the products that could clog the review pipeline there. But be careful. Make sure you check out the reputation of the rep you're dealing with before making any commitments. A rep will charge you from 5% to 12% depending on the product, the expected sales volume and the effort involved. If you fill out the Product Evaluation Form located on page 310 I will be happy to evaluate your product, send you a report and forward to you the name of one of the reps who could assist you. There is no charge for this service.

Method Three. Find out when the company will be in your area. QVC, for example, had what they called their "50 in 50 Tour." A product evaluation team would go to a particular state and rent a hall in which people from that state could put their products out on display for QVC buyers to select from. The buyers would select the products they felt would appeal to a national audience and then QVC would do a remote broadcast with a special show from that particular state a few months later. Although QVC no longer has the 50 in 50 Tour, they feature a

"Local Flavors Tour" displaying the most popular food products found throughout the U.S. Call the QVC Product Search toll-free number 888 NEW ITEM (888 639-4836) to learn of similar local events to effectively present your new product.

Method Four. Go to the company in person with your product and camp out in the reception room until a buyer sees you or you are evicted. This is certainly bold and quite chancy but it has worked before. I'm not encouraging this, but if you happen to be driving through West Chester, Pennsylvania or Clearwater, Florida and have complete details on your product, you might just stop by. There is one problem, however, and that is finding a parking spot near QVC. Plan on parking a few blocks away and walking. I've never seen more cars in a parking lot than those around QVC.

Method Five. Another way that will make your presentation go a lot faster is to have a successful infomercial. Both HSN and QVC now realize that if you have a successful infomercial product, it should work very well on the home shopping format and you'll literally find an open door.

The methods presented above give you a clue as to the ways you can get your product on QVC or HSN. They have all worked before and could work again. The easiest are Methods One Revised and Three, filling out the Vendor Relations Form or showing up at one of the companies' trade shows in your state. If you have something of interest to them, they will generally spot it and take action. Use Methods Two and Four only if you feel so strongly about your product that you're willing to involve a rep or take the drastic action I've suggested by showing up at the company door. Method Five will get you on the air the quickest, but then you need to have an infomercial product that has already been successful on TV—which is far from an easy task. (Of course, it doesn't hurt to be related either.)

In the next chapter I go into greater detail on what is involved in getting your product into QVC once you've had it selected for possible purchase. I am assuming that the process is very similar for HSN.

One day in July 1997 the customer service department at our office received a call from one of our QVC customers who was very upset. She claimed that she called a company that sold products on QVC and was told that the company was leaving QVC for another home shopping network—HSN based in Clearwater, Florida. But what really upset her was that the very same company was not only bum-rapping QVC, but also telling her that a lot of other vendors were defecting from QVC and joining HSN. She was also told that my company, BluBlocker Corporation, was one of them. She was very upset and wanted to verify this. The rumor wasn't true.

It's a fact that if you are on one of the home shopping networks, it is rare that you can be on the other as well. So, in general, vendors would first try to get on QVC, the bigger of the two networks, and if that failed they would end up on HSN. HSN was the early leader, but they were eventually surpassed by QVC. When I joined QVC in 1991 they were actually smaller than HSN. Today they are twice the size.

Some Were Defecting

One of the QVC vendors indeed had been talking to me about HSN. It seems that HSN was encouraging companies to leave QVC with offers of more airtime for the vendor's products. Although I decided to remain at QVC, the vendor who talked to me was evidently passing around false rumors of people defecting from QVC.

I felt that it was only a matter of time before QVC would find out about the rumor, so I wanted to go right to the top and squelch it completely. I called Doug Briggs, QVC's president, and told him of the false rumor. I also suggested that QVC might be having vendor problems that would be causing these defections and that he should look into it seriously.

A few weeks later, I received a call from Marilyn Montross

of QVC. She received my name from Darlene Daggett—one of QVC's top merchandise heads and the lady who supported many of my promotions in the past. Marilyn was calling to invite me to attend a special vendor meeting in August to discuss ways QVC could improve their vendor relations.

Selected for the meeting was a cross section of the people who have had a great deal of experience presenting products on QVC. Some were on-air guest hosts from companies that had been on the network for several years. Others were behind-the-scene companies that supplied product for QVC's hosts to present, and some were either manufacturer's representatives or vendors from specialized categories.

There were eight people who were going to give important feedback to QVC to help them improve the flow of product through their system, which was one of the reasons some companies were defecting. If QVC could avoid some of the confusion that the product flow may have caused among other vendors, then maybe there would be fewer defections and possibly a better QVC system. Apparently Doug Briggs was taking this very seriously.

As the Company Grew

Things had changed at QVC through the years. It once was a relatively simple thing to get a product selected and then approved and on the air. As time went on and as a bureaucracy was set up to handle the rapid growth of the company, there emerged a maze of intermediate steps that a vendor had to traverse before his or her product was accepted and put on the air. As the maze grew, it started to affect the older vendors in the way they were being treated. Soon, a few vendors, totally frustrated and seeing greener pastures at HSN, started to defect. The meeting with Marilyn was to find out what was happening from the vendors' perspective.

At the meeting Marilyn laid out a flowchart of the various steps required to have a product flow through the system to an appearance on TV and then all the way through the reorder phases. Indeed, it was a complicated maze that took you from the time you presented a product to the time a check was cut and you were paid.

I will take you through this maze, which is now much more refined and streamlined. Incidentally, I've heard through the grapevine that those who have defected to HSN are not very happy in their new home. Remember, QVC at this writing is doing $2 billion in sales compared to HSN's $1 billion.

The Product

Let's assume you have presented a product to QVC for acceptance. As you may remember, there are five ways to get your product accepted by QVC. Let us say you have taken the one they recommend and submitted forms to the Vendor Relations Department. (See Appendix A.) And now let us assume that QVC has called you and asked you to send a sample. You send the sample and if the buyer is efficient, he or she will call you and possibly request a meeting. Sometimes, if it is a simple product, the buyer may simply talk to you over the phone and work out all the details.

The Buyer Meeting

You now fly to Philadelphia, rent a car and drive out to QVC in West Chester, Pennsylvania, about 40 minutes from the airport. At QVC you find a place to park and you go to the large reception room where you announce yourself, sign in with security and get a badge. Security calls your buyer, who then comes into the reception room and escorts you to one of the many conference rooms in either the buyers' office area or the lunchroom. You then formally present your product if you haven't previously sent it, and you negotiate price, terms and delivery. Once that's arranged, you leave and the product then enters the formal approval stage.

Quality Assurance

Your product will now be put through one of the most rigorous tests it will ever go through—it now goes to the Quality Assurance Department. The department has some of the most state-of-the-art testing equipment and is staffed by a team of dedicated and aggressive technicians/detectives who will totally go through your product, check your instructions if they are required, read the statements on your packaging and, in short, make sure that what you deliver is packaged, produced and presented to the consumer properly. If there is one little correctable flaw, it is rejected and you correct the flaw and resubmit it to the

QA department again for approval. Requirements vary for each department. For example, clothing requires that all clothes fit specific parameters so that a QVC customer who orders a medium can expect a medium regardless of which manufacturer supplies it. But let us say you finally get your product approved.

The Purchase Order

On some occasions a verbal purchase order is issued so that the vendor can produce enough product in enough time to meet QVC's time schedule. Later a purchase order will arrive at the vendor's office. QVC has been pretty good at honoring their verbal commitments, so the written purchase order becomes just a formality. Typically, a product won't go on the air without first having $10,000 in inventory for a conservative test and a lot more for a product in which they have a lot of confidence.

The Planning Department

The product is then presented to the Planning Department where they firm up the TV requirements. Does the product have or need a video clip to explain it? What will the set look like? All of this is decided in advance.

Shipping

No product appears on QVC without first being received in their warehouse. So you ship your product to arrive at least a week before the on-air date.

Loading

After the goods are received, the information about your product is loaded into the vast computer network at QVC so the phone operators who take the orders have all of the information they need. The quantities are also listed in the computer so as they are sold, they can be subtracted from the inventory. The buyers usually prepare what are called "Blue Cards" for the hosts—description cards that the hosts refer to on-air when presenting a product.

Show Planning

This department then assigns you an on-air date and time. They get your approval to make sure that you can be there and you formally approve the times.

You Fly to QVC

For your first show, I recommend you arrive the day before and check into a nice hotel that I've stayed at for the past six years—the Great Valley Desmond Hotel in Malvern, Pennsylvania, close to QVC's corporate headquarters in West Chester. Call (610) 296-9800 and tell them that you want QVC's corporate rate of around $100 a night. It's a full-service hotel and the staff is very helpful and friendly. If you've got some extra time, go to the King of Prussia Mall—one of the biggest I've ever been in— or visit some of the many historic sites such as Valley Forge National Park.

Tip: Don't cut your time too short for the trip. I once did and my flight was delayed because of a major thunderstorm that was hovering over the airport and wouldn't go away. So my plane diverted and finally landed at the Baltimore airport. I then chartered a private plane and told the pilot to fly me to West Chester, Pennsylvania. The pilot only heard "West Chester," so when I started seeing the New York City skyline and realized that I was not flying to QVC but instead to Westchester, New York, I told the pilot to fly back down to West Chester, Pennsylvania. I arrived at QVC with only five minutes to spare. Since that time, I always arrive early.

You Wait in the Green Room

This is the moment you've been either looking forward to or dreading. But it is all part of the job. You arrive about an hour before the show and sign in at security. You are then escorted to the Green Room, which is what most broadcast studio lounges are called. You wait to go on the air. In the Green Room you'll find a computer with sales results for the products that are on the air, another computer showing the length of the queue or number of callers waiting in line to place their orders, washroom and makeup facilities, refreshments, a few telephones and a clothes closet.

There are a number of comfortable chairs for you to sit on and a page to coordinate your visit. The pages are usually freshly scrubbed, bright college students who are looking to make a career in marketing or broadcasting. They add a nice touch to the hospitality QVC offers you. If you're smart, you ask the page to take you to the setup table where your product is located and prepped before being given to the host who presents it on the air. You want to make sure everything is there and that your product is clean, functioning and ready to go on the air. Then you return to the Green Room and wait for your turn to go on the air.

If you're nervous, don't worry. I always have tremendous compassion for first-time guests, and I try to provide some support and advice. I reassure them by saying, rather facetiously, "Just talk to the camera and ignore the millions of people who are watching their TV sets and judging you."

One little warning: As you sit in the Green Room there is also a TV set with the current QVC broadcast being shown. If you're like me, you'll watch the TV and see a product that you'd like to buy. You simply step outside the Green Room, give your order to one of the operators and step back into the room. I have bought thousands of dollars worth of products this way.

You're Wired Up

Then about 10 minutes before you go on the air, the page walks in with your lapel microphone and clips it to your suit or dress and then attaches the transmitter to your belt. If you're going on the air, it helps to realize that a belt is very helpful for holding this device. Another device they hook on you is called an IFB— the device through which you'll hear the phone callers when they are put on the air. A plug is put in your ear and the wire is taped to your neck and hidden under your clothes, out of the way.

You might also be visited by your host to discuss your product and any last-minute suggestions you may have. The hosts on QVC are among the nicest people with whom you'll associate and they want to help you sell your product. They'll remind you of your next-door neighbor, and you'll find, as do millions of other QVC viewers and customers, that you'll have no problem relating to them.

Ready for Prime Time

You are now ready to go on the air. You are escorted to the correct soundstage, step next to the host, the camera's red light goes on and the red "Live" bulb glows on the monitor. It's now prime time for your product. Just talk to the host as you normally would to anybody else and forget the millions of people examining your every word and looking at your every facial blemish.

Forget about the way you appear in the monitor. Don't be distracted by the IFB sticking in your ear and the flashing sign that tells you a phone call is waiting. Let the host do the talking and when it's your turn, answer as clearly and concisely as possible. The host will also introduce each caller and have the caller say hello to you. Remember the names of the callers, as it is nice to refer to them by name during a conversation. Smile a lot. Be as natural as you can with the host. Just keep reminding yourself that this is the moment you have worked for all this time.

Sales Results

You step off the soundstage and the page takes off your IFB and microphone. Simply go to the Green Room, look on the computer monitor and see how you've done. If you've done well, congratulations.

Reorder

If it is your first time and your buyer is very conscientious, then he or she might be there to greet you after the show, especially if you have a smash success. You'll hang around a little while, call your office or loved one to tell them the results and then after about a half hour leave the Green Room for your hotel or a meeting with the buyer. It's now time to discuss a reorder.

Getting Paid

If you don't have a success, you'll probably get all the product back that hasn't been sold and a check for what you have sold. If you are successful and sell out, you'll just get a check plus any returns that come back from dissatisfied customers. Usually a few days before you receive your payment, you will receive an accounting report detailing how your payment was computed. You have to rely on their inventory count and what has been sold, as that is all you are usually paid for. Participants in the "50 in 50 Tour" (when QVC visited a state with their roving bus) usually had the option of receiving full payment for their shipment except for estimated customer returns.

General Points

The system usually works well, but people can make mistakes. There are so many steps that need to be taken that foul-ups are always possible. It is therefore important that the vendor be vigilant and work with the buyer and the rest of the QVC staff to make sure that everything is followed up and moves along. A buyer can be lazy or use poor judgment. It's up to you to be frank with the buyer and explain your position. Remember, QVC is your partner and you need to communicate and work with them as a partner.

Since that meeting with Marilyn Montross and the eight other participants, the entire atmosphere at QVC has changed. I learned that there were many more meetings between vendors and QVC after ours. It was obvious that QVC was quite serious about making changes and indeed there were many. Much of the bureaucratic atmosphere has been dramatically reduced. The buyers are now doing so much more to make your experience at QVC less stressful that the contrast between the old and the new is really apparent. They recommend new product ideas, work with their senior managers to maximize the potential of your product line and—the part I like best—there's no more of this secret stuff where you get a directive from "above" but with no explanation and no idea of who made the decision. Of course, this is only my observation. But I have talked to other vendors and they are telling me about the changes they are noticing too.

Buyers Are the Key

The buyers are a very important group at QVC. These men and women are among the most dedicated, committed and overworked individuals on the staff. They often must screen thousands of products, make the decision to accept or reject each one and then live by that decision.

If you are fortunate enough to have a product accepted by QVC, it is the buyer who becomes your most frequent contact. Treating the buyer correctly could make a difference in how successful you are with QVC, not to mention how frequently you appear on-air and how long you last there.

There are many tips to getting along with a buyer. First, realize that each buyer is different and they come from many different backgrounds—some from direct marketing, some from retail and some are very experienced at QVC having been buyers there since the inception of the company. Understanding their background is just as important as understanding the QVC process. The more experience they have, the more they will instinctively know what will sell and what won't, how to present your product and what you need to do to be successful as a presenter or guest co-host. And since there is nobody who always knows whether a product will do well or not, they could be wrong too.

Once you start working with a buyer, the first thing you must do is respect their time. When you phone them and get their voice mail, make sure your message is very short. State your name and phone number clearly at the beginning of your message. Give the purpose of your call very quickly and briefly. I have sat in many a buyer's office and watched them race through their messages listening to them from their speakerphones. You have just a few seconds to hold their attention and get across the purpose of your call. I've seen them erase a long message without even listening to it in its entirety simply because it was too long.

In fact, all of your communications should be short and to the point. Use the fax often and keep your faxes short. Put things in writing to confirm conversations. And simply realize that your buyer is not only your contact with QVC but other vendors' contact as well. But once you understand how to get through the various channels at QVC and have earned the respect of the buyers who know they can trust you and that you deliver on all your promises, you'll find them not only easy to work with but open to any future product you may want to present.

I've had buyers tell me after they've been transferred to another department, "Joe, if you ever have another product in my category, I want you to know that my door is always open to you." In fact, some buyers who have learned that they can rely on you are genuinely sorry to lose you as a supplier when they are transferred.

It's Not Easy

It's tough getting on QVC, it's tough staying on QVC and it's even tough when you succeed on QVC. But I've had one of the most enjoyable experiences of my marketing career. Not only do you learn and grow from your experience of dealing with QVC but you get the opportunity to meet other vendors, sports stars and celebrities from the music, exercise, cooking, movie and car-racing fields as well. There is a lot of cross pollination that takes place.

I once walked into the Green Room and sat down. There were three people already talking and I was on next, so I left, went on the air and then after I was finished, went back to the Green Room. When I returned, one of the men in the group stood up and shook my hand. "Nice job, Joe. I just want you to know that I've been wearing your sunglasses and I love them."

The man congratulating me was Tommy James of "Tommy James and the Shondells" fame—a rock-and-roll star during the '60s. The coincidence was that I had once hired him 30 years earlier to perform for me when, in an earlier career, I ran music clubs in the Chicago area.

Section Two

| **The Three Acts of an Infomercial**

You've already had a taste of the power of television to do everything I've promised and more—all conveyed through my own experiences. Now it's time for us to get to work and see what it takes for you to make your own infomercial. We'll also look at some of the subtle yet important lessons you need to learn to win at this high-stakes game. That's what the rest of this book is all about—what it takes to win and win big with your very own successful infomercial.

During the years I was doing the BluBlocker infomercial, I had three hit BluBlocker shows in a row that ran for a total of four and a half years. I soon developed the confidence to try a new concept—something different.

If you recall from Chapter 4, I shot a complete show from each of three cities. What I didn't mention was that I was hoping to eventually create a 13-show series. Then I could rotate these shows during my time slots to make watching our commercials more interesting.

The Idea Was Flawed

But my idea was flawed from a direct marketing standpoint. First, we could probably test all three shows and one of them would be better than the other two. So if one show outpulled the other two, then what? Do we run the other shows simply for variety? Or do we continue to run the winning show until it doesn't do well and then go to the next one that would appear fresh to viewers and see if it produces more sales?

If you're a direct marketer you already know the answer. You run your strongest show until it no longer is the strongest show. And you continually test your next show against the stronger show to make sure you are always running your strongest show. So the concept of a show series didn't make sense unless the series had a high viewer rating and had outside national sponsors—highly unlikely for an infomercial. However, when we found ourselves competing with the networks and their sitcoms, we often had comparable ratings.

But of course, I was so wrapped up in my wonderful concept that I didn't realize how stupid it was until long after I did all three shows. And when it came time to test them, I discovered that the best of the three—the show from Maui—did not make that much profit and wasn't nearly as successful as I had expected. This meant that I had three shows I tested and I didn't even have one that I could run and expect a lot of success with.

The Suggestions Were Many

Dan Rosenfield, my ad agency president, had all kinds of suggestions for me. They ranged from ideas about techniques we used in the show to getting a handsome show host to replace me. "I hope you're not too insulted with my suggestion," said Dan, "but remember, you are not a professional actor and maybe a real hunk is what we need to boost sales."

Dan had some other suggestions which violated many of the direct marketing principles I had known and taught for years. When things go wrong, it seems everybody has their theory of why something didn't work. Dan was sincere in his advice and truly meant well, but as a direct marketer, I knew that many of his logical recommendations would not work emotionally in a selling-type show.

I remember sitting alone thinking to myself, "OK, I know direct marketing. I know what should work and what shouldn't work. I have read all of Dan's suggestions and tried hard to be open-minded. I know how to create and how to test. I've been on TV with three incredible shows. What is there that I am missing?" Maybe it was something in the art and not in the science of TV. Maybe there was something I could learn about the structure of a TV show that would help in the commercial application of that knowledge.

I Learned About My Craft

So I went to a bookstore and got a book on screenwriting by Syd Field—one of the gurus in the art. I learned that practically every movie and play is divided into three acts and that within each act there are plot twists that change the direction of the characters and of the plot. I then looked at my infomercials

It's the most critical act in the entire show.

and realized that I too should be breaking my infomercials into three acts.

But what should the nature of each act be? What should be in the first act and what should be in the second and third? What were the plot twists in an infomercial and what elements paralleled those of a screenplay?

I then deduced that all infomercials should be looked at in three acts and that each act could be defined as to its purpose. Once I realized this, I named the three acts as follows: Act One was called "Entertainment," Act Two "Selling" and Act Three "Closing," as in closing a sale. And if the play was to have a name, I'd call it "How May I Serve You?"

The purpose of "How May I Serve You?" was to sell my product, and if I looked at the selling process and transferred the principles of a screenplay to infomercials, I would then be using the correct tools for the medium. Or to put it another way:

Theory 1

An infomercial is simply a three-act screenplay whose purpose is to cause your prospects to exchange their hard-earned money for your product or service.

This meant that I had to look at my three previous infomercials, see what was missing and then restructure them to fit the format of my new play.

I looked at the entertainment portion of each of the three infomercials I shot and realized that I was missing a lot of really entertaining characters that I used to have in my other successful shows. And I realized that if I did have these entertaining segments, they should be during the first act, or at the beginning of the show. I also saw segments that could be used in each of the remaining two acts. But I was missing some elements and decided to go to Venice Beach, near Los Angeles, where I could always find something new and entertaining to film.

The shoot went exceptionally well. I shot a street vendor selling knockoff BluBlockers and then, on camera, I showed both the knockoff pair and the BluBlockers to passing tourists who extolled the difference between the two. I shot a bare-chested guy who was wearing a famous pair of sunglasses but loved ours. Then when he thought he was off-camera he told me how much he *really* liked BluBlockers. Of course we were still running the camera and we captured him saying that as well. His off-camera comments made his testimonial even that much stronger.

The Day Went Quite Well

I shot enthusiastic and animated BluBlocker fans who were wearing the sunglasses when we approached them and were very pleased with their purchase. We took great testimonials of some customers who wore prescription glasses and used our clip-on BluBlockers over their prescription pair. But one of the most impressive performances was done by a street performer by the name of Dr. Geek. He saw us filming, walked up to us and we handed him a pair of our sunglasses. He then went into an impromptu rap song as if he was doing a commercial for us.

When I returned, I had plenty of great footage to complete

One of the scenes we saved from our Maui shoot was of this strong testimonial.

my show. I knew what I wanted for Act One and much of what we shot was indeed used. I also had some great stuff for the remaining two acts.

We always took plenty of footage to establish a scene. This windsurfing shot was used as background footage in our beach interview segment.

When I assembled the show, I took the best parts of each of the three previous shows along with my Venice Beach footage and put together a show that incorporated everything I knew about selling, direct marketing and my new knowledge of the three-act screenplay.

Each segment did exactly what the name of the act implied. I entertained during the first act, sold during the second and was very persuasive during my close for the product in the third act. In fact, my close was a dead serious strong presentation filled with credibility and a strong call for action—all the elements you would want if you were selling in person.

When the final BluBlocker infomercial was completed, it turned out to be the biggest blockbuster in our history. I went from the throes of near defeat to a major hit show—all based on the new principles I learned on how to write a screenplay called "How May I Serve You?"

In the following chapters, I will explain some of the techniques I learned and how they should be used when you do an infomercial or any long TV production designed to sell a product. Some of the principles may surprise you, but they all have been proven or are logical extensions of proven direct marketing principles.

Chapter 20 | The Glue Factor

I like to break things down into the simplest components to explain them. For example, in my book on copywriting, *Advertising Secrets of the Written Word*, I state that the main purpose of all the elements in a print ad (such as the headline, subheadline and pictures) is to get you to read the first sentence. And the purpose of the first sentence is to get you to read the second sentence. But when you're on TV you have a different purpose for every element in an infomercial.

Theory 2

The main purpose of every element in an infomercial is to get your prospects to take one action—namely, to put down their remote control channel changer.

I know that may seem a rather simplistic approach to defining the main purpose of every element in an infomercial, but keep this concept in the back of your mind. You'll soon appreciate its relevance.

In the previous chapter I described the three-act play you create for your product or service called "How May I Serve You?" I also said that Act One is called "Entertainment" and that you should spend the first act entertaining your prospects. Put everything else aside for the moment such as revealing all the features of your product or service. This doesn't matter right now.

When entertaining your prospects you will need something that grabs their attention (as you would in a headline), causes them to pause for a moment (as you would with a subheadline) and then become glued to the TV screen and unwilling to change a channel (as they would do if they started reading effective copy).

Becoming glued to the TV screen is the real goal of Act One. But what causes this to happen? And what do you do in order to ensure that it does happen? Let's start by talking about the "glue factor" first.

Simply put, the glue factor is anything that you can put at

the very beginning of your show that is so captivating, curiosity-building or enjoyable that it will hold your viewers' attention and give them a pleasurable emotional feeling. The viewers then hope that they will see something repeated again later in the show that will give them more of that feeling. Let me cite the experience that caused me to realize this and explain why it's so important.

The Family Test

After I sent the raw footage of what I had shot at Venice Beach to my ad agency president, Dan Rosenfield, in Kansas City, he brought it home with him to view with his family. At the beginning of the tape was a small segment with Dr. Geek—a rap musician and street performer that we captured in a spontaneous rap for BluBlocker sunglasses. As the tape played Dr. Geek's performance on Dan's TV, his children walked into the room and started watching. They were so enthralled with what they saw that they stayed to watch the entire raw footage—over an hour of viewing.

Dan called me and told me about his family's reaction to what we shot. "My kids never stay for very long to watch anything, but they were so enthralled with Dr. Geek that they stayed glued to the TV. They were hoping to catch some of the other characters we shot who had appealed to them like the good doctor. Dr. Geek is definitely somebody we've got to include in our show."

This was a major revelation to me—if you put something that is very compelling in the beginning of your show, people will watch your entire infomercial with the hopes of experiencing the same type of entertainment or feeling later on in your show. I call it the "glue factor"—those elements that glue you to the TV screen for extended periods of time.

People watch TV to be entertained. That is what the medium is about. Even documentaries or biographies are entertaining while they educate, inform and teach. If you watch *The Tonight Show with Jay Leno* or saw his predecessor, Johnny Carson, they would always start their show with a monologue in which they tell some of the funniest jokes you'll hear during the entire show. They then grab you right after the monologue with a skit—again to entertain you and get you into the format of the show. This is performed before any commercial break. Twenty minutes might elapse before you hear the first commercial.

You Keep Watching and Hoping

If you've watched *Saturday Night Live*, you know the show starts out with a funny skit which lasts a few minutes before the program's opening credits. And then after the credits, they take you through a few more skits before they present the first commercial break. Some of their shows have been devoid of great humor, but you keep watching hoping to catch some really funny bit. You know you've been entertained before, you remember the good feelings the show left you with and you're hoping to be entertained again.

Theory 3

The "glue factor" is a powerful attention-getting element at the beginning of an infomercial that causes viewers to watch the entire show in hopes of encountering a similar experience later in the infomercial.

In comparing copywriting to selling on TV, I talk to my classes about the "slippery slide" theory, in which reading the first sentence compels you to read the second sentence. Before long you are sucked into the copy and slide down this very slippery slide unable to stop reading until you reach the end of the copy.

In the beginning of the ad it isn't important what you even say about your product. It's totally unimportant. The main purpose of the first part of a print ad is to get your reader to read. Simply getting the reader into a reading momentum is critical to the success of what you are eventually going to sell.

On TV you basically want the viewer to keep viewing—to put down that channel changer and focus on the images you are showing on the screen. The product or service is irrelevant at this point. You want to focus on just one goal and that is to create viewer momentum—to cause that viewer to keep watching. And one way you can do this very effectively is by using entertainment as the glue factor.

Sometimes it is an intense interest in your product that will cause the viewer to "stick around." Sometimes it's a series of images, or in the case of the BluBlocker infomercial, maybe it's Dr. Geek and our entire Act One of the show.

In our BluBlocker infomercial I put in several segments that could be considered examples of the glue factor. The first was a

The purpose of the glue factor is to keep your prospects from changing the channel once they land on your show.

series of images introducing the show—scenes flashing across the screen during the first few minutes. Then I showed Dr. Geek doing his rap. Then I showed another funny scene—all of this designed to entertain and to cause the viewer to stop changing channels and stay tuned to my 28-1/2 minute message (the actual length of an infomercial).

The glue factor could also be expressed as simply that one segment that attracts your viewer and causes that viewer to put down the TV remote control.

It has nothing to do with selling your product. It has everything to do with establishing the start of viewer momentum. And if you can stop the viewer long enough to establish the glue factor, chances are good you will develop good viewer momentum all the way to the end of your show.

Chapter 21 | The Entertainment Factor

Once you've created a powerful glue factor, you've then got to realize an important element in any TV broadcast—entertainment. That is the main reason people are watching their TV sets. You might think that TV news is not designed to be entertaining, but think about it. If you don't like a TV news broadcaster for any reason or if the news he or she is broadcasting is not entertaining or interesting, chances are you'll tune in to another broadcaster you enjoy watching. Even TV news (a serious subject) has got to be entertaining. Networks have even created newsmagazine shows which take news stories, explore them in depth and make them fast moving and more entertaining.

Theory 4

People expect to be entertained on TV and if you want to do well in the medium, you've got to entertain them.

In my copywriting book, *Advertising Secrets of the Written Word*, I emphasized the importance of creating reading momentum rather than selling your product at the early stages of the copy. As long as the reader was reading and couldn't put your copy down, then that gave you the perfect opportunity to start the sales process. On TV you want your prospect to keep watching your show by putting down the remote control.

Your show should be presented in the three acts described in Chapter 19 with the first act called "Entertainment." And the primary purpose of the first act is to get the viewer to put down his or her remote control channel changer. Period. And, of course, with that remote control device sitting safely on the table, you are hoping the viewer will watch your entire show. The concept is parallel to the print example I just described. You must devote all your skills to presenting a fast-paced and very entertaining beginning to your show.

This doesn't mean that you neglect showing the product. Quite the contrary. You work at tying your product into the entertainment. A good example was the rap song that Dr. Geek sang for

It's important throughout the show to entertain your viewers.

BluBlocker sunglasses. Another example in the same show was a practical joke we played on a balloon sculptor on April 1st using the sunglasses as a prop. We gave him a pair of BluBlockers and after the interview, we asked him what day it was. He replied, "April 1st, April Fool's . . ." We then remained silent. You could then see his reaction as he realized that our camera crew may have been an April Fool's joke. Of course, it wasn't, but his reaction to our crew was quite entertaining.

There are car care shows where the host creates car-cleaning competitions, sets a really expensive car on fire or sprays paint on the surface of a car's hood—all to entertain and get the value of the car care product conveyed to the viewers. This is entertainment. This is show business at its best and it is salesmanship in its full glory.

In my infomercials for our Miracell wrinkle pill, I hired a group of women who looked 20 years younger than their actual age, taped them in interviews where they announced their ages and ran this segment at the beginning of the show. This not only proved to be an excellent glue factor but it also provided a lot of entertainment. The women were fun, interesting and they looked much younger than their actual ages, which amazed the viewers and kept them glued to their TV screens waiting for more.

The Glue Factor and Entertainment

There is a difference between the glue factor and the entertainment element in the beginning of the show. The glue factor refers to those really special scenes that rivet attention. Entertainment is a more general term that covers the glue factor and everything else that makes the show entertaining.

Entertainment can be created by the characters you use as your host or in testimonials. Infomercial producers have used men who were extremely hyper to entertain such as Tony Little, outspoken women who have shaved their heads to give them a unique entertaining quality such as Susan Powter and finally, the animated Richard Simmons. There are a lot of ways to provide entertainment utilizing your product or its many features in entertaining segments of your show. The more entertainment, the more positive you can be that people will watch not only your first act, but your second and third acts as well.

The Entire Show Should Entertain

Just because you call the first act "Entertainment" doesn't mean that you don't entertain throughout your entire show. It simply means that the first act should be primarily entertainment whose focus is not necessarily your product. It's better to involve your product, but it is not mandatory.

I have given many speeches during which I have played the first few minutes of my infomercials. I can always expect a lot of laughter and sincere interest from the audience, many of whom come up to me asking where they can see the rest of my show.

When I taught copywriting, I always taught that humor in the selling process is very dangerous and should be avoided. There are exceptions, however, which involve either presenting yourself as human or using humor to attract attention. You can then get serious when you start the selling process. The same applies to TV. In the case of the BluBlocker infomercial, I had a

Using likable characters and "beautiful people" provides entertainment and tends to stop the channel surfers. This scene appeared in one of our more successful infomercials.

very entertaining segment in the very beginning of the show that caused audiences to laugh. Later in the show I got very serious during the process of closing the sale.

Theory 5
If you have a number of segments to present in an infomercial, present the humorous portions early in the show.

You want to attract viewers, but after you've gotten them to put down their remote controls, you must then get them involved in the presentation of your product and the serious side of what you are doing—getting them to exchange their hard-earned money for your product or service.

In the next chapter I talk about another trick that will help you tremendously in keeping the flow going after you've finished Act One of your screenplay.

Curiosity is one of the most powerful motivators you can use as a marketer. In copy, it helps develop the reading momentum that makes your prospect read your entire message. A typical piece of copy might say, "But was I surprised at what I was about to discover," and the reader will feel compelled to read further to find out what indeed you discovered. Curiosity is used in a print ad to motivate somebody to continue reading.

The use of curiosity on television is also powerful in a very similar way.

Theory 6

Plant seeds of curiosity throughout your show to cause the viewer to be curious enough to keep on viewing.

The seeds should be presented as incentives or as a "tease" to keep a viewer watching your show. It is similar to the use of curiosity in a print ad to keep a reader reading the copy. Let me cite some examples.

Learn to plant seeds of curiosity throughout the show.

In my BluBlocker commercial I knew that Dr. Geek singing his rap song was a really good introductory segment and would be popular with viewers. So after his little rap song, I stated, "We've got more from Dr. Geek later in the show," to tease the audience and to make them curious so they would stay with us. And at the end of the show, we replayed part of his original rap song to fulfill the promise I had made. We played it at the very end after the close and while the toll-free number was showing to keep the viewer watching.

Another use of curiosity is between each segment or break in the show. For example, I would be on camera with my co-host and say something like, "Watch what happens when we walked up to an outdoor stand selling a pair of knockoff BluBlockers." This would create enough curiosity so the viewer would at least watch the next segment.

In news broadcasts you'll find similar uses of curiosity before the commercial breaks. A newscaster might say, "And when we come back, we'll show you the latest fad sweeping the city and it may just surprise you."

Whenever I watch *CNN Headline News*, they're always teasing the audience with what they're about to show later in the half hour or even in the next half hour to keep the viewers interested and watching. CNN does it with curiosity and they do it very effectively.

Whenever we used a celebrity as in this BluBlocker commercial, we teased the audience in the beginning of the show to create curiosity and get them to watch the full show for the celebrity segment later.

In your infomercial you should use the same techniques. Talk about an experiment that you might be trying later in the show or tease the audience with something that is coming up. Be careful not to say too much to keep the curiosity heightened. Watch commercial television broadcasts and be aware of how they use tease or curiosity techniques to encourage viewers to keep watching. Simply by being aware of the tease you will

*The main purpose
of the beginning of
your commercial
is to get your
prospect to
put down that
remote control.*

notice it more often during regular broadcasts, and you will see how to use this technique effectively.

Curiosity Sells Sunglasses

I've also used the technique of curiosity to sell the BluBlockers. In scene after scene I show people trying on a pair and reacting in some surprising fashion to the effect they see when looking through the lens. But nowhere do I show the viewers what it looks like when you look through a lens. The reason involves the use of curiosity and the technology of the camera lens. The only way viewers can experience what the people I interview experience is to buy a pair and see for themselves. In short, I use curiosity as a strong motivating factor to buy the product as there is no other way viewers will be able to satisfy their curiosity than to buy from me.

If I would show the camera looking through the BluBlocker lens, I would in essence have shown too much. And one of the keys in the use of curiosity is to not show or tell too much or you lose the power of curiosity. Another factor is one of human physiology. When you put on a pair of BluBlocker sunglasses, your brain adjusts to the color shift that you see at first when you look through the lens. This adjustment makes all the colors appear more natural after a few seconds and you don't notice the yellowish tint that you do when you first put them on. But on a TV screen, you just see the yellowish tint.

In the BluBlocker commercial, curiosity was the strongest motivating factor in the entire show. In the next chapter, you'll see another application of curiosity and why it really is important that your viewers watch your entire show.

Your competition is not another TV channel, but rather the viewer's remote control. You want to keep the viewer watching your show and not touching that remote control. Only by having somebody watch your entire show are you really going to complete your three-act screenplay and reach the powerful close at the end of your show. Curiosity is a powerful tool to make sure this happens.

Chapter 23 | Important Creative Principles

Now that you have the basic structure of an infomercial, it will be a lot easier for you to develop your show. But there are a lot of other principles that should be expressed in your show and they are practically the same as those you'll find in print mail order advertising. And these similar principles are what I want to share with you in this chapter. In fact, I will take the most salient points from the first book in my series, *Advertising Secrets of the Written Word,* but will focus on the important aspects of these points as they pertain to the infomercial business and video in general.

Honesty

If I had to pick the single most important creative element of all of the creative principles, I would pick honesty. Your advertising must be honest.

The consumer is very smart—smarter than you think and smarter collectively than any single one of us. With all the experience I have in the marketing of products and with all the product knowledge I've gained over the past 35 years, take my word for it, the consumer is quite sharp.

The consumer can tell whether somebody is truthful in what he or she is communicating. And the more truthful you are in your advertising, the more your message will be accepted by your prospects. When I did my BluBlocker shows, I would include a few of the negative comments people made. Consumers were so impressed with this approach that they developed a special trust in us. When I was doing print advertising, it seemed that the more truthful and frank my ads were, the more the consumer responded. I soon realized that simply telling the truth was one of the best advertising "gimmicks" I had ever used.

Consumers really appreciate the truth. And since they are smarter than you or I, you can't fake it. They'll pick out a phony statement every time. In every communication I make to my customers about my products I insist on truthfulness, whether it be on national television or in my print ads. And the more truthful I am, the more responsive my customers.

Satisfaction Conviction

Seeing the above heading, you might think we are talking about the trial period. Indeed, a trial period could be defined as a form of satisfaction conviction. "If you aren't totally satisfied with my product within one month, you may send it back for a full refund." But that isn't what I mean here. Sure, every direct response offer should have a trial period. After all, the consumer needs to touch and feel a product to make a decision about whether to keep it or not. So the trial period provides buyers with a level of confidence that they can change their mind if they're not happy.

Theory 7

A satisfaction conviction is more than a trial period. It basically conveys a message from you that says, "Hey, I'm so convinced that you will like this product that I'm going to do something significant for your benefit to prove just how incredible my offer really is."

If your potential customer, after reading what you are going to do, says something like, "They must really believe in their product" or "How can they do it?" or "I bet they are going to get ripped off by customers who are going to take advantage of their generosity," then you know you've got a great example of a satisfaction conviction.

Let me give you an example. When I first offered BluBlocker sunglasses, I said in my TV advertising, "If you're unhappy with BluBlockers, I'll let you return them anytime you want. There is no trial period." A lot of people thought to themselves, "That must be a good product or otherwise they wouldn't make that offer." Or they may have said, "Boy, are they going to get ripped off." In either case, I conveyed a conviction that my customer was going to be so satisfied that I was willing to do something that was really significant and for their benefit.

In one print ad, I stated, "If you aren't happy with your purchase, just call me up and I'll personally arrange to have it picked up at my expense and refund you every penny of your purchase price including the time required to return the product."

Able to Test Its Power

One time I was able to test the power of a satisfaction conviction. In an ad I wrote for a company I created called Consumers Hero, I was offering subscriptions to a discount bulletin showing refurbished products at very low prices. But rather than just mail the bulletin to prospects, I formed a club and part of the membership was a subscription to the bulletin. I tested various elements in the 700-word ad. I changed the headline and tested it and my order response increased by 20%. I tested a $5 price point against a $10 price point and got twice the number of orders for the $5 offer as I did for the $10 offer, but ended up with the same dollar volume. But when I changed just the satisfaction conviction, the response rate doubled regardless of any other factor.

In one ad, I said, "If you don't buy anything during your two-year subscription, I'll refund the unused portion of your subscription." In the second ad I stated, "But what if you never buy from us and your two-year membership expires? Fine. Send us just your membership card and we'll fully refund your five dollars plus send you interest on your money."

In the first example, you see a basic, simple trial-period type offer. In the second version, you see one that goes well beyond the trial period and can be classified as a satisfaction conviction.

In the test, the response doubled even though the satisfaction conviction was at the very end of the ad. This meant that people read all the copy and then, at the very end, when that important buying decision had to be made, the satisfaction conviction removed any remaining resistance to buying into the concept. If you are applying this principle to an infomercial as a three-act screenplay, then obviously you would want this element to be in the very last act called the "Closing."

Theory 8

The ideal satisfaction conviction should raise an objection and resolve it, going beyond what people expect.

It was effective in my Consumers Hero example because it tied perfectly into resolving any last-minute resistance. First it raised the objection, "What if I don't buy from your bulletin over a two-year period?" And then I resolved it with a satisfaction conviction—something that went beyond what people expected. In my BluBlocker infomercial, the objection might have been, "What if I receive a pair and I don't like them?" And then I resolved that objection with a satisfaction conviction that gave people the opportunity to return their purchase anytime they wanted to. No questions asked.

The satisfaction conviction is a critical part of the sales message and few realize how important it really is. Yet, if you create a powerful satisfaction conviction, this simple device will do a great deal for the success of your offers and would be a great way to supercharge Act Three.

The Desire to Belong

The desire to belong is such a strong motivational factor in marketing that it is often not appreciated or even recognized as a factor. Think about it.

Why do people own a Mercedes? Why do they smoke Marlboro cigarettes? Why do certain fads catch on? It all could be related to the basic premise that these people buy a specific product because they subconsciously want to belong to that group that already owns that specific product.

In the case of Marlboro, the smokers subconsciously want to join that group of smokers who have responded to the rugged western image that the cigarette's ad agency has created.

The people who buy a Mercedes often want to belong to that special group of people who drive a Mercedes. Do you think it's because of the special braking or suspension system? Forget it. They're going out and spending megabucks to buy something that's maybe slightly better than many of the other automobiles. The other cars can take you to the same places at the same speed and yet these same people—all very intelligent—will go out and buy a Mercedes.

And the list goes on. You name a product that has an established image and I'll show you consumers who, somewhere in their subconscious value system, want to belong to the group of people who own that product. Fashion, automobiles, cigarettes, gadgets, whatever the category, the consumer who buys a specific brand has been motivated to buy that brand by virtue of the desire to belong to the group of people who already own that brand.

When Volvo discovered that its customer base had one of the highest education levels of any of the car manufacturers, they went out and publicized this fact. They then noticed that when the same survey was conducted a few years later after the advertising campaign, the percentage jumped even higher. The percentage jump was caused, in my judgment, by the association that other educated buyers wanted to make with the educated Volvo owners. They wanted to belong to that group.

I've had my students say to me, "Well, what about hermits? Don't tell me they have the desire to belong."

And my answer was that they want to belong to the group of people who are hermits. To belong to the group means you don't necessarily have to be with anyone or be very social. And maybe the best word here is "identify." The Mercedes owner wants to be identified with the class or group of people who also own a Mercedes.

In California owning a Rolls-Royce in the '70s was the ultimate status symbol. I couldn't believe how impressed people were with other people who owned one. Being a midwest boy and not growing up in the car-conscious West Coast, I experienced culture shock when I realized how much a Rolls meant to somebody from the West Coast. Yet when you look at the car, it is one of the most conservative and old-fashioned-looking automobiles on the road today.

Theory 9

The desire to belong and identify with a group of people who own a specific product is one of the most powerful factors in why people buy.

Therefore, show your product being used by people they might want to identify with. Good-looking actresses with perfect skin would be ideal for a skin care product, and a friendly-looking and personable older gentleman for a car care product. If the viewers relate and identify with the people in your commercial, you've established that special relationship with your prospect and his or her desire to belong. Make sure, then, that all your characters are appealing, that the product is displayed in the best possible way and that your show host is somebody with whom the masses want to identify—either because of her beauty, his good looks or an endearing quality. People want to belong and identify. It's a very strong human psychological trait.

In our BluBlocker infomercials, we interviewed a number of people who gave incredible testimonials about our sunglasses. These interviews created a subconscious sense that everybody wanted to belong to the group who bought this product, thus further enforcing our message.

Sense of Urgency

You might have already figured this one out. You've sold the prospect. The prospect believes in your product and is ready to buy. You've come up with an incredibly powerful satisfaction conviction. But like many of your customers, this one says, "Well, let me think about it."

It is a proven fact that when this happens, chances are the prospect won't buy. And the reasons are really very logical. First, in time that excellent sales message you wrote and was seen on the screen is forgotten. It disappears like vapor. Second, if you're lucky and it isn't forgotten, it doesn't have the same impact it had when it was first seen. That old saying "out of sight, out of mind" holds true in a case like this.

To avoid the delaying tactic by the prospect, you've got to provide him or her with an incentive or reason to buy now. In fact, if you do your job right, that customer has to feel guilty not to buy right now. But how do you do it?

First, here's what you don't want to do. You've spent a lot of time with the prospect and you've convinced him or her to buy. The one thing you don't want to do is blow your integrity at the very end of the ad by making a statement that is not true. A statement like "If you don't respond within the next few days, we'll be sold out" or some other untruthful statement will actually cause the prospect not to buy. Remember, not only are you in Act Three, you are at the very end—just before the curtain drops—and your audience is ready to reach for the phones. So be careful. Whatever you say should be the truth and should be crafted in such a way that you maintain the same integrity you expressed throughout your entire commercial.

How Can You Give a Sense of Urgency?

Now, what can you do to provide a sense of urgency? Some ads that I've written in print had a sense of urgency that I expressed in my offer. For example, I ran a retraction which said that the price listed in a previous ad was the wrong price and that the new price was $20 higher—but you only had a few days to purchase the product at the old price before the new price went into effect. That approach was an integral part of the concept and provided a sense of urgency that was obvious and very real.

Another good example of how to create a sense of urgency is in the way QVC and HSN sell their products. They may mention something like, "If you're thinking of ordering, half our quantity is already sold, so I would suggest you call soon." Since the QVC viewer is used to seeing a product get sold out, they have learned that if they want to buy a product, they must act quickly. Another way QVC does this is by showing a time clock on the screen to indicate how much time the product will be shown on the air before the next product will be shown. And still another is the "amount sold" counter which sometimes creates a buying momentum and a sense of urgency.

You can use the sense of urgency in many different ways—low supplies, closeout opportunity, price rise, product shortages, limited-time price opportunity or limited-edition opportunity. And then there's "If you buy a pair of BluBlockers within an hour of this show, I'll send you a second pair absolutely free." That's the message we gave in our last two BluBlocker infomercials with great success.

The number of possibilities is limited only by your imagination. The sense-of-urgency statement always goes at the end of Act Three and is one of the most critical parts of your entire show.

Simplicity

In print, you must keep your advertising copy simple. The positioning of your product must be simple. Your offer must be simple. In short, you want to keep your entire presentation as simple as possible while still getting your message across. The same is true for television.

What does this mean in terms of your message? I like to tell my students to focus. Focus on what you are trying to accomplish and eliminate things that either complicate your presentation or aren't necessary.

Always remember to keep it simple.

This doesn't mean that your dialog must be so simple that the youngest child can understand it. That's not what we mean by simple. But the dialog should be comprehended by the least educated of people as well as the most educated and still come across clearly. It is not good style to talk "down" to anybody or "up" to anybody either.

The use of big words to impress is totally uncalled for and is simply an ego trip. Remember, you are talking to the mass market. Use simple, easy-to-understand words. Words are, after all, stories—emotional images, each having an impact sometimes greater than we think. Using simple words has the greatest impact. Using words that everybody can understand has a greater impact than words that some people have difficulty with.

And keep your sets simple with few distractions. A good example of how simplicity works in direct response happened to me when I was selling the Swiss Army watch in a print campaign. There were three styles and three colors in each style for a total of nine different watches. One style was a men's watch, the second was for women and the third was for children. The colors: black, red and khaki. I examined the watches, learned the history and in general became very knowledgeable about the watches themselves. Then came the big question from the president of the watch factory: "Mr. Sugarman, you've examined the watches. What do you think?"

I looked over the watches, thought for a few minutes and answered, "I'd like to run just the men's black watch in *The Wall Street Journal* to test the concept."

He Looked Perplexed

The watch company executive looked perplexed. "Why don't you offer all the styles? Look at how many more people you'll appeal to if you offer nine different styles. You'll reach women and children in addition to men and you'll give them all a color choice."

I told him that in my experience, keeping it simple was the best approach and that offering a customer too many choices was a very dangerous thing. But no matter what I said, he would not agree. "Logic says that offering more of a choice will result in more sales," he said.

I then came up with an idea to prove that I was right. I offered to run two separate ads in what is called an "A/B split." That is where *The Wall Street Journal* will print two separate versions of the same ad—version A and version B—to be delivered in the same area at the same time. So one home will get one version of the ad and the next-door neighbor will get version B. This is a very good way to test two different ads to determine the winning approach.

I offered to do the test and eventually ran the two ads with almost identical copy and graphics. One of the few differences was that in ad A I showed the men's watch along with the child's watch for size perspective, whereas in ad B I showed just the men's watch. I then listed each one of the choices—nine in ad A and just one in ad B.

Simplicity Wins Again

When I finished the ads, the A version even looked better than the version with only one choice. But when both versions ran, the ad that featured only one men's watch outpulled the other version that featured nine models with a surprising 3 to 1 ratio. In short, for every watch we sold from the ad that featured the nine styles, we sold three times as many in the other ad that showed just the one black watch.

I knew almost instinctively that to give the consumer a confusing array of choices or to keep the choices complicated would make the consumer back off and not buy.

When would I show all these nine watches? In my catalog. Once I'd located those people interested in Swiss Army watches,

I would then show all nine models in my catalog, because by the time my catalog reaches my customer, he or she has been qualified as a good watch buyer who already owns a Swiss Army watch. I can now offer a larger selection. The same is true on TV. Offer the strongest of the products you have in an infomercial and then offer the entire line on a home shopping format.

Another good example of the power of simplicity occurred during the production of the infomercial I was doing for the product called Miracell that I described in Chapter 5. Of the two offers I created for the show, it was the simple offer that worked and produced a profit and not the complicated one.

A Single Pair of Sunglasses

Even our BluBlocker offer was quite simple. It was a single pair of sunglasses. At one point, a competitor did an infomercial on sunglasses and offered three different styles. Seeing that, I knew it wouldn't work. Like the Swiss Watch company president thought, it seems logical, but in marketing, logic often doesn't work. Simplicity in direct response is critical and quite necessary. These are just a few of many examples that I have heard about or personally experienced during my many years in direct response.

Specificity

Being specific in your explanations is very critical and can affect the credibility of your entire show. Let me first give you an example. If I were to say, "New dentists everywhere use and recommend CapSnap Toothpaste," it sounds like typical advertising lingo or puffery designed to sell a product. It's so general that it will probably cause a viewer to discount the statement you have just made and maybe everything else you say. But if I say, "92% of new dentists use and recommend CapSnap Toothpaste," it sounds much more believable. The consumer will feel that we did a survey and that 92% was a scientifically generated figure.

People tend to regard general statements as puffery or typical advertising babble, and at best, those statements are discounted or accepted with some doubts. On the other hand, statements with specific facts can generate strong believability. I once wrote an ad for a company I created called Battram Galleries—a collectibles company. In the ad I stated my exact cost of running the ad, my exact manufactured cost of the product and clearly demonstrated through specific figures that we weren't making any profit from the offering. It was so successful, it was oversubscribed. I've used this technique on video as well.

Always Be Specific

In my BluBlocker infomercials, I state the specific reasons why blue light isn't good for your eyes. I explain that blue light focuses in front of the retina (which is the focusing screen of the eye) and not directly on the retina as do the other colors. So when you block blue light, you block those rays that don't focus on your retina and therefore objects appear clearer, sharper and more defined. I'm specific. It sounds believable. And the statement is a lot better than just saying, "BluBlocker sunglasses block all the blue light and so you see clearer, sharper and with more definition."

If you're describing a product that is designed for the circulatory functions of the body, you can talk about "242 miles of blood vessels" instead of "miles of blood vessels." When you talk about the bottom of your feet, instead of saying, "There are a lot of nerve endings at the bottom of your feet," you can say, "There are 72,000 nerve endings at the bottom of your feet." You are stating a specific fact as opposed to a vague statement. You are more believable.

There's one other benefit to being specific. By being specific you sound like you're an expert in what you're selling. You sound like you've really investigated your product and are knowledgeable about it. This too builds trust and confidence.

People are very skeptical about advertising in general and often don't believe the claims. But when you make a specific claim using exact facts and figures, your message is more credible and is often trusted primarily because it has been broadcast on TV. The perception is that you wouldn't lie about a fact.

Objections

No product is perfect. And in the process of presenting a product in a sales presentation, it is often possible that your prospect is thinking of an objection to your product. A good salesperson selling face-to-face will anticipate this objection and raise it right at the beginning of the sales presentation. The same goes for selling on TV or in print.

In print, whenever I took a picture of a product and realized that the product did not look good or had some obvious imperfections, I called attention to those imperfections. In my ad for the Magic Stat thermostat, I stated up front in the ad copy that the product looked ugly. In my ad for the Energaire ion generator I talked about that piece of fuzz at the top of the very sleek-looking unit and used "Miracle Fuzz" as the title of my ad. These are just a few of the many ways I've recognized objections right up front, as candidly as I could, and then resolved them. This is not genius. This is very much common sense. Bring up the objection early and resolve it, and the client opens up and is more receptive to accepting any resolution you have. The same is true on TV. When you're presenting a product and you are trying to hide an objection, it will certainly come up in the minds of your viewers. And if you don't resolve it, it will kill the sale.

Raise It and Resolve It

In our Miracell food supplement commercial when we thought an objection might come up in the minds of the viewers, we resolved it. For example, one of the questions in the minds of the viewers might have been, "Is it habit forming?" At one point in the show, I had one of the users comment that it wasn't habit forming, thus resolving a possible objection that might prevent a large part of the audience from ordering.

In infomercials using a *Larry King* type interview format, very often the host will raise possible objections throughout the show in almost a skeptical or questioning format. This skepticism, once it's resolved, is amazingly powerful in making the prospect feel comfortable. And, since it is a screenplay in which the two actors are in constant dialog, the objections can be resolved immediately after they are made.

If your product or your statements about it may raise a question, then you've got to answer that question no matter how negative the answer may be. And it is in the answer where you have the opportunity to turn the objection into a powerful advantage.

One of the issues I brought up when I was once selling a home pinball game was the issue of service. I brought it up because I knew that my customers were probably wondering who was going to fix such an expensive and large machine if it should break. Would they have to send the whole pinball game back for repair, and what would they have to do if they didn't like the product on arrival? The answer to this objection was that the integrated circuit board was removable and could be mailed in for replacement—which represented 90% of any problem that might occur. And if the customer didn't like the game after it arrived, no problem there. We arranged to pick it up at our expense.

On TV, if you're selling a piece of exercise equipment, the question of what consumers need to do if they don't like it when it arrives should be addressed very clearly somewhere in the show—usually near the end in the "Closing" part of the screenplay. If your product needs some type of installation, bring this out and explain how easy it is or what procedure will make it easy. Don't hide anything.

Even failing to give the dimensions of a large piece of exercise equipment is an example of not resolving the possible objection: "Will that unit fit in my closet?" I know that many a time when I've personally taken phone orders, a number of people would call not to order, but to get some piece of information that I failed to put in my ad because I thought it wasn't even important. Had I answered their questions in my ad, I would have gotten orders instead of questions.

Since many other of these principles can be found in my book *Advertising Secrets of the Written Word*, I urge you to pick up a copy and read it. It's the type of background that will make a big difference in your ability to recognize opportunities as you write a script and plan the infomercial.

Chapter 24 | Writing the Script

You should be ready to write the script once you understand the basic structure of an infomercial (the three-act play), the goals of each act (entertainment, selling and closing) and have some of the creative concepts in mind.

There are no differences in principle between writing the copy for a print ad and writing the script for an infomercial, but there are of course differences in the execution and in the format in which you express yourself.

In a print ad, the entire copy is a dialog between you and your prospect. In a TV script there are also the elements of scene description and camera direction in addition to dialog. For example, you might have a studio setting where two people are sitting on a couch talking. That is the scene. Then you may want a tight head shot of the host, so that would be considered a camera direction.

A Multi-Dimensional Expression

In a TV script you use these three elements of dialog, scene and camera direction to create a multi-dimensional expression of what you create in a print ad. There is less left to the imagination, as you are creating a visual, mental and audio impression in full color and in full motion for the viewer to apprehend.

You are also enhancing one of the driving forces behind the selling process—namely, emotion. You are creating an emotional feel with your message. And in selling, emotion is one of the key selling elements you need to accomplish your goal—that of causing your prospect to exchange his or her hard-earned money for your product or service.

TV creates the ultimate emotional climate. You, as the producer or writer, can create emotion from the people you choose for your commercial. You can create an emotional sense from the scene. You can bring out the emotion in the spoken dialog—something that can be done in a print ad but is very difficult. There are many opportunities to create emotion on TV.

Your goal is to create as much emotion as possible.

When writing your script you should have some basic knowledge which can easily be found in a library. First, you should have a good comprehension of camera angles. You should know what a "tight shot" is and what a "wide angle" looks like. Then you should know other terms such as "dolly-in" or the many terms that refer to the physical requirements to create a camera angle or effect. All these terms and the resulting visual appearances can be found in many books.

It is necessary if you are giving camera direction that you speak the same language that everybody else in the industry speaks, so pick up a book of terms and study them. You should study why these angles are used and the emotional impact that they have.

Before I wrote my first script, the first thing I did was read several TV scripts and then I studied a few books on camera direction. Having a background in photography as well as copy-writing gave me a head start, but we are not talking brain surgery. If you have any background in writing and photography, this will all come easy.

Once you understand the terms and the technique, then the next step is to create a script yourself. A script has a specific format that differs from the way you write copy for a print ad. You have on the left side of your page the scene and camera direction and on the right side the dialog. On one side, you direct the director and the cameraman and on the other side you direct the actors.

Many Software Programs

You can get the format for a script from many different sources. There are also many software programs that automatically format your script so you can simply type all this information into your computer and spit out a completed, properly formatted script quite quickly. A program called "Final Draft" is available for both the Mac and the PC computers.

What I do when I create a script is work the entire show out in my head first. I can visualize the types of scenes I want, the flow of the show, the dialog in general. In print you do pretty much the same thing. Very often when doing a print ad, I've thought out almost the entire text and it is simply a matter of sitting down at the computer and letting it flow onto the screen. George Lucas, when asked about his future installments for *Star Wars*, commented in an article I read 20 years ago, "I'm working it around in my head." So take a walk, relax in an easy chair and visualize all your scenes and the sequence in advance. It's more of a thinking process as opposed to the mechanical process of putting it on paper.

Let It Flow onto a Computer Screen

Once you've studied the terminology and the techniques, once you've worked the script out in your head, you're ready to let it flow onto a computer screen. But before you do, make sure that you've incorporated the key elements necessary for your selling screenplay. Are there three acts? Do you have the glue factors at the beginning of your show? Is most of the entertainment at the beginning of your show? Have you used enough curiosity throughout your show to cause your viewer to put down his or her remote control? Is your close a strong, serious message that will cause your prospect to exchange his or her hard-earned money for your product or service?

If you can say "yes" to all of the above, you are then ready to visualize your show as you transcribe all that emotion onto a sheet of paper for all your production team to share, comprehend and use.

My first script was created pretty much along the lines of what I've just described. It was the first BluBlocker show and it was scripted except for the testimonials and the experts that we interviewed. But later when most of our show was totally impromptu, the only scripting was for the host and myself.

The dialog should be written and performed in everyday real English. The worst thing you can have is dialog written or delivered to sound like it was scripted dialog. When I did my last BluBlocker infomercial, I had shot all of my interviews and edited them, and then all I had to do was shoot the host shots. I hired an actress by the name of Kimberly Horn who had not seen the scenes I had edited but who had to introduce them on the show. When she introduced each segment her delivery was so real and the script so natural that those watching the show could swear that she was actually familiar with each segment. In reality she had no idea what she was introducing.

Script as a Guide

One of the bits of direction I gave her was to use the script only as a guide. She was to read it, understand what I wanted her to say and if she wanted to make any changes so it would sound more real to her, she was to make them. And I read my script the same way. In the end, we followed the script closely enough to get our points across, but not so it sounded like a script.

This brings me to another bit of advice regarding hiring somebody to read a script. An actor or an actress knows how to improvise or make your script sound natural. A non-actor usually does not. So dealing with the problem of using a testimonial expert or other non-actor is one of experience. What I will typically do is brief the person on what to say as opposed to giving them a script. This way, they will use their own words, usually be more natural and not sound like they are reading a script, which of course they are not.

Remember that interview I had with that gorgeous model to be the show host for my BluBlocker show that I mentioned earlier in Chapter 4? To make sure she was the right person for the part, I arranged to meet with her for dinner and discuss the show and see if she would fit the bill. She was attractive, had a great personality, was glib and had a great sense of humor. She seemed perfect for the part. But when it came time to read the script, she couldn't read it without sounding like she was reading.

She Just Plain Froze

So I had her put the script down and just ad-lib the parts. She couldn't do that either. I ended up with an expensive lesson. First, audition before you go on the set, and second, hire a professional—one who has done this type of work before. The model was a great model but not qualified to act.

Once you've crafted your script and finished it, have somebody read it aloud. You'll be amazed at how different it will sound when somebody else reads it. Don't be afraid to constantly make changes. Many times, I've made changes that veered from the script—right on camera—and really enhanced the show. Your script is simply a blueprint for constructing a show. And if you've ever built a house, you know how many times you can deviate from the blueprints and make changes that occurred to you only after the walls were up and you could see the spatial relationships of the interior elements of the home.

I produce shows that seem to flow because the comments are real, the people are real and the dialog sounds like somebody's true emotional expression.

Having somebody else write your script costs around $7,000 to $15,000 depending on the complexity of the show and how much dialog and camera direction is required. Some agencies charge as much as $40,000 to write a script. And when you write the script yourself, of course, it won't cost you more than your own time. If you do write one yourself and it's your first one, hire a consultant or a scriptwriter and have him or her critique it.

Script writing is an art. But with the tips I've given you in this chapter and in the rest of the book, you'll have the basis for doing a pretty good job the first time out.

When you write that script, make sure that the ordering information is not given too early in the show or you might be in for a surprise, as I've illustrated in the next chapter.

Chapter 25 | When Do They Buy?

Steve Dworman is the publisher of *The Infomercial Marketing Report*—a monthly newsletter on the industry. By virtue of his position, he is a pretty knowledgeable guy who makes it a point to know everybody in the industry. He also knows what shows are working and making a handsome profit for their producers.

Steve also has a keen interest and some experience in TV production, so it was merely a matter of time until the infomercial bug was going to bite him. I also had many discussions with Steve about the techniques I used in my infomercials, and one of them was the overriding curiosity technique in my BluBlocker commercials. The concept so intrigued Steve that he wondered what he could do to come up with another product that might lend itself to the power of curiosity.

One day Steve called and told me that he had the idea of producing an infomercial that sold perfume. "I'll create so much curiosity about why this perfume is so good that women will jump at the chance to buy the stuff."

Add to His Knowledge Base

Steve followed up on his idea. After all, he knew the industry and many of the techniques and he felt that it would add to his knowledge base if he actually went through the entire process of producing a show of his own.

The first thing to do was to find a perfume that really produced the effect that he wanted. Then after he did that, he had to come up with a name. He was totally stuck after a variety of fancy names he had proposed were refused at the trademark office—all of them were already taken. So he called me and I suggested naming the perfume "Curiosity"—which he did. It was available and the trademark office gave him the registration.

Then he created the packaging for the product and produced the infomercial using many of the curiosity techniques I used in my commercial but applied very cleverly in a perfume format.

Testimonials from pretty women and interesting comments from men all added to the curiosity about the product: What did it really smell like?

Results Were Marginal

Steve tested the commercial and the results were marginal. Often, after you run your first tests, you do what is called "tweaking" to get the show to work a little better. I have found that if a show as produced is basically a good show but the product doesn't sell, it is often the product that is the reason the show doesn't work. In this case, tweaking the show doesn't help that much unless there are some major flaws in the show that can be corrected.

If you only have one product and you must make it work, then you indeed play with the show and get it to work by simplifying or otherwise changing the offer or by changing or enhancing certain segments. Steve looked at his commercial and then interviewed several people. The biggest complaint about the show was that the sell portion (the portion with the toll-free number, price and ordering information) came so late in the show that the viewers were getting impatient and wanted the ordering information to appear earlier. In short, they wanted to buy very early in the show but had to wait too long to get the toll-free number.

Steve called me with the results of his research and I warned him, "Steve, if you advance the ordering information to the very beginning of the show, you've removed another form of curiosity. You've got to keep people glued to the TV screen for as long as possible, and by keeping the price a mystery as long as possible, you are using one of the best techniques of curiosity. If you reveal the price in the first five minutes, you don't need a half-hour show to sell your product but rather a five-minute commercial."

We Disagreed on Research

Steve disagreed. "But Joe, you should hear the comments I'm getting. It's not a matter of selling the product. It's already sold. The viewers just want the ordering information."

I had done a lot of research into when people buy and even had a survey done by my order-taking service. We found that over 80% of the orders were placed at the very end of the show despite the fact that we had the ordering information presented twice before the end of the show. This confirmed my position that selling my sunglasses in a three-act play, if properly structured, required enough time to allow the selling proposition of my play to be effectively acted out.

Steve changed his commercial to place the ordering information after the first seven minutes of the show and tested the results. "They were terrible," he confided in me. "There was a dramatic difference between the way we had it before and the way it is now with the ordering information up front. Our sales are now cut in half."

So Steve reverted to the original approach and with enough experience found other ways to improve his response. The point that Steve's example makes is also the point of my research—namely, that withholding price information acts as a form of curiosity to keep the viewer watching the show. If the show is viewed as a three-act selling play and viewers only see the first act, the viewer is not likely to get the complete buying message. And finally, as I've indicated, the purchase of your product is usually made at the end of a half-hour show. The dynamics of your selling proposition should conform to this important bit of research.

In the *Larry King* type interview shows where the price is never mentioned, you have to call the toll-free number to find it out. So curiosity works for you throughout the entire show.

Once again, remember that if you are using a half-hour format to sell your product, you must use the entire half hour to do the most effective selling job. That half hour must be viewed not as a half hour, but as three segments overlaid with techniques, such as curiosity, to compel the viewer to watch your entire show. Do this and you'll see the difference in your infomercial results.

Chapter 26 | The Product as King

Let's make a few assumptions right now. You understand the importance of creating a three-act screenplay with the first act called "Entertainment," the second act called "Selling" and the final act called "Closing."

You also understand the importance of the glue factor and the effect it has on causing a person to keep watching your commercial to the very end. You also know how important curiosity is in keeping your viewer watching your show with his or her remote control safely out of reach.

You also just learned that indeed you need the entire half hour to do the effective selling job that your product requires. You also realize that you're producing a screenplay and you can't cut the play off in the beginning or even in the middle. Your viewers must watch the entire play from beginning to end to make your infomercial really effective.

Determine If Product Makes Sense

With this much information you have some valuable insights into what it takes to script and produce an infomercial. But obviously, there are a lot more steps involved and a lot more insights needed to make an infomercial into a very effective and profitable marketing tool.

First you have to decide if your product even makes sense for an infomercial. Then you have to write a script, decide on a format—video or film—select a production house to assist you, hire the talent, rehearse the talent, shoot the footage, edit the footage into a show, and possibly arrange for an audience if you need one for your show format.

Then you have to test the show, buy media and run your commercial throughout the country. And then there is the matter of fulfillment. You have to take the orders through a phone order-taking company, process the orders, ship the product and if it is something you are producing yourself, manufacture the product.

It's not an easy process and there is a lot to it. And quite frankly, unless you have megabucks to make this happen, a tremendous amount of previous experience in TV production or a sizable company that can organize this, you shouldn't even attempt to do an infomercial.

You can, of course, have a wonderful product, approach an infomercial producer and work out a deal to have him or her take care of producing your show and marketing your product. That certainly is a good way to go and I will discuss this approach a little later in this book. But simply by reading this book, not only will you be able to determine if your product is suitable for an infomercial, but you'll know if the company you are dealing with is using the proper techniques in producing your show.

First the Product

I will now take you through the rest of the process in a logical fashion so you can grasp some of the important marketing insights that are so critical to success in this field. The first of these concepts concerns the product itself.

What products work best in an infomercial? How important is the product to the overall success of the show? And what kind of margins do you need to make a successful go at producing an infomercial? Let's take the importance of the product itself.

It is my experience from working with all forms of direct marketing that there are times when certain products are ready for the public and other times when they are not.

Theory 10
When the product is right for the market, it is priced right, it appeals to the broad audience for which it is intended and it is in a form that harmonizes with the needs of your audience.

When this point is reached, chances are that if the product is presented in a reasonable way in accord with correct principles for selling on TV, it will sell well. If the product is not ready, is priced too high or doesn't harmonize with the needs of the audience, it will not sell and there is little you can do to make it sell. It is the public who decides whether you have a successful product or not.

Later, in Chapter 31, I will discuss the testing process and describe how you can inexpensively test to determine if a product could be sold effectively on TV. But let us assume that we must now decide on a suitable product.

The first thing I would look at is the size of the market for the product you are offering. Does your market encompass everybody who watches TV, or what is called the mass market? If so, it is an ideal TV product. After all, everybody watches TV and this means people in all age and income groups.

If your product appeals only to women, the product still has a very good chance to succeed, but you are losing half your audience and therefore you are paying twice as much for each prospect than if your product appealed to the masses—both men and women.

Smaller Market Requires More Profits

You can then follow this logic even further. Let us say you have a product that appeals to both men and women but it is very expensive. Although your product appeals to both sexes, those in your audience who can afford the product may represent only a small fraction of your potential prospects. Once again, you are wasting a lot of money to hit just those high-income people, but then again, they may be worth it if you have enough profit built into your product.

Your market could be all older men or older women or younger men and younger women (still a pretty good market). If your market is all golfers, you limit your market in two ways—to only those who play golf and probably only those in a higher income group. Would such a product succeed? It might, but you are wasting a tremendous amount of your money reaching the rest of the mass market who can't afford your product and who don't play golf.

Theory 11   *The closer you get to matching the demographics of those who are watching TV to the demographics of your product, the greater your chances for success because the larger your potential market the more efficiently you can reach this market.*

Even though you are reaching a mass market, there is one way to attract an audience that has the demographics that match those of your product. If your show has a game show feel with audience participation, it will tend to reach a slightly lower-income demographic group than if it were a one-on-one type of talk show. Why? Because typically the type of viewer who watches the one-on-one talk show is more intelligent and has a higher income than the viewer of a game show. So simply by picking the type of theme or format for your show you can determine which segment of the audience you will reach with your product.

One of the other elements that you have to look at is the margins in your product. If you are pricing a product around $39.95 and you hope to cover your TV advertising costs, the product should cost you not much over one-tenth of that price. In short, the $39.95 product should cost you from $4 to $6 to make it profitable in an infomercial format.

The Higher the Price, the Less the Margins

For the more expensive products such as the popular exercise devices, the margins could be less, with a four-times markup for the retail price, but that is the lowest limit—from four times the cost of a product on some items to 10 times the cost on others.

There are some exceptions to this rule, but in general, these are margins you need to shoot for to succeed. When I sold vitamins in the early days of infomercials, I sold them for double what the vitamins cost me. But I had a continuity program in place and my customers kept buying from me. It was during the early stages of the infomercial industry when practically anything that had half a chance to succeed would make it. This is no longer true today.

Now let's look at some of the product categories and see how they would fit into the infomercial format. First, there are the intellectual property products—cassette tapes, books, software programs—the types of products that cost very little to duplicate yet have their real value in the unique intellectual talent and effort of the author. The self-improvement tapes and books which may cost around $17 to produce sell for $170. The real estate and direct marketing courses, for example, sell for a very large multiple over their cost of production. Once the raw cost to produce the product is covered, then the profit margins really make for an impressive infomercial product.

Direct to Consumers

Sunglasses are another category. You can produce a pair of sunglasses inexpensively using the best of materials and they will compare with or be even better than many of the expensive pairs on the market. The difference is simply in the number of hands a pair of sunglasses goes through before it reaches the public—the wholesaler, the jobber, the retailer and then eventually the public. Producing them yourself, as I have done, and then selling them directly to the public is a very efficient way to offer a quality product at a good value and earn a respectable profit.

Another example of a good product category is chemical products such as cleaning liquids, car additives, face creams or anything that is manufactured from chemicals. There are two reasons they make good products. First, they often have large margins and can sell for many times their cost. Second, they are often consumable and therefore have large reorder potential or what is commonly called continuity. You need this continuity to supplement your income during the time your product is being sold on TV or to develop a nice future business at retail after you get off TV.

One of the things I noticed about BluBlocker sunglasses was that indeed there was an aftermarket for my product. People were often so pleased with their purchase, they bought extra pairs to keep in their car or give to friends. In many cases they bought pairs to replace the BluBlockers they lost. On QVC, many of the viewers buy several over the course of a year. They were either developing a collection or buying different styles to wear on different occasions.

Health-Related Products Sell Well

Another example of a good product with large margins is vitamins or other health-related items that come in consumable form. They can be sold along with a continuity program, which means that people are automatically shipped the product each month and then automatically charged on their credit cards. You might not make a profit on the first shipment, but the average life of a customer might be more than several shipments and therefore you earn your profit on subsequent automatic sales.

I have sold health-related products—sunglasses, vitamins and wrinkle pills—on infomercials with relatively good success.

Some of the other product categories that seem to be doing very well on TV are beauty products. These often have great margins somewhere in the 10 to 1 range.

Exercise devices that develop a specific part of your body (such as the popular abdominal devices) seem to do quite well. In these products, the margins may not be as great as with some of the other products, but these products appeal to the mass market so you are achieving more efficiency in terms of reaching the people who can use and afford your product.

If you have the opportunity to price your product, you must price it not so much to meet the margins I am recommending, but rather so that the product appears to be a good value. Consumers are not stupid and they know good value right away.

There are three major elements to remember about the selection of an infomercial product, and they transcend all other issues by far. The first is the size of the market to which the product appeals and the second is the ratio of the cost to the retail price. If you have a broad enough market and the right profit structure, then you have the two strongest elements required to be successful in this difficult but very rewarding medium.

But even if you have both of these elements in place, the final element and the most important is the consumer. For if the consumer feels that your product is not of interest, you have nothing. If the product is king, then the consumer is truly the king of kings.

Chapter 27 | The Production Issues

You've got the right product, you've got a script in mind that is like a screenplay with three acts, you've got some great ideas for your glue factors and you've got enough entertainment and built-in curiosity to hold the attention of a viewer with even the shortest of attention spans. Now comes the part where you have to put all this together and create the show.

There are three ways to produce your infomercial. The first is to go to one of the infomercial production companies. Check Appendix D for the *Adweek Source Book,* which lists these companies. They are equipped to take your product and do everything from writing the script to videotaping the infomercial. You're on your own after that, but they will hand you a completed show after they finish.

The second choice is for you to write the script and hire an agency that specializes in videotaping shows. You would be the writer and director. The third choice is for you to go to an existing infomercial company and have them do it all. You just supply the product and earn a royalty or a percentage of the profit or gross sales.

Many Approaches Possible

If you have none of the skills to produce your infomercial and don't have the time to organize it yourself, then you can choose the last option. If you have some direct marketing experience but don't have the time or inclination to undertake the production of your own show but have some money to invest in an infomercial, I would suggest the first approach of hiring a full-service agency to do the entire project. You'll need all the expertise you can gather and a full-service agency is the best route to take. But a full-service agency will cost you a lot more than if you do it yourself. You're probably looking at a minimum of $250,000 or three times what it will cost to do it yourself.

What I did in my career is use a combination of approaches.

I hired an ad agency by the name of Rosenfield & Lane out of Kansas City, and they assisted me in organizing my productions. With a midwestern ad agency, I had access to reasonably priced, local on-air talent and lower production costs. My production costs often dwarf those of the big full-service agencies operating out of New York and Los Angeles.

When I do a studio shoot, they set up the props and organize the team to support the shoot. They also place some of our media time and arrange for a camera crew to accompany me. In short, they play a support role while I focus on the script and the directing as well as the editing.

The Support of an Ad Agency

Could I do everything myself and organize it within my own company? Probably. But it is nice to have the support of an ad agency that really cares and whose pricing is very reasonable. And Dan Rosenfield, president of the agency, has been somebody I've always been able to count on.

If you're interested in going with a full-service agency you might be interested in reading *The Complete Guide to Infomercial Marketing*, by Timothy R. Hawthorne ($60, NTC Business Books, Lincolnwood, IL). Tim is the founder of Hawthorne Communications and has had a lot of experience with infomercials from the very early days. He was truly a pioneer.

The book is written, in my judgment, as a good promotional piece for his agency, and his examples tend to support hiring the type of agency he represents and paying for very high production values. The book has a lot of good information, but I disagree with many of the points he makes about costs and production issues. You can produce great infomercials at very reasonable prices if you do them yourself. If you don't have the desire or the skill and you use a full-service agency, expect to pay a lot more—maybe triple.

The next issue is the style of show you want to shoot. Will it be similar to a *60 Minutes* format, a *Larry King* format or will be like *The Price Is Right* or even *The Tonight Show*? In other words, to really tune in to the TV market you want, tune in to a show format that matches something that is popular with the TV audience and appeals to the type of viewer you are trying to attract. For example, if I were doing a golf show, I would want my show to look like a golf sporting event. If I wanted to reach a very upscale viewer, I might do a *Larry King* format. And if I wanted to reach a mass audience, maybe an *Oprah Winfrey*, soap opera, or sitcom type approach might work.

Theory 12   *When you pick the show format, you also pick the demographics of your audience.*

Regardless of your choice of show format, you must now decide what image format you will be shooting in—film or video. The quality of film far exceeds that of video but the cost of shooting with film is almost four times that of video. But there is also a feeling you get from video that brings the viewers closer and gets them more involved in the scene than with film.

Let us say you choose video. You've chosen a less expensive format as well as one that will be more "endearing" to your audience. It will have a "warmer" feel to it. It will feel more "real." I realize that some of these terms may not make sense to you, but after shooting 13 infomercials with video and having people compare my productions with those shot in film, these are some of the terms they've used to describe the difference.

I have another way to express the difference. People are used to watching TV, and on TV most of the shows are shot with video. People are used to seeing films in a movie theater on a very large screen. By doing your show in video, you are more closely matching the format that viewers normally experience when they watch TV at home.

When you shoot in video, typically you shoot with an expensive camera system like the Sony Betacam or something similar. And in a studio, that is the best format to use. But for many of the scenes that I've shot I used the High-8 format, which is the same used by many amateurs and which can be bought inexpensively in any video store. In short, I found that the quality of the shot was not as important as what was actually shot. Some of the most successful shots we took—such as the one with Dr. Geek, the rapper who appeared in our BluBlocker infomercial—were shot with the High-8 format.

Too Much Attention

In addition, if a full-blown camera crew would create too much attention, I simply used my own video camera and shot it myself. And with the new crop of digital 3-chip cameras, you would be hard-pressed to tell the difference between the best $30,000 Sony Betacam video camera and the low-priced digital models. If you're hiring a crew or doing a studio shoot, always use the best, however, as it won't cost you more in the long run.

When would you use film? I would use film if I were a major U.S. corporation concerned about my image and didn't care what the infomercial cost to produce. I might use film for certain segments of a show where clarity and crispness are important for a shot. But in general I wouldn't use it, as I don't believe the difference is worth the extra cost nor does it relate as strongly to my audience and their viewing habits.

On the other hand, if you are an infomercial producer and have a hit show, then even if you spent $500,000 to shoot a show in film, the cost of the production could easily be covered within a very short time. The problem is determining whether you have a big hit, and one never knows until the show runs.

My Lowest-Cost Infomercial

In my experience, I have spent approximately $40,000 for most of my BluBlocker infomercials. The exception was my last one, which cost me only $20,000 because I already had most of my footage from three previous shows.

In my last BluBlocker infomercial, I broke even overall on the production costs of the three city shows and the new show on the first day it ran as a test. And from then on, my major risk was eliminated. I have also had a few that totally bombed, but in the long run the winners more than compensated for the losers.

Now that you have gotten the product, written a great script and chosen the production company or the group to assist you in producing the infomercial, it's time to videotape your show. What are some of the insights I can share with you about my shooting experience that might help you? That's my next subject. Remember, you have already done a lot of work in preparation for the shooting of your commercial, and how it translates into video will be an important part of this process.

Chapter 28 | The Shooting Experience

If you are directing your show, I have two suggestions. Have a background in photography and be knowledgeable in video. If not, find somebody who is.

When I say "knowledgeable in video," I am not necessarily referring to experience. I certainly didn't have much when I started. But I knew photography, I knew what I wanted to achieve and I had read enough about the terms and techniques in video to be familiar with the art.

Knowledge Leads to Success

As in print photography, you can make or break a scene with the wrong camera angle, a poor microphone or a bad sound system. The more knowledge you have, the more potential you have to succeed.

Let me share with you some of the insights that I have learned from my 10 years in this medium. I'm certainly not the ultimate expert on this subject and don't pretend to be, but a few insights from my experience might help you.

Hiring a camera crew to cover an event or tape an interview is a relatively easy thing to do. You simply locate one from the *Adweek Source Book* (see end of Appendix D) or look in the Yellow Pages. Generally you want to locate a company that has a Sony Betacam or similar equipment. I'm not averse to lesser formats, as I've discussed in the previous chapter, but in general if you want to do the best job possible and have a final product with the best possible production values, go for the top-of-the-line equipment.

A crew will often consist of the cameraperson, an assistant, a sound technician, and a lighting technician if required. That's all you really need in order to get the best shot possible. A simple setup like this only costs, on average, from $1,200 to $1,500 a day. You could add additional lighting people if required and a makeup person. A makeup person often enhances the subject you are shooting and removes a few blemishes that might be obvious on camera. The extra lighting people might be needed if you are shooting indoors and lighting a large area or lighting a subject.

The Big Show

In my experience, I rarely use a makeup person except in a studio shoot or when lighting is required where you really want your subjects to look their best. I've been to remote shoots done by other infomercial companies where they have two cameras, 20 people running around preparing the scenes, doing the makeup, supporting the support people in charge of the microphones, lighting and catering—and, in general, creating the impression that you're on a movie set. What I often find is that much of this activity is a show, possibly to impress the client or the high-profile personality they are shooting. The additional benefit gained from all these people can be quite small when compared to the simple, relaxed set where the minimum number of people are present.

Another tip I'd like to share involves directing. If you are the director, you want to be in charge. You can listen to suggestions from people who come up to you and whisper in your ear, but never allow anybody to blurt out directions or suggestions within earshot of the talent. You are in charge and you've got to act that role and make sure everybody else knows this as well.

Only one person can be the director or else there is a lot of confusion.

I was on a shoot at a sheep farm in New Zealand with some-body I had along as my assistant. I was training him in the art of directing a video and he had very little experience in video. Whenever he had an idea, he would either direct the action or shout out his suggestions to me. The participants were getting confused. They didn't quite know where their orders were com-ing from. I had to take the student aside and tell him to whisper any suggestions in my ear. He realized what he had been doing and stopped, thus reducing the tension on the set.

For the people who are the talent, there is enough stress from simply being on camera. They don't want to be confused and they don't want to have to take orders from more than one person. The cameraperson may have a suggestion, the sound technician may want to give some advice—all that is OK as long as it is directed only to you.

And that brings me to another point. Listen to your camera-person and sound technician. They often have a wealth of expe-rience. If you aren't sure about a shot, ask for advice. It is one thing to be in charge and another to be humble enough to ask for advice when you are not sure. Nobody will think less of you as a director. In fact, the crew will have more respect for you.

Avoid Any Surprises

Review your production from time to time while it is still in the camera to make sure it is being shot right. The worst night-mare in the world is to shoot something, go home and find that something was wrong with the camera. Sometimes a cameraper-son will bring along a small portable monitor in which you can see the action. If you are in one location long enough, it is handy to have and will often save you from having to review the video by looking through the camera viewfinder while the videogra-pher replays the scenes. If you are constantly on the move, though, sometimes the monitor is not practical.

Also make sure you review the sound. In one of my shoots at Venice Beach, I just had a cameraman and no sound technician because of the candid nature of the shoot and the requirement for mobility. Larry Brewer, the cameraman, had a microphone mounted on his camera and a remote mike for me to use. Half-way through the shoot the remote mike failed. Fortunately he somehow sensed this and we had it replaced.

If you hire somebody to interview people, make sure the person has a nice smooth way of talking with people. Make sure the interviewer is relaxed and can relate to the person he or she is interviewing. I once asked a person who was assisting me to interview a few subjects for my BluBlocker commercial. He was so hyper that the subjects felt very uncomfortable during the interview. Once again, there is a knack to everything, and often an audition is the best method of determining how a person will act in front of the camera and interact with other people.

Cost of Camera vs. Quality

As I mentioned earlier, you can have some beautiful video shot with a simple video camera that you can buy in any camera store for around $500. And you can get some pretty lousy shots from the most professional video camera if the cameraperson goofs.

This happened with a new crew I was using in Chicago. The cameraman was not paying attention to his focus and his white balance control, and some of the video quality was horrible. But the shot that he took was so important and effective in its content that we were forced to use it. Content is much more important than technique.

Some of my other shooting advice is limited to my personal experience only and by far I'm not an authority on the subject. A lot of it is based on common sense and knowledge of video in general.

For example, one of the subjects that should be discussed here is budget. How much do you budget for a shoot? If I were preparing a budget for a client, I would provide a very extensive detailed breakdown of expenses to cover all contingencies and every possible cost. But since I'm the director and the guy paying the bills, I'm mainly concerned with the costs of outside services such as the camera crew. I always get a quote from a camera crew for a shoot before I start. Usually it is a per day or what is called per diem cost that includes support people and all other expenses. It is the easiest way to go unless you only need a little footage and the shoot will last only an hour. But typically, you hire a crew for the day if you are going on a remote shoot or even doing a studio shoot.

Nature as My Background

If you need to create a set for your show, you can do it either through a professional set designer or by yourself in a very simple way. For example, I used nature as my set designer when I shot my BluBlocker commercial, as I shot it in Maui with a beautiful ocean and palm trees as my background.

A set designer gives you a budget for the set design and drawings for approval and then constructs the set, buys the components and puts them all together for you in time for your studio shoot. You should always have enough time to make any corrections in the set and even shoot a segment on video to see how the set shows up. This will give you a chance to make any last-minute changes in either props or lighting.

Some final bits of advice: Feed your crew. One of the things you don't want to forget are the logistics associated with supporting your team. Often a shoot will go a lot longer than you expect. Be prepared for it. Give everybody ample breaks. If the energy doesn't feel right to you on a shoot, take a longer break.

Shooting is like anything else in life that you want to master. The more you do it, the better you get. The more you practice, the better your score.

Chapter 29 | The Editing Challenge

You've now got hours of raw footage that you must review to select those special cuts that will go into your infomercial and be assembled in a seamless fashion. How do you prepare for the editing process?

The first thing I do is get time-coded tapes of the raw footage and then I review them on a simple VCR that I have at home. A time-coded tape contains a small window at the bottom of your tape showing a reference point of the exact minute and second and even fraction of a second of the footage you've taken. By looking at the time code shown on your screen, you can select the exact cut and sequence you want in the final production. I study all the tapes, take notes and write down time codes of the takes that seem the best and could be used in the final cut.

Frame-by-Frame Advance

A good VCR will do. I use one that has a remote control and a pause button so I can stop and rewind to make sure I have the right time codes. Some VCRs can advance the tape frame-by-frame. This is helpful, as often you need to select the exact moment to stop the action or dissolve into another scene.

In a well-scripted show where there is little impromptu conversation, it is simply a matter of reviewing which is the best of several takes. It's like editing a movie. For my BluBlocker commercials, however, I never knew what I would end up with because practically the entire show was spontaneous.

I then will review what I have edited and make more refinements. It's about now that I might end up with more than 45 minutes of possible takes to fit into a 28-1/2 minute show. Either I'll transcribe the audio portion for each of those cuts and then sort out what I want and their flow or I'll continue to refine my selection until it is complete.

I then send a complete listing of the cuts and takes and the order of the cuts to the editing studio and they produce what is called a "rough cut" of the segments that I send them. I then review the rough cut and make slight alterations, send it back to them and they return the final version to me.

Just like Editing and Refining Copy

Sometimes I do this directly in their studio. This gives me more flexibility as I can make last-minute changes while editing. But I always first review the tapes on a simple VCR and reduce them to the best footage I can before I go to the rough-cut stage.

Once I have a rough cut, I generally go into the studio or the "edit suite" as it is called and put all the pieces together that make up the final show. This may take from a full day to two or even three days. Typically with my BluBlocker shows it would take a good day and a half, and many times sessions would go late into the evening. You don't want to stop as all the pieces are familiar and stopping may interrupt a good flow. Edit suite costs are very high compared to what is called "off-line" editing, which involves your rough editing of the commercial. A typical cost would range from $200 to $300 depending on the studio.

There is a new development in computers and software that allows you to edit your own show right on your computer. In addition, there are advances such as the all-computerized Avid video editing system that many of the big studios are now using. The price of the Avid system is coming down, and the computers that can almost replace it are now multiplying. It won't be too long before you'll be able to create your own shows on your PC or Mac right in your own office.

The Future Is Here Right Now

I've worked with the Avid system. It is too complicated to learn quickly, so you rent the equipment and hire a competent operator who comes with the equipment. You tell him or her what you want and the scenes just flash across the screen. I've done this off-line for some of the more intricate editing when I'm trying to tweak a show.

Just as in editing copy in the copywriting process, you have a specific goal in editing an infomercial:

Theory 13

In editing, you want to get the full emotional impact out of the time you've been allotted to sell your product or service.

In editing, you've either got the talent for it or you don't. It's an instinctive feel for knowing emotionally what to cut and what to leave in. And age plays no role either. My daughter April, when she was in her early 20s, had that "emotional feel" for editing. I sent her to Kansas City to do the editing of my last BluBlocker infomercial and she did an incredible job putting all the pieces together within two days with Dan Rosenfield and Larry Brewer from my ad agency. In fact, that one commercial turned out to be the most effective BluBlocker commercial we ran in our series of four.

During the editing process you will be presented with many options for moving from scene to scene. For example, there might be a lap dissolve or an abrupt cut. This subject is important to the seamless flow of the infomercial, and it is something that can be found in books in many video stores. You can also get a lot of guidance from the video editor you work with. Often he or she has a wealth of experience and can provide you with quite an education in the process.

Once you understand the techniques for going from scene to scene, your goal is simply a matter of refinement. You should already have in place all of the entertainment, selling and closing elements in your screenplay. It is then up to you to make the tough commonsense choices of what to cut and what to run.

Theory 14   *The most important part of the editing process is your ability to retain and enhance the emotional appeal of your product and your characters. You edit for emotion.*

When I worked on my Miracell wrinkle pill infomercial, I refined the show to such an extent that it was three minutes short. I could have gone back and added a few scenes from the footage I eliminated, but I decided against that. If I felt it didn't add to the show, then I wasn't going to corrupt the emotional flow and nature of what I had already accomplished.

In this instance, I repeated the strongest emotional segments from the earlier part of the show and also showed biographies of some of the characters who appeared along with their ages while I showed the toll-free order number on the bottom of the screen. The repeat cuts reinforced the sales message and the biographies kept viewers' attention while the toll-free number encouraged them to call up and order.

When you complete the editing process, the next step is to take your final video, which is now exactly 28-1/2 minutes long, and test it on a TV station or series of stations. But before you can do that, you have to buy media. And that brings us to the next chapter.

PSST! WANNA BUY SOME CHEAP TV TIME?

TV media is one of the most negotiable of all the forms of advertising.

There are several different approaches to buying media just as there are several different approaches to producing your infomercial. You can buy your own time, work through a media buying service or do a combination of the above. At JS&A I elected to do both—buy media through a media buying service and buy media directly.

We bought all of our media directly during the early stages of our experience with infomercials. And we got pretty good at it. But we also were offered some very good time slots or what are called "avails" from a company called New Day Marketing— a buying service out of California. So we started slowly buying from them. Vikki Hunt, the company president, often could get us pretty good deals and even though we had a very good rapport going with many of the stations already, Vikki had a pretty good rapport with stations we weren't familiar with.

Eventually we turned a good chunk of our media buying over to her and she earned a portion of the 15% agency discount. We still dealt directly with many stations with whom we had previously dealt because either they were local, we had great rapport with them or they were important in our testing procedures.

One of the steps we took during the buying of media was to create a manual for anybody to follow—a real how-to for the buying of media. That was my daughter April's responsibility since she did some of the buying for our shows. But before we go into the actual process of media buying, you need to understand the strategy of media buying and the importance of this critical step in the infomercial process.

As in print, it is extremely important to get the best possible rates. If a TV station charges $20,000 for a half-hour time slot and you produce $20,000 gross profit from the sale of your product, then in essence you have not earned any money. You've just broken even.

But Negotiate Correctly . . .

But if you are able to negotiate a deal on that media and buy a slot for only $10,000 and you made the same $20,000 in gross profit, then you have earned $10,000. Now that's a big difference.

It therefore becomes imperative that you buy media correctly. You can have the best margins and a great product, but if you pay too much for media you can lose your shirt.

Theory 15   *TV media is one of the most negotiable of all the forms of advertising.*

First, it is finite. A station only has so much time and the last thing they want to do is run public service announcements to take up that time. So they have to balance the demand with the time available.

It is the ideal example of supply and demand. In fact, when infomercials first started appearing in the mid '80s on just a few stations, rates were very low and most anything that ran did well. Later, at the start of the '90s, we had a mini recession and many

WELL... WE CAN EITHER RUN "MY MOTHER THE CAR", WITH PUBLIC SERVICE ANNOUNCEMENTS, OR SELL THE HALF-HOUR TO BluBlocker FOR $27. CALL AND TELL 'EM THEY GOT IT!

Sometimes you get the most incredible deals.

of the stations felt the effects and reduced their time costs to attract business. That is when the infomercial industry really took off. The recession encouraged many advertisers to reduce their advertising expenditures, leaving a tremendous amount of open time to be bought by the infomercial companies. In addition, the networks who were not willing to allow infomercials to be run on their affiliates had a change of heart and started accepting them. During this period, infomercials were a very profitable growth business.

Then, just as the economy started to improve and we pulled out of the recession, demand by marketers for infomercial time and advertisers for broadcast time caused rates to soar. In addition, some of the companies running infomercials weren't interested in making a profit off the infomercial. They wanted no part of the accountability associated with direct marketing as they were running their infomercials to create brand awareness and not sales. Major corporations like IBM, Apple and Volvo Corporation started using the media. And although they saw sales increase, there was often no way to know whether the increase was due to the infomercial.

Cowboys Mess Up the Market

Another factor that started driving rates higher was the new marketers known as "cowboys" in the infomercial industry. Not knowing the importance of negotiating media, they would simply either pay higher prices or bid up the prices when they had a new show that worked very well. They would buy at any price just to get their show on the air, and as a consequence, they set a higher benchmark which other infomercial producers then had to match.

Combine the better economic climate, the major corporations getting into the fold, increased demand for the limited amount of airtime and the new cowboys entering the field, and you set the stage for an escalation of media prices that continued for several years.

Let me cite examples of some of the events that were going on in the industry during these periods of rate escalation. A station in San Diego that was normally selling a time slot for $2,000 to infomercial buying services was approached by a mainstream ad agency representing a major national infomercial advertiser. The station quoted $20,000 for the same time slot they had been selling for $2,000 and the ad agency accepted the price and consequently preempted the infomercial that was scheduled to run at the same time. The station then got wise and its rates nearly tripled within a very short time. And whenever the station in San Diego was approached by an ad agency representing a major corporation, their rates were very high.

There Are Always the Deals

On the other hand, a major network approached JS&A directly and said that one of their advertisers had just dropped out of a major time slot following an NFL football game and that the rate was normally $100,000 for a half hour but because they loved our infomercial, they were willing to sell this prime time slot to us for $20,000. We took the time slot and did very well. Obviously, we were asked to keep our transaction confidential.

We are dealing with supply and demand, and rates can fluctuate tremendously based on circumstances and timing. When we hit our next recession, that will be a great opportunity for people already in the infomercial industry. Their rates will go down, more people will be at home as opposed to out shopping and response rates should do very well. Infomercials should be recession resistant.

Spot media is also bought through media buying services. Generally, it is a completely different media buying agency than the agency that buys infomercial time. Long-form commercial time (infomercial time) is usually bought by agencies that specialize in this type of buying. They know how important it is to get the lowest possible rate for the advertiser.

Everybody Must Make Money

Advertisers must make a profit from each show, and if they don't, they won't be buying much media in the future. It is therefore imperative that the agency not only is good at media negotiations but also knows the profitability for each show so they can use that as a bargaining tool when negotiating rates with a station. It also helps to provide boundaries based on that station's effectiveness in the past. For example, the media buyer knows how much the infomercial company can afford to pay for the time slots based on their profitability with similar stations, and therefore they can negotiate within boundaries.

Each show must be profitable, and you must account for how much profit each show makes. You can't run on 20 stations and then average the responses and come up with a net profit and say, "Well, we did well on our weekend run." You must know to a penny what each station did on each exposure. Separate accountability for each station and each show is possible by simply using a different toll-free number for each show. If you are using an outside order-taking service that specializes in this type of activity, they have the toll-free numbers and the computer facilities to separate all your orders and report back to you on how many orders you've received. Then it's up to you or your media buying service, armed with the figures, to determine the profitability of all your media selections for your time slots.

Two-Week Cancellation Clause Necessary

Media response can vary. But generally, when your show starts to fade on a station it doesn't take long to realize it. Response will start to drop and then fall below a certain comfort zone. It's then a good time to pull your commercial off the station or replace it with another show. I always make sure that we have a two-week cancellation clause in our station contract whenever possible. I can then get off a losing station rather quickly without too much damage. The only exception is where you get a good deal for a certain block of time and have other shows that you can substitute for the show that isn't working. Anybody who buys a block of time for a single show might be making a big mistake as that show can die and you're stuck with the time. Or maybe not.

Let us say you do commit to a large block of time over an extended period such as 13 weeks and you have only one show. When time becomes tight and unavailable, sometimes it pays to buy a block of time as a defensive measure. And let us say the time was sold to you at an incredibly low rate so that you knew you could use at least half the time profitably. You can always contact your agency and have them sell the time to somebody else.

One word of caution when dealing with a media buying agency. You must always know your stations and their history with your shows. Just because you surrender your media buying to your agency doesn't mean you surrender your oversight responsibility. You must always be vigilant. For example, your media buying service has committed for a block of time and they're stuck with it. You ran on that station before and it didn't do too well. But your media buying service slots you into that poor time because you are doing well enough on other stations to mask a loser in that one time slot. If you were watching the results, you'd know that you were being taken advantage of.

Clearly the lesson here is to always watch your results and get off the air when your commercial stops pulling. In our case we were using New Day Marketing, who practiced "client-specific" media buying and therefore never got "stuck" with bad time slots. Most agencies operate that way too. But again, it is up to you to inquire and be sure that you are getting the right attention to *your* needs from a service that buys time just for *you*.

Theory 16

Each time your infomercial runs, consider it a test.

One of the tasks you might have is negotiating media. How do you go about doing it? First of all, negotiating media is such an important part of the infomercial scene and so unique to it that to neglect it would be leaving out an important piece of a puzzle.

Second, there might come a time when indeed a station calls you directly, as often happened to us, where we had to make a snap decision and negotiate a deal at the last minute. This information then becomes quite valuable.

One of the important elements in buying media is to have a data bank of all the stations you've run on, what they've done in the past and how profitable they were. If you're just starting out, you'll learn which stations pull and which ones don't—but it can be costly. That's where a media buying service can really make a difference.

Database Made a Difference

JS&A not only had a database, but we had enough input to cover the 700 stations we dealt with all over the U.S. We also had a computer system that held our information and several years experience in buying media.

The first thing you do when you buy media is to obtain the *Television and Cable Factbook* and the publication *TV DataTrack* (Media Market Resources, Inc., New York).

Decide on a specific market and find that market in the *Factbook* and get its rank and call letters. You can use the *DataTrack* to find the videotape size requirements and audio and video wattage. A lot of this was already in our computer.

You should always consider the small markets as well as the big markets. When you're running a national campaign, it is easy to overlook the smaller cities and go for the big ones, but in the long run, the smaller stations will be just as valuable in your overall strategy.

Channel Position Is Very Important

Channel position is critical in buying media. The ideal channel position is below channel 12. That's where all the affiliates are located. From the *Factbook* get the affiliate (NBC, ABC, CBS, Fox) and net weekly circulation, or what is called "net cume." Checking a number of stations to compare their channel position and net cume gives you a good start. Look for low channel position and high net cume for your ideal station.

If you're buying cable time, watch out. First, the channel position is determined by the individual cable companies and there is no one source from which to get this information. Second, the same cable company can have your show on different channels or change the channel position without notice. And finally, your show can be broadcast from the same cable company but appear on several different cable channels. To cite an extreme example, KADY out of Ventura, California, broadcasts on channel 63, is carried on Sonic Cable in San Luis Obispo on channel 10, Cox Cable in Santa Barbara on channel 14, East Ventura Cable on channel 8, Lompoc Cable on channel 41, Comcast Simi Valley on channel 29 and . . . well, the list goes on.

Let us say you find a good station and you look up the name of the rep organization that handles it. You call them on the phone and ask for the "avails," or the available time slots during which you can run your show.

The rep will give you a rate but you've got to check this rate against your past experience, other stations in similar markets and similar times. If the show was used before on the station, you have a pretty accurate history already, so it is simply a matter of estimating profitability based on past results.

Based on Experience

If the show did not do well before, you advise the rep of what you can afford to pay based on previous results and negotiate the type of deal that makes sense for you to go on again. The facts should be clear. Let's say you didn't earn enough money because the time slot was too expensive. The rep either comes down in price to meet your profit requirements or you don't buy the slot. It's just that simple. The rep may have other offers for the slot and may not be anxious to discount it too much. He or she may sell it to you for a good price and then along comes another infomercial company who bids up the price and preempts you from running your show. It's all part of the media buying game.

If you're calling a new station in a new market and have a comparable rate used in another market, then inform the rep for that station how you reached your figure. The rate you select comes from experience but it is based on all the data you have gotten from the *Factbook*, the *DataTrack* and from past history.

It doesn't take long to actually build up your experience and instinctively know what to pay. You want to pay far less than the station is willing to let you have the time slot for and yet you want to be flexible enough to work out a buy.

Once the negotiations are complete, you issue a "time order" to the station and send along with it what is called a "view tape." A view tape is simply a VHS tape of your show for their review. Assuming they approve it, you need to know from the rep what size tape the station takes—1 inch or 3/4 inch.

Then comes time to send the tape. We dealt with West Telemarketing, the company that took our toll-free calls and entered our orders into their computers. Before we would send the tape, we would have our duplicating service add the toll-free number that West gave us. West usually had several numbers to give us. For example, if we were on several stations in the same market, we usually received several different toll-free numbers so that we could determine which stations and which time slots were working and which ones were not. The same phone number can be used over and over, as long as the stations it is assigned to do not overlap in their coverage area. The *Factbook* can help with this determination.

Payment Up Front Is the Norm

Then we would send the tape to the station and monitor the results when the show ran. Stations insist on payment up front although there are a few companies that have now established payment terms with a few of the stations.

When you buy media, be reasonable with the rep but be firm with what you can and can't afford. It takes practice, but before long, you'll be making good media buying decisions.

We had a weekly budget based on the results of the previous week, and after we analyzed the results over the weekend, Mary Stanke, our chief operating officer, would allocate a budget for the following week and our media people would then call the stations to either cancel, increase time or simply let the existing time play out. Remember, every run of our commercial was a test, as you will find out in the next chapter.

Chapter 31 | Infinite Testing

Testing is just as important as media buying, and even more critical. And testing doesn't just mean the first time you run a show to see if it works. You are always testing.

Theory 17

Every time you run your direct response commercial you are conducting a test. You are testing that commercial in a specific market at a specific time during specific financial conditions and during specific news events or political conditions at a specific place in time and space.

Conditions can vary and news events can have a tremendous impact on the buying mood of the public, but in general, we have a fairly homeostatic society and things don't change that much.

So with the above facts in mind, you now have your final commercial and have selected a media buying service and you now need to test the commercial to see if your product or service will sell profitably. What do you do?

The media buying service can help you a great deal with selecting the proper stations to test your commercial. There are some criteria you want to use when testing, however, to guide you when approving your testing budget. First, you want to use a very responsive station and a very responsive time slot.

Theory 18

One of the goals in testing is to make a profit.

Your chances of earning a profit are better when you test on a proven and very responsive station.

The second thing you want to do when you test is to test across a good cross section of the economy. In short, there are stations that truly represent the "average" American TV viewer, and the media buyers at your buying agency have a pretty good idea of which stations these are.

The third thing you want to accomplish is to obtain a level of confidence in terms of your "rollout" potential. The act of rolling out is simply taking your commercial and sending it to stations all over the country for broadcast. If your test indicates a tremendous winner, you want to definitely expand your media schedule as quickly as possible. If your response is good but not tremendous, you want to be more cautious.

The next step is to determine the amount of money you want to invest in the testing process. If I gave you a dollar figure here, it could be outdated in a few short years. With our BluBlocker commercials and many of the other successful shows, I was able to easily determine a winning show after spending only $10,000. If the show was tremendously successful (our $10,000 investment made us $30,000 or more), I knew right away that we could roll out our infomercial throughout the country.

A Shift in Consciousness

If it was marginal, then we spent another $10,000 to see if there was a fluke during the days we tested. Maybe the consciousness of the planet shifted for that weekend. Generally, when we retested, we got pretty much the same results. It was then back to the drawing board to determine what wasn't working and why. If our test showed good promise but wasn't a great big success, we expanded cautiously, spending maybe another $50,000.

You can get by with spending only $3,000 on a test on a few stations and get a pretty good indication of the success of your half-hour show. But if you are successful, then the next step will be to continue to test cautiously with another $20,000. By spending only $3,000 on a test, your next step should be just that—a step.

Remember, regardless of how much money you spend to create an infomercial, there is always the possibility of the show failing and ending up with not enough sales to pay for the cost of advertising. It is always prudent to test. Nothing is a sure winner as I learned many times.

In the end, the customer rules and testing is the only way to find out what His or Her Royal Highness really wants.

There are tests you can make on very small stations that cost only $200. Or you can blow the entire amount on big-city stations that can cost you up to $20,000 or more. The key here is to have a variety of test stations in a variety of markets representing the best cross section of the TV audience and to rely on the advice of your media buying service. They want you to succeed as much as you do.

The Wild Days of the Pioneers

The pioneers in the early stages of the infomercial industry did not have much experience in direct marketing and especially in testing. One minute they could be making a fortune and the next month they were in Chapter 11 bankruptcy. Then one month later they had earned enough money to get out of bankruptcy. They did not look at each insertion as a test. And when it came time to stop running a show on a station, they didn't know it. Today, with the tight margins and high media costs, the infomercial companies are considerably more knowledgeable in direct marketing.

I mentioned earlier how events can change the response rates during a test and this brings to mind a few examples. Although I wasn't testing any commercial at the time, I was running my BluBlocker infomercial during the outbreak of the Gulf War when everybody was watching TV to see the latest news. When the war broke out, for about a day or two our response was not good at all. But around the third or fourth day, as the war dragged out, viewers were getting tired of watching the Gulf War reports (especially as they knew we were winning) and they started looking for other venues on TV. Since all the networks and news organizations were busy covering the war, our infomercial had a tremendously large audience and we did quite well—more than making up for the poorer response during the early stages of the war.

Another example happened to me when I was appearing on QVC doing one of my hour-long BluBlocker shows. During the first half hour, sales were quite brisk. In fact, we were doing quite well. Then it was like the bottom dropped out. Very few sales. As I stepped off the stage after finishing my full hour, I was approached by Roger Elvin, one of the producers, who said, "Joe, don't feel bad. The Waco compound was just burned to the ground and all the networks are covering it."

Typical Evaluations

Once you've tested your infomercial, you gauge your results in a lot of different ways. Typically you determine the cost of advertising with respect to the total sale price of your product. For example, a typical result would be a $20 cost of advertising for a $40 retail item. This means that 50% of the retail price your customer is paying for your product goes to cover just the cost of advertising. You can now see why the cost of the product needs to be low. If a product costs you $4, that still leaves you with a $16 profit per sale. Then from that figure you would deduct your other expenses including overhead and processing costs, which hopefully are covered by your postage and handling charge.

Then you have to factor in your return rate. And this is a very critical step. The return rate is simply the percentage of customers who are dissatisfied with your product and want to return it. You can test a product and get a great response but then be surprised by the high return rate. For example, hair extensions became a big infomercial product. Soon every major infomercial company had their own hair extension program and there literally was a war going on in this product category. When the smoke cleared and the final results were in, the return rate was a staggering 30% and the companies that had expected a 10% return rate found themselves with little profit and in some cases a major loss.

When we launched our first BluBlocker infomercial in 1987, our advertising cost per order was only $3. This was extremely low for any product during those early years and one of the lowest in our history. But from that figure, we knew we had a big winner and rolled out nationally as quickly as we could. Our cost per order inched up through the years until it reached around $20 for a $50 item.

The COD Problems

If you sell your product via CODs, you can expect to get back almost 50% of what you've shipped out. The typical COD customer either is not home during the day, is too busy to pick up the product at the post office or has just plain decided in the intervening time not to accept the package. You therefore have to charge your customers more for the COD shipping and handling to make up for all those packages that come back.

You must also account for the very high return rate and the cost of processing in determining if COD shipments even make sense for you. Again, if you have the margins in your product and you do your own order processing, accepting CODs could work.

However, if you use outside service bureaus to handle your fulfillment and your margins are minimal, then usually the costs are too high to accommodate a COD transaction.

Testing means not only determining if you have a successful product, but also making sure you've factored in the correct return rate. You must determine whether or not you can profitably accept COD orders and figure out the exact advertising cost per order. Once you've gotten the results and have examined all the variables, you are ready to make a decision on what your next step will be. Do you step up the media expenditure or do you simply retest or do you even drop the show? A good test should tell you all that and, if you're lucky, make you a good profit.

If you'd like to see how all these figures are factored into a product-specific profit and loss statement, turn to Appendix B for the sample Cost Analysis Worksheet that New Day Marketing provided their clients.

If you think that you have to make all your profit from the sale of your well-margined product, get ready for another surprise. There is another way to earn money that hasn't been covered yet called the "back end." It will be covered in the next chapter.

Chapter 32 | The Back End

The "back end"—what a funny name for one of the most important aspects of running an infomercial.

Simply stated, the back end is everything you need to do to cause your prospects to reach into their pockets and exchange more of their hard-earned money than they thought they were going to exchange in the first place. Obviously this can cover a lot of ground and it does.

I have mentioned that you don't really make your money from the sale of your product but rather by how effectively you buy media. In short, you make your money from your *savings* as opposed to your *sales*. This is not true with the back end where you make your money primarily from more sales.

Theory 19 | *Money is made at the back end of your business from selling more of your product to those who respond to your infomercial.*

There are many ways to mine a lot of profit from the back end and each one is critically important to your success. Why? Because there will be times when the basic offer you are making will just break even or be marginal and the only profit you can generate will be from the back end. The second reason is that even if you are making a fortune with the infomercial as it is, it is always nice to take advantage of the opportunity to make even more.

The most common form of back-end sales is done right on the phone while your prospect is actually placing an order. It is an offer, called an "upsell," for another related product or service that the prospect might want. You can use any one of several approaches. For example: (1) the upsell could be a supplement to the original product, such as a lens cleaning kit for our BluBlocker sunglasses; (2) the upsell could be the purchase of more of the product for a lower price; (3) the upsell could be an incentive to enter into a continuity program to receive the product each month, as in the case of a regularly consumed product such

"MRS. ELLINGTON? I HOPE YOU LIKE YOUR NEW 'RAY-O-MATIC'.
I HAVE EXCITING NEWS ABOUT HOW YOU CAN USE IT!
HAVE YOU HEARD OF OUR 'FROZEN PIZZA-OF-THE-MONTH' CLUB?..."

The real money is made at the back end of your business.

as a food supplement or vitamin; or (4) the upsell could be the offer of a continuing or higher course of study, as is the case with personal development programs or business opportunity schemes.

Always Offer the Most Expensive First

The above approaches to the upsell generally take place when the product is first ordered on the phone. At JS&A we offered a $10 lens cleaning kit as our upsell and then if the party didn't order that, we offered a matching child's pair of BluBlocker sunglasses. This brings up another point. There could be several upsells—each one tied nicely to the main offer. Here's another important tip when making an offer. Always offer the most expensive upsell first and then go down the line in price. The lower you go, the more of a bargain the next upsell will seem.

The most successful upsells usually are less in price than your original order. It makes the upsell more of an impulse buy. Put yourself in the place of a typical buyer purchasing a $60 item. If you offered an accessory item as an upsell that would cost only

$10, the prospect would be inclined to look at the purchase almost as adding sales tax. Start increasing the price and you reach a point where the prospect "has to think about it." Once again, this is a good example of where testing comes into play. Test various price points and find out where the resistance levels start. Every product is different and every upsell is different. There are no hard-and-fast rules other than the rule of testing.

There is a new infomercial format that presents a product but does not reveal the price. You have to call a toll-free number and ask for the price. You then get a sales pitch for the product and if you decide to purchase the product, you then get pitched on the upsell. The person who started it was Kevin Trudeau, who made his fame selling his Mega Memory course in the late '80s. His new show format created a very simple concept that cost him very little to create. His set looks similar to the *Larry King Live* show on CNN. The show was basically a one-on-one type interview format with some interesting person being interviewed by either Kevin or a personality he selected.

He Started a Trend

It was so simple and involved such a low investment in terms of production costs that very shortly others started following the format and began calling it the "Trudeau format." Today there are at least three other copycats. Trudeau realized that the closer his format came to one of the many popular formats on TV, the more he could relate to his audience. And the production costs allowed him to produce several shows for the same cost necessary to produce one expensive infomercial. In fact I would estimate his cost per show to be around $10,000—a great price for the person with a low budget.

Basically, his entire offer required creating enough interest in the product and enough curiosity on the part of the viewer to find out the price of that product. People were compelled to take an action—namely, calling on the phone. That action was an involvement device. It involved the viewer immediately in the buying process and resulted in a number of successful shows and a good profit for Trudeau.

The back end doesn't end with just the phone call. There are other ways you can cause your prospects to keep digging into their pockets and exchanging their hard-earned money long after you have taken their order and sold them an upsell. The first is through contacting them again with another related offer.

When I first launched BluBlocker sunglasses, it was through print advertising. At the time (in 1986) the word 'infomercial' did not even exist. I spent over $1 million in print ads to sell over 100,000 pairs of sunglasses at $59.95 and then decided to follow my print campaign with a mailing. I first sent out a test mailing to 10,000 customers and it was so successful that it paid for the next mailing of 90,000 pieces. When I finished the campaign, it was one of the most profitable direct mail campaigns I had ever run.

I then went on TV with our first BluBlocker infomercial and discovered that the medium was explosive. Whereas it took me six months to sell 100,000 pairs when I was doing print, I was now selling 100,000 pairs in one month on TV. As I accumulated my customers' names, I started sending them the same direct mail package that I sent to my print customers. But I barely broke even. I then sent a similar mailing to my old print customers and the mailing did quite well even though it was the second time I had sent them the same mailing. I then realized that there was a difference but didn't fully appreciate it until I found out from list brokers that TV names don't work well in print but do quite well with telemarketing.

TV Is like Vapor

I then discovered that TV names will work fairly well with a direct mailing if it is mailed within a short period of time after a customer buys—usually within three months.

Why don't the TV names work well? I could appear on TV before millions of people dozens of times a year and make much less of an impact on them than if I appeared in one of my print ads. Why? TV is like vapor. Once you've finished seeing me on TV I quickly disappear from your mind. In print, you see a still visual image. You involve yourself in the mental process of reading that ad. And you remember it for a longer period of time. And so when that corporate logo and mental image of the print ad is duplicated in a direct mailing, the customer remembers that impression and feels comfortable responding.

When a TV customer gets something in print as a result of

buying a product from an infomercial, he or she doesn't relate it to the TV show. It is a different medium. It appears like just another piece of mail. There is nothing to correlate the TV image with the print image and even if there was, the customer has forgotten the TV image. On the other hand, a telephone call is very interactive. The customer can be asked directly, "How do you like your pair of BluBlocker sunglasses?" Then the conversation can take off from there. There is a direct connection to the product.

TV customers can also be good video buyers. Instead of calling them, send them a videotape presenting a single offer and sell them as you would in an infomercial. The only problem with this format is that it is expensive to produce the tape, reproduce it and then mail it out. You have a lot more flexibility on the phone. You can respond to a customer quickly with practically no production costs. You can change the selling script as new concepts are uncovered. Telemarketing is really the way to go.

Don't Want to Be Bothered by Phone

The print customer is a pretty lousy telemarketing customer. He or she is print oriented and doesn't want to be bothered by the phone.

Also remember that with TV lists you are dealing with the masses, and the masses in general may not all be mail order customers. It is a lot easier, however, for them to talk on the phone than to read a letter or promotional mailing.

When JS&A uses telemarketing to sell a TV product, the item does much better from a cost standpoint than when we sell it through direct mail. But I would never totally ignore direct mail either. I would test both direct mail and a telemarketing program. It might also mean a combination approach—sending a mailing and following it up by phone. Here is where testing comes in. You work on creating a combination of approaches to determine the ones that work and the ones that don't work using many of the techniques you've learned as a direct marketer. You also test a variety of products and pitches to see which ones work as well.

But there is one more element to the back-end puzzle that shouldn't be overlooked. As you advertise your product, you develop brand awareness. More and more people are recognizing the name of your product and you are developing a pent-up demand for it at retail. There is a percentage of the population that simply won't buy via mail order. They were either burned from a bad experience by some mail order merchant or they just would rather hold and feel the product before they buy.

Once you've established a level of success with your product, you then take it to retailers and have them offer it in their stores. They'll want to test the response too and chances are you'll do quite well. Retailers have learned that infomercial products do quite well at retail and they are anxious to give your product a try.

Complete Departments Have Been Set Up

When we offered our BluBlocker sunglasses at retail, the Walgreens drugstore chain was the first to take the product. They ordered only 30,000 pairs as they weren't sure it would sell. Within a few days after they announced the product they were sold out. Now complete departments called "As Seen on TV" are springing up at retail stores and feature many of the products sold on TV.

You could develop other back-end opportunities. Affiliating with many of the infomercial companies that have a presence in foreign countries is another way to go. Chances are if your product works in the U.S. and does not conflict with local laws or customs in other countries, you can expand your market worldwide. BluBlocker sunglasses have been sold all over the world and with great success. My voice has been dubbed in German, French and even Japanese.

Once your product becomes recognized, another back-end venue would be on the home shopping channels. They too have learned that infomercial products sell very well and they are anxious to test them. And once you test successfully, you are not limited to home shopping in the U.S. BluBlocker sunglasses are sold in London on QVC, in Germany on the QVC German affiliate and in Canada on the Home Shopping Club. Japan has opened a home shopping club and other countries all over the world are doing the same. In short, the proliferation of home shopping clubs is creating additional international venues for your product.

In Section One of this book I related the BluBlocker story and you saw the many ways you can sell a product once it is a success on an infomercial. But the biggest lesson you should learn from this chapter is that many opportunities are available to you once you create your infomercial. The infomercial is only the tip of the iceberg. There is so much hidden opportunity available to you once you have a successful show.

However, the biggest achievement you can reach as an infomercial producer is to have your product become a nationally recognized brand name which can be successfully sold at retail and throughout the world. The infomercial and the associated back-end sales afford you that opportunity.

Chapter 33 | Some Powerful Tips

I was asked to speak at one of Steve Dworman's Infomercial Marketing conferences and my topic was to cover some powerful concepts to increase sales and profits. Many of these techniques have already been discussed in earlier portions of this book, but there are a few tips I gave the audience that you should consider while you are planning your infomercial.

Match the Medium

I mentioned the format that Kevin Trudeau used for his one-on-one *Larry King* style infomercial productions. They were short, simple and inexpensive. But the impressive thing to me was how he used a format that had received wide TV audience acceptance and related it to his presentation. If you were inclined to watch the one-on-one type shows, you'd stop to see what was being broadcast when you came across one of Kevin's shows while scanning the channels.

If you were a fan of *America's Funniest Home Videos*, you might enjoy our BluBlocker shows as they were often spontaneous and unpredictable. I once even came up with a great idea for doing a game show in an infomercial format where the contestants and the audience participated—the contestants winning prizes and the audience at home able to buy those same prizes. I used a game show approach and knew that many people who typically watch game shows would probably stop and watch my new show idea long enough to get hooked.

I presented it to King World—the company that syndicates *Wheel of Fortune* and *Jeopardy!*—and they put one of their top game show experts on the project to refine the concept. It was a great idea as nobody was doing a game show in an infomercial format, but there were a number of operational issues that killed the idea.

Keep Their Attention

There are many techniques used to keep a person's attention and we talked about a few of them earlier in this book. To understand a few more techniques you need to realize three things about your audience: (1) their mass market level of comprehension, (2) the changing nature of your audience and (3) the fact that more and more adults have grown up watching MTV. Let me explain.

MTV pioneered the rapid-fire sound-bite type of broadcast TV that has been picked up in commercials and even in some TV series. Action is quick, movements are fast and production techniques are used to excess. Images are flashed across the screen in rapid sequence and you are left gaping at the TV with your mouth wide open totally captured by what you are experiencing. Well, my friend, that is something you'll have to contend with when you do your infomercial. The attention span of your audience has diminished. The producers who edit the TV news footage grew up watching MTV so sound bites have shrunk. In short, get ready to tightly edit that show of yours to make it a fast-moving flow of images or you'll lose your audience.

A newspaper article dated January 25, 1992, reads:

TV News Sound Bites Shrinking

In 1968, the television news sound bite was as filling as, say, a large pizza slice with mushrooms. A presidential candidate spoke for 43 uninterrupted seconds in the average appearance on the evening news. But a New York Times study has found a drastic reduction in the sound bite time since the '60s.

In 1972, the average bite shrunk to 25.2 seconds. In 1976, the bite shrunk to 18.2 seconds. Then, in 1980, to a mere 12.2 seconds.

In 1984, 9.9 seconds. By 1988, the bit had shriveled to 8.9 seconds. All told the sound bite has lost 34 seconds in two decades or 1.7 seconds per year.

If the rate continues, the average sound bite will soon be two seconds long or, observes the Times, enough time to say, "Me president, you voter."

In reviewing my earlier infomercials and comparing them with the ones I did a mere six years later, the older ones seemed slow. In short, I had picked up on the need to make them flow faster by using shorter sound bites and keeping the action moving through tighter editing.

This doesn't mean that every show should be fast-moving with short sound bites. Certainly the one-on-one format wouldn't qualify for that type of treatment. But it is clear that your editing should be tight and concise and that you must be very concerned about not wasting any time in conveying your message. Just as in a print ad where space is at a premium and you must measure each and every word, so too should you consider the same approach when you edit your show.

Shoot the President

Hey, I don't mean the president of the United States. That's illegal and besides you could get thrown in jail. What I'm talking about here is filming the president of a company offering the product. It is and will be among the most important moments in the infomercial. Having the president speak on camera with belief in his or her product, unless he or she is a total dork, is an effective way of conveying the strongest emotional message possible about your product. Sure, testimonials are strong and often very powerful at conveying an independent opinion devoid of any personal prejudice the president might show in favor of his or her product, but the president says something else.

The emotional message the president conveys should sound something very serious like the following: "I'm the person who heads my company and makes my product and I totally believe in my product and I'm totally standing behind what I've produced. I've created my product with a lot of work and effort thinking first of you, the consumer, and I personally guarantee your satisfaction."

This is the message that will contain the most emotion, and as you already know, emotion sells. It is the talk that says to the consumer, "Welcome to my store. Come in and I promise you my utmost attention and respect as you browse the products I present." Too often there is no presidential message. On many of the home shopping shows, rarely do we hear from the president of the company. But I bet if we did, the selling pace would go up. That is why I have my byline at the start of each print ad. That is why I personally sell each one of my products both in my infomercials and on the home shopping networks on which I appear. That's why Ron Popeil is so effective when he gets on the air. People feel the emotion when the top gun makes his pitch.

Think about the president of the United States during a crisis when he stands before his constituency and addresses the nation. Those speeches are relevant, important and emotion-packed. Your selling message is certainly a very serious moment in any infomercial. And what you say must also be relevant, important and emotion-packed when it comes to your constituency—that potential buyer who has to decide whether or not to exchange his or her hard-earned money for your product or service. When you create your infomercial and you are the president of your company, make certain you personally appear on your show to appeal directly to your prospects.

Theory 20

There is no better way to reach the emotional center of your prospects than by the personal appeal of the president of a company selling his or her product or service.

In print, you put a byline in your ad. That makes the message very personal. You don't put your picture in the ad unless you are in a crisis situation or running for political office. Your picture might cause a negative reaction in some print prospects and kill the sale. On video your image may turn off a few consumers, but in the long run, the powerful emotional impression it makes through what you personally say is a powerful tool to assist in selling your product or service.

Read My Lips

If "Read my lips" is good advice, I've got an even more powerful bit of advice: "Read my books." Read the other two books I've written in this series. One is called *Advertising Secrets of the Written Word* and the other *Marketing Secrets of a Mail Order Maverick*. They contain so much more information that will help you as a direct marketer in understanding the entire process of creating an infomercial, even though they concern print advertising. If you're serious about TV marketing, you should definitely read them.

If this is the only book you'll read on TV marketing, you'll be getting a wealth of information on the subject. All my books are designed to stand on their own. But since many of the principles of print mail order advertising closely relate to TV advertising, reading these books will prove quite helpful to you in understanding the sales process on TV.

To help you understand the relationships between print and TV, I have come up with a number of comparisons for you to study, and these I discuss in my next chapter.

Chapter 34 | Direct Marketing Relationships

I've given you some valuable tips on producing an info-mercial and creating a brand name for your product. There is certainly a lot more to making an infomercial than I've conveyed so far, but I've related many insights that may help the experienced professional as well as the person just starting out.

The purpose of this chapter is to emphasize the importance of certain parts of an infomercial and show you how the different parts relate to print advertising. By understanding the significance of each of these elements, you will have a better understanding of the marketing process.

The first comparison is the infomercial itself. What does it compare to in print? The infomercial compares to the print mail order ad. Both the mail order ad and the infomercial are designed to appeal to a mass audience. They attract from a mass audience those people who are very interested in your product or service, so interested that they are willing to do something that requires a lot of trust—namely, to exchange their hard-earned money for your product or service.

There Exists a Mass Market

Sure, magazines can be targeted to specific groups much more easily than TV. But even within those targeted magazine groups there exists a mass market from which you've got to cull those interested readers willing to buy your product. Your offer has to be simple, compelling, priced right and easy to order.

It is critical, however, that once you've attracted a group of customers from your infomercial, you've then got to develop your back-end business to maximize your profits. The same goes for print. Once you've attracted your prospects and have turned them into print customers, you develop your back end of the business. That might mean sending your print customer a mailing or a catalog.

What compares to the print catalog in a TV format? The

answer is the home shopping format such as QVC, HSN, Value Vision and the home shopping networks opening throughout the world.

The print catalog will be effective since you are sending it to your own customer base. But a direct mail letter will also be very effective. In a print ad you focused on just one single product or product concept. In short, you kept your message really simple. In the direct mail letter you focused on a single product too, but you added dimension to the product through the use of a full-color brochure, an involvement device or return reply card. And you've mailed that letter to everyone who has taken the big leap of faith and bought from you.

A phone call to your TV customer offers a single product in a very clear and easy-to-understand offer. Now what is the next step? Do you form your own home shopping club? You can if you are big enough, but it can be very costly and will take years to accomplish. And here is where the parallels diverge.

The TV Version of a Print Catalog

Home shopping is the TV format where you can offer many different products. Home shopping sounds and feels exactly like a TV version of a print catalog but with one important difference: It is very easy to transition from a print ad or direct mail piece to your own catalog, but extremely hard to transition from an infomercial or telephone call to starting your own home shopping channel.

But all is not lost. You don't need to open your own home shopping show. In fact, it would be a lot easier to look at putting your TV product on somebody else's home shopping show such as QVC or HSN. In this way, they have attracted for you all the TV buyers who would be willing to buy through a TV offer. And they have provided you with a forum under some theme such as "home improvement," "jewelry," "cooking" or "car care" to name just a few. And through their customer relations, they have established the authority and the credibility for your product by providing excellent customer service and a generous return privilege. If your product did well on an infomercial and later through telemarketing, chances are your product should do well on a home shopping show.

Another reason that a home shopping channel is an extremely difficult thing to launch is not just because of the logistics of putting together all the capital and personnel required to create the company. It also requires buyers to build a customer base.

When QVC started in 1986, there was no customer base. And the response started slowly in the beginning. You had to wonder if they would ever make it. But through patience and a lot of capital, they eventually did. And today, they do $2 billion in business and have a customer base of over 10 million viewers. For you to do that would require many millions of dollars.

Comparing Spots to Print

What about TV direct response spots? Where do those 60-second to two-minute commercials fit into the picture and how do they compare to print? They parallel the print ad just as the infomercial does but with a different type of ad—the small print ad selling a cheaper, simpler product which is usually an impulse buy in the $19.95 or below range.

If I were selling a cheap product or a product that was simple and easy to understand and whose price represented an impulse purchase to me, I would use the direct response spot as opposed to the infomercial. We discuss this topic in the next chapter.

The important point to remember here is simply this:

Theory 21   *TV and print are totally different media whose similar attributes, when understood, reveal powerful concepts about ways to market your product or service.*

I've shown you that the infomercial format parallels the print ad. But what can we also learn from this relationship concerning product?

First, product is king. The product is going to represent anywhere from 70 to 90% of the infomercial's success. Second, the offer has to be simple and focused on a single product or service. The offer can't be too complicated.

Now the similarities start to go out of parallel slightly. The infomercial product must provide a profit margin or cushion of 4 to 10 times its actual cost. In a print ad, the margins need not be that great. Typically in a print ad you can target your potential prospect by selecting a magazine or newspaper that goes to a specific market segment. With an infomercial, you will hit the mass market and your product should appeal to a large segment of that mass market—all women or all men or all animal owners or all people over 40 or all balding men or all women interested in a beauty product. You get the picture—the masses.

You can throw a print ad together rather inexpensively and test it rather quickly for little cost. With an infomercial, you'll spend a fortune—from $10,000 for a Trudeau-type one-on-one show to $250,000 for your more expensive production, and you won't have a clue if it will be successful until you spend anywhere from $3,000 to $20,000 on a test. In short, it's not a game for somebody unfamiliar with direct marketing.

Once again, you make your money not on the product or on the tremendous margins you make from your product, but on the effectiveness of how cheaply you buy media. This is something I learned rather early in my print advertising career and it applied directly to TV as well.

I've already given you many ideas on how to make an infomercial. In the next chapter, I discuss the other form of TV— namely the "short form," as it is called, or the 60-second or two-minute mail order spot. Even if you have a successful infomercial, you still want to take a look at the short-form TV offer as another way to sell on TV.

Chapter 35 | Short-Form TV Formats

As I explained in the previous chapter, a short-form TV spot is parallel to a very small ad in print. In print we could be talking about a want ad or even a 1/3-page ad. The print ad could flash the features and benefits of the product in short concise bullet form with very little copy and a low price that creates the environment for an impulse buy. The same goes for a short-form TV spot.

In a TV mail order offer in 60, 90 or even 120 seconds, you flash the highlights of your product and you jam everything you can into a very short period of time. Your offer has to be almost an impulse buy (unless you are asking somebody to call a toll-free number for more information).

Although the infomercial is a powerful direct marketing concept and has been the focus of so much attention, the short-form format has been around for a lot longer and has done exceptionally well.

Spots Sometimes Make More Sense

There are products and concepts that make more sense run in a spot than in a full-fledged infomercial, although you can use both the short form and the long form for the same product and run them at the same time.

When we did our BluBlocker shows, we always also created short-form spots and have had many occasions to use them even though our infomercial was doing very well. We would often work out a package deal with a station and part of the deal would be a few free spots. We always had them ready to ship with our infomercial.

With the infomercial and spot combination, we were able to sell our BluBlockers at a much higher price in the spots than otherwise would have made sense if we were doing only short-form spots. The price was too high for an impulse buy, but we still managed to make some sales through the short-form spots because there were enough viewers who had seen but not bought through the infomercial who then acted when they saw the shorter spot. And of course, these spots hardly cost us anything as they were often thrown in with the infomercial package buy.

But there were other occasions when having spots handy made sense. We were broadcasting our infomercial when Burl Hechtman called me from King World—one of the top syndicators in the country (syndicating shows such as *Oprah*, *Wheel of Fortune* and *Jeopardy!*). Burl was president of their new direct marketing division and he knew we were doing well with our BluBlocker infomercial. He asked me if we had a one- or two-minute spot.

"Joe, I've got a wonderful situation, if you're interested. We've got this weekend show called *Inside Edition* and we own some of the commercial time on the show. I was wondering if I could run your spot in these time slots at no cost to you, and we could work out a joint venture and share profits."

I didn't see a problem with the idea. We had the spots, they wouldn't cost us a thing to run and according to Burl, they could run for 13 weeks or as long as the spots were pulling or nobody else had bought the time.

We Worked Up an Agreement

I agreed and we worked up an agreement. King World was just getting into direct response television and Burl was put in charge. This was his first venture into direct response and he wanted to make sure he had a winner since top management was watching him very closely. The spot worked well and Burl and King World did quite well. He later confided in me, "This was the first project we did and it was very important that it succeed because that would help us expand our entire division and really go forward."

The two examples I mentioned above both involved opportunities that were available but did not normally make sense for a short-form spot.

What are the types of products that would work in short-form spots? Simply watching TV and seeing those spots will tell you. Music collections often do well. You can't buy them at retail and they usually sell in the $20 range. Products such as household gadgets or items that help you do a simple job better and are able to be demonstrated—for food preparation or for cleaning your home—all make good TV items. Lately I've noticed that math and reading courses have done well too.

Simply looking at a list of Ronco products (from Ron Popeil's company) would give you a good idea of some of the items that have worked quite well on short-form TV in the past. Ron was the king of this type of advertising for many years. If you're interested in learning more about this form of advertising and Ron himself, I'd suggest reading his book, *The Salesman of the Century*, which I've listed in Appendix D. Another master of this format was Alvin Eicoff—one of the pioneers in TV advertising. His books are well worth reading and are listed also in Appendix D.

Find Out What Is Working

If you want to know what is working, just tune in to your local TV or cable channels. Watching TV will tell you. Don't rely on what worked in the past and then copy the product or the sales message because chances are it may not be working now. And there's even a danger with doing something that is working now. The product you see on TV now may be at the tail end of its life cycle, or the product's back end might be the only profitable part of the offer. You can't often tell simply by watching somebody else's supposed success.

Another use of the short form is a "combination play." You put a TV spot on the air that normally would be a mail order spot but instead of showing a toll-free number, you put on a tag with the name of a series of retail outlets that carry the product. A tag is simply the part of a commercial that is added to the end of a spot and it is often not part of the spot itself. For example, we often tag our spots with our toll-free number. The spot has no toll-free number at the end in its generic form, but adding the tag of a toll-free number then completes the spot.

A big player in this business right now is Joe Pedott out of the San Francisco area. He's best known for his Clapper light switch and his Chia Pet household plant. His distribution is at retail and his spot drives his retail business.

BluBlocker Corporation now uses a 30-second spot to promote its products at retail and tags its stores too. But these spots are less mail order spots and more simply informing the public where they can find BluBlocker sunglasses.

A few last hints if you have a product that would make a good short-form TV mail order product. Deal through media buyers who handle this type of format only. Just as there are experts in the long form there are experts in the short form as well and you want to deal with them exclusively. They can be found in the *Adweek Source Book* listed near the end of Appendix D.

What happens when you decide to take your product to a retail chain to sell? And when should you take it? These questions and more are discussed in the next chapter on how TV advertising can drive retail sales.

You've already discovered how successful we were when we first sold our product through Walgreens drugstore chain. BluBlocker sunglasses represented the fastest-selling promotional item in Walgreens' history. And its success was primarily generated by the pent-up demand created by the TV exposure the infomercial gave the product.

The same is true for many of the other infomercial products that make it to retail. In the case of BluBlocker sunglasses, we had six years' worth of national awareness to help create the demand. In the case of other infomercial products, it is usually quite shorter than that—a year at the most. But that's all it takes to give a product enough awareness to make it a success at retail.

Support Your Product at Retail

Once your product gets into retail, you want to support it through spot advertising so the public knows it is there. If your infomercial is still running on TV, it will also help move your product at retail, but you will find that your infomercial sales will now start to dwindle.

Continue to run your infomercial as long as possible even if it reaches close to breakeven as it is helping to support your retail sales. But don't keep running the infomercial without retail support if your infomercial is no longer working.

There is a figure that I've heard around the infomercial industry that after you run your show for a while and decide to go into retail, you generate five to 10 times in sales over the sales you've done on TV. And it was this figure that inspired me to present our product to Walgreens.

I also had another thought. If this were true and we were selling around 300,000 pairs of BluBlockers a month on TV, then with a conservative figure of five times TV sales we were looking at 1.5 million pairs per month. We only had about two months of inventory as that is all we ever needed. Product would come into our warehouse and within a few months it was out the door. With only a half-million pairs in stock when we started to ship to Walgreens, we alerted our factories to be prepared to really gear up. We didn't want to commit to anything until we were absolutely sure this figure would hold up.

Walgreens ordered a conservative 30,000 pairs. They were burned by one of the copycats who sold them 30,000 pairs of BluBlocker look-alikes with a retail of $6.95. The knockoff pairs stood on their shelves for months and the last thing they wanted was a repeat of this. And besides, our sunglasses were going to sell for $19.95—a much higher price point.

To top it off, it was December and they were insisting that if they didn't sell all their inventory by March, they wanted the right to return everything. In short, what they wanted was a "guaranteed sale"—the right to return any unsold product after their test promotion was over. They also agreed that any reorder would not be on a guaranteed sale.

It Blew off the Shelves

The product was offered a week before Christmas and disappeared off their shelves within a few days. We eventually resorted to shipping to stores directly in what turned out to be one of the biggest successes in their history. But now I was faced with an important decision. How many do I make to support the retail effort? It was obviously a success, but how many do I produce to fill the pipeline?

I eventually decided to use three times our sales as a figure upon which to base production. And when I called my factories, they claimed that they had already been gearing up and as a matter of fact were well into production. How many were they producing for me without any instructions from me? "Oh," said our factory president, "about 5 million pairs."

"What," I said. "You're kidding me?"

They weren't. They had bought supplies for 5 million pairs and were planning to supply me with over a million a month. I did order 2 million pairs and told them to hold off until we had some really solid figures. Their predictions never panned out. Retail, although it has been good, never reached the figures we had achieved on TV.

SURE THESE ARE THE REAL THINGS YOU'VE
SEEN ON TV!... HAVEN'T YOU HEARD OF THEM?!!

It was starting to get ridiculous.

Part of the reason probably was that our TV exposure had created so much pent-up demand without our filling it that anybody with a pair of sunglasses that blocked blue light could set up shop and make some money.

Small street-corner vendors were buying cheap sunglasses from importers, loading up their trunks, going to busy street corners and putting up a sign saying, "Authentic Blue Block sunglasses—as seen on TV—only $5." People were stopping, picking up a pair and driving away.

In addition, importers were bringing in knockoff sunglasses by the containerful and selling them to whoever would buy them at any price. At one point 25% of the imported sunglasses had lenses that blocked blue light and were in some way a knockoff of our product—that's almost 50 million pairs.

Customs agents were catching some of the flagrant knock-offs that used names like "Blue Block" or "Blue Blocker." But for the most part, with only so many customs officers, plenty got through.

In retrospect, it is possible that the market was eating up 10 times what we sold on TV, but they were buying the cheaper sunglasses and not ours. We had not filled that part of the market demand and there were others very eager to fill it for us.

Facing a Frustrating Situation

The street vendors were perplexing to me. There was no way we could enforce our trademark on these small guys as they would simply close their trunk, remove their sign and drive to some other location. And the state fairs throughout the country were replete with booths and stands featuring similar signs and similar sunglasses. I had inadvertently created a cottage industry of vast national scope. This was a big problem and I tried to figure out what I could do to turn this into an opportunity.

My sense was that these street vendors were really providing a good service to their community. Imagine driving down the street and not having your sunglasses with you. You see a street vendor selling these nationally famous sunglasses. You realize that you don't have to stop and park at a drugstore and go inside to buy a pair. It was convenient and the perfect small business that served a real purpose.

I then came up with the idea of creating an opportunity for small entrepreneurs wanting to start their own sunglass business. I went out and purchased a really attractive folding booth and created the sign, "Authentic BluBlocker sunglasses." I arranged to import the knockoff styles—the same styles that were being sold by my now competitive street vendors. Hey, if you can't fight 'em, join 'em.

We Tried an Experiment

The plan was to offer the cheap pairs just like the vendors were doing now but to also offer the option of the authentic BluBlocker sunglasses, which none of the other vendors had.

We tried an experiment and sure enough, it seemed like it could be a lucrative little business for the income opportunity crowd. But I also realized that as good an idea as this was, it meant setting up an entire army of vendors throughout the country, which would be frowned upon by those same drugstores that were being robbed of our business right now. I then very quietly killed the idea.

Having many people take advantage of our advertising and our brand name has been a persistent problem that has plagued me all my marketing life. In the next chapter, I briefly describe some of these companies and what it was like to fight them while maintaining the validity of the brand name we had worked so hard to create.

Chapter 37 | Copycats and Knockoff Artists

As you can see from the previous chapter, the problem of copycats was a big one. Not only were we suffering the consequences of reduced sales, but our brand name was being hurt as well.

When you own a famous trademark, it is your responsibility to maintain and protect it against anybody illegally using it. If you don't, then not only do you lose business as a result, but it is also possible that you could lose your trademark protection.

We had to run this ad warning other companies that if they copied our trademark, the U.S. Customs agents and our company would go after them. Copying became a way of life.

Let us say that somebody who uses your trademark and then is sued by you proves that you aren't protecting your trademark. The Patent and Trademark Office can actually revoke your product name. That's why companies like Xerox run full-page ads advising people that improper use of their name is illegal. How many people do you know who have said, "Let me xerox this page," using the trademark name "Xerox" as a verb?

Whenever we received a newspaper clipping of a knockoff using our name or a similar name, we turned it over to our attorneys and they fired off a strong letter requesting that the infringer stop using our name. We have spent thousands of dollars a month doing that in order to protect our rights. We even ran an ad in various trade publications warning drug chains about the illegal use of our trademark and the illegal sale of knockoff BluBlockers.

In the infomercial industry, it has become common practice to knock off certain types of pioneering products. When hair extensions first came out, it wasn't long before there was a "hair extension war." Everybody was falling over each other to copy the successful promotion.

A hair extension is a strand of hair a woman can place in her hair to supplement it without having to wear a wig. They just clip into your hair and make your hair fuller. And American infomercial companies were importing this hair from the Far East where millions of women were selling their hair as part of a major new Asian cottage industry.

It Turned into a Nightmare

Millions were being sold. And for good reason. First, look at the market. Hair extensions appealed to all women—young and old. Far more women watch TV than men. The three main companies competing in this market had prices that would appeal to the entire mass market. And all were doing well—until, that is, women started sending them back by the carload. The return rate was over 30% and what seemed to be a copycat's dream turned into a nightmare.

The infomercial industry is known to be really flagrant at knocking off products. If a product is a success, it doesn't take more than a few weeks before a new show has been shot and a new product has hit the market. Some infomercial companies have perfected the art of knockoffs. Some companies actually specialize in taking the products of others and copying them without remorse or conscience.

It is therefore imperative that you realize this fact when you are ready to launch a new product idea never before seen on the air. You have to anticipate that somebody will come up with an exact copy or something similar to what you are selling and sell it for less after you have done all the pioneering work.

A Strong Brand Name Is the Best

So you either have to have a strong patent and have the financial reserves to back up a long and expensive lawsuit or you've got to have a strong brand name, which is usually a lot easier to protect. In either case, it is a sad commentary on the conduct of business and the costly and lethargic court system we have in this country.

I am an innovator, not a copycat. I can't copy. I will walk away from a situation rather than copy somebody. My life has been always focused on innovation and it is my theory that the copycats don't win in the long run anyway. They eventually trip and fall.

Recently a new war broke out. It is the ab war ("ab" meaning abdominal muscle exercise device). There are at least four companies selling similar products and there is a major lawsuit against a few of them. Who knows how this all will turn out, but I've observed that the innovator who really made the product category usually wins the battle—at least in the beginning.

We've had three lawsuits against infringers or trademark abusers or knockoff artists. We've settled all three and won close to a million dollars. I am relentless against infringers.

They Copied Our Packaging

In one instance, the infringer used the name "Blue Light Blockers" and copied our packaging so closely, you would think it was actually a pair of BluBlockers. The product was actually being sold in a major drug chain and they had to pull all of their product. In another case, a company copied our infomercial format closely and used dialog from our infomercial in theirs. We sued them on copyright infringement as well as unfair business practices. In another case, an infomercial company misrepresented their product and demeaned our product on-screen. We sued them and received a settlement. All of the above cases were settled out of court before they went to trial.

It is truly sad that this knockoff activity occurs, but knowing that it does, you must plan a strategy for minimizing it or anticipating it as I did with our BluBlocker Viper sunglasses. We had been copied by so many people that when we announced our new Viper style sunglasses and saw immediately that it was a major hit, I contacted my factory and ordered close to a million of them. I also called one of the low-priced producers and ordered a knockoff of the Viper and was prepared to enter the market at the low end the minute I saw somebody knocking us off. I ordered 250,000 of them. Guess what? Nobody knocked us off. And I ended up having to liquidate the entire inventory to Wal-Mart.

Knockoff artists are a sore spot for me. There are other times, however, when I had within my grasp the opportunity to make a tremendous success, only to let it slip through my fingers. Was I upset? What were these opportunities? I've got some interesting stories to share on the next subject—the ones that got away.

Chapter 38 | The Ones That Got Away

When I started my adventure into video production, I already had a very successful and extensive background in mail order and print advertising. Since many of the same mail order principles applied to TV, it was easy for me to produce effective shows that sold product.

The Popeil Food Dehydrator

On the other hand, if you take Ron Popeil, the very successful infomercial producer, and study his life, you'll find a different type of background that also lends itself to a successful career in infomercials. Ron started out as a carnival pitchman and a department store demonstrator and salesperson. He then went on TV and sold a variety of his family's products in direct response spots. Ron had none of my background in print and I had none of his in TV, but we both had a firm grasp of the principles of salesmanship through our respective experience.

In fact, if anybody had a good chance of making it in infomercials, it was Ron. Not only was he familiar with all the selling principles, but he also knew direct response television and how to use it effectively as a sales tool.

I had known about Ron and his products but had never met him and had no idea what he was doing. The only thing I had heard about him was that his company, Ronco Teleproducts, had problems with a bank that had pulled their financing, leaving Ron and his company with no choice but to declare bankruptcy.

In June of 1988, *North Shore Magazine* (a Chicago magazine distributed throughout Chicago and its suburbs) did a cover story on me entitled "Perennial Pitchman."

The author, George Harmon, referred to me in the article as "the 1980s version of Ron Popeil." A few days after the article appeared, I received a call from Ron Popeil himself. When I heard that he was on the phone, I thought that indeed he had read the article and was calling me to comment on it. I was totally wrong.

Ron had not even heard of the article. He was now in Los Angeles and simply wanted to talk to me about a proposition for a few product inventions that he wanted me to sell in an infomercial for him. In a pleasant chat, he explained that he had followed my career, just as I had followed his, and liked my approach to marketing both in print and on TV. He thought that I'd be the perfect home for his product. By coincidence, I was going to Los Angeles the following week, so we set up a meeting.

When I arrived at Ron's home, we talked for a while and then he took me into his kitchen and showed me his product—a food dehydrator. He explained that he was going through a rough time when his company went under. His marriage had fallen apart during this period. We shared a little beef jerky and some small talk and I explained the amazing coincidence with the article and his phone call.

"There are no coincidences," said Ron. "I really feel that this product was meant for you. In addition, I can supply a bagel cutter as a free gift to go along with this and I have enough in inventory so you could do a really good test."

I looked at the product and then asked Ron, "Why don't you do this? I mean, you're one of the nation's top pros in the direct response TV industry. You've got the product already. Why don't you do it?"

Ron Wanted to Retire

Ron then explained that he wasn't that anxious to get back in business with all the inherent headaches. No, it wasn't for him. He was willing to give me the product and take a reasonable royalty and relax.

I thanked Ron and told him that I would think over his proposition and get back to him. I left and thought about Ron's proposal and decided not to go ahead with it. Why? I was not a cook. I didn't know a thing about the kitchen other than where the dishes, glasses and silverware were located. I couldn't use a kitchen gadget, couldn't cook much of anything until the microwave oven was invented and always had my meals cooked for me by my mom, later my sisters and then my wife. There were too many cooks in my family for me to ever take an interest in cooking. I just didn't emotionally connect with the product and couldn't sell something that I couldn't connect with. I called Ron and told him. "From an integrity issue, I can't relate to your product. But I still think *you* should do it."

Ron took my advice and got into the infomercial business starting with his food dehydrator. The rest is history. He's made one of the most successful infomercials in the business and has expanded his product line to include newer versions of his dehydrator, a pasta maker and several similar products.

He's taken these products to QVC where his success continues, and we've often bumped into each other in the Green Room. I'm always amazed at how carefully he prepares his products before he goes on the air. I've often seen him in the QVC kitchen personally preparing the food for his demonstrations. He's a true professional in every respect.

Kevin Trudeau

There have been other products and people I've turned down that have gone on to do very well. Kevin Trudeau is one of TV's bright new stars and has developed and refined the one-on-one *Larry King* talk-show type format for infomercials. He was also one of the early success stories on TV with his Mega Memory System—a memory training program for anybody who wanted to improve his or her memory.

One of the effects of a successful infomercial is that you will attract other products and other people. It was the same thing for me in print. I would run a calculator ad and other companies with calculators would approach me to handle their product. If I ran a telephone product, other companies with telephone products would want me to offer their products. I found the same to be true with infomercials, although there I attracted many different types of products. And people too. Like Kevin.

Kevin's background was as a self-taught student of sales, marketing and motivation. He was bright, articulate and read everything he could get his hands on regarding selling. He read Joe Girard's book *How to Sell Anything to Anybody* and was so impressed that he decided to become a car salesman while he supported his habit of attending seminars and studying. After the Mega Memory hit, Kevin was rolling in money. But he lost a relationship, had some business setbacks and soon lost almost all of his money. It was in 1992, shortly after Kevin started to pull himself up, that he called me.

Take Over Marketing of His Product

He stopped by our office with his attorney, Jeff Salsberg, and presented his Mega Memory product to me to see if I would take it over and sell it as part of our stable of products. Kevin was also willing to partner with me to produce several infomercials while leaving the media placement and the fulfillment to our organization. In short, he was looking for a home.

Kevin sat down and we talked about possible arrangements. At one point I asked Kevin if I could see the videotape he was sending out as part of his memory training program.

"No," was Kevin's reply.

"You don't understand," I said. "I want to see the tape you produced that you use to fulfill your orders so I can get a sense of the program."

"No," said Kevin again. "It's not necessary."

Kevin then proceeded to tell me a story as to why he wasn't going to show me the tape. He related the following:

"I'm going to tell you the story of a tuna salesman and you'll understand why it is not necessary for you to even see the tape. The story starts out in New York. A man pulls up to a produce market with a truck full of canned tuna. He offers the tuna to one of the buyers there for 50 cents a can. The guy he sold it to then goes out and sells it to another dealer for $1 a can. That guy goes out and finds somebody who is willing to pay $2 a can and is ready to sell him the truckload when the buyer asks the seller if he could open some of the boxes and examine the contents of the cans. The seller agrees and the buyer opens up the first can and he says, 'Hey, this tuna is rotten.'

"He then opens a second can from a different box and sees that it's also rotten. Finally, he opens a third can and sees that it is rotten too. 'Hey,' says the buyer, 'you don't expect me to buy all this tuna—it's all rotten.'

"'Hey!' says the seller, 'This tuna's not for eating—it's for selling.'"

After Kevin finished the story and made his point, I told him that I would get back to him after I thought about it. Kevin and Jeff left and Mary Stanke, JS&A's president, who was also in the room, looked at me and smiled. I told her, "Kevin has great potential to be a pretty successful guy, but I don't think we relate to his type of approach."

It was this kind of approach that hurt the entire industry, but Kevin wasn't alone. In the early days, there were many producers who would ship anything if it would sell, and long-form advertising quickly developed a bad reputation. In short, we never consummated a deal and Kevin went on to become one of the most prolific infomercial producers in the country with some very successful shows. The whole industry seems to have improved since those early days, and I'm sure Kevin has grown and learned as well.

The ThighMaster

Then there was Josh Reynolds, the inventor of the mood ring—a fad during the '70s—and the ion generator that JS&A ran in print for several successful years. Josh was a very clever inventor who was low-key, very honorable and a pleasure to do business with. Incidentally, inventors are typically among the toughest and most frustrating people to deal with, but Josh did not fit that mold.

One day in 1990 Josh called me and said that he had an exercise device that was very simple, produced very good demonstrable results and was ready to be marketed. He indicated that the product was invented by Anne-Marie Bennstrom from The Ashram, and wanted to know if I would be interested in selling it. "What's it called?" I asked.

"It's called the V-Bar right now, but you probably could come up with a better name."

Josh sent me the product. It was a simple spring-loaded device that you put between your legs and squeezed. It conditioned your thighs and really gave you a good workout. I then called Josh back and told him that I decided not to take on the product. "Normally I would, Josh. I really like the product and it's perfect for a direct response spot. My problem is that BluBlocker sunglasses are doing so well and it's like I've got a tiger by the tail and I don't want to devote any energy to a new product right now."

One of the Biggest Successes of 1991

Josh went on to name his product the ThighMaster and together with a company called Ovation, its CEO, Peter Bieler, and Suzanne Somers, created one of the biggest successes of 1991. In fact, after he created the success with his partner Ovation, I consulted with Bieler on some of the production problems he might experience overseas.

Was I disappointed that I missed big opportunities in the above three examples? I've never looked back and regretted it. I based each decision on an honest evaluation of the situation. In the case of Ron Popeil, I could not accept a product for which I had no feeling simply for the sake of making money. In the case of Kevin Trudeau, I did not feel that Kevin at that point in his life held the same convictions as I did nor that he would end up with us in a long-term relationship. And finally, I was just plain honest with Josh Reynolds. I didn't want to take the focus off my sunglass company for any new product. Things were going too good.

There are always going to be products that "get away from you." Nobody is a Solomon when it comes to picking winning products. And if you're actively playing the game, you're going to miss a few balls while you're juggling others.

One of the things that many people don't realize about the infomercial business is the major risks. They say that only one out of every 10 to 20 infomercials makes it. The rest are complete losses. Yes, that's an obvious risk. But what happens when you have a major hit? It might be more of a curse, as you will discover in the next chapter.

Chapter 39 | Hidden Land Mines

A wise man in the infomercial business once said, "The worst infomercial experience is to have a huge success."

Now reading that, you might be thinking, "I should only be so lucky." But there is truth to what this man said. Let me explain.

Let us say you run your infomercial and it is a huge success. I mean, it is so successful that you throw a celebration at your office for the entire company. You're now looking to roll out nationally as quickly as possible. But you don't have that much product in the warehouse. And you also know that if you don't start to advertise very quickly, some scumbag knockoff artist will copy you and beat you to the punch once he or she learns you have a success.

So the temptation in the industry is to throw caution to the wind, start advertising the product and then go out as quickly as possible and manufacture the thing you're already selling.

Big Mistake

Jumping the gun by advertising without having product in your warehouse is very dangerous. First, it's illegal. You can't advertise knowing you won't have product within 30 days without revealing that in your infomercial or at a minimum when the order is placed. Second, you have to pay for the advertising in advance so you are tying up your working capital for a longer time than necessary. (There are usually no terms for infomercial time.) Third, you are not shipping product so you aren't making any income. And fourth, since you aren't shipping, two things may happen.

The first is that your customers may, because of the delay, cancel their orders or forget they even ordered your product and you'll experience a high cancellation rate. The second thing you may later discover only after you ship your product is your customer dissatisfaction return rate. And both of these things can cause big losses.

But, hey. You're getting a billion orders. No need to worry. Right? Wrong.

Suddenly all the money you need to manufacture the product has been spent on TV and there is little left to make the product. And then once the product goes into production, there is usually a learning curve involved that causes many further delays and false starts.

Let us say you do have enough money to manufacture the product and you even make it past the production stage and you are actually now shipping product. You ship the product and wait. It's been a few months since you've gotten your orders and just as you ship—just as you finally start turning all that advertising money into sales and cash—that scumbag knockoff artist you expected has just launched a hot infomercial knocking off your product. Combined with the late shipments and the high cancellation rates, you've got to worry about people now seeing your competitor's product and ordering from him or her and canceling your order.

Accused of Knocking Off a Product

But hey, no problem. You had the jump and you're doing so well that nothing can stop you now. You'll take the cancellations as simply a cost of doing business. Until the process server knocks on your door and hands you your first lawsuit from the inventor of the product who claims that you knocked off his invention.

Finally, three months go by and you find your return rate is only 15%. That's a little high but still no problem. Then comes the problem. You get a call from the post office. "What do you want us to do with these 400,000 cartons that we've been holding here at the post office from all your old customers looking for refunds?"

All of the problems I've just mentioned here are taken from actual experience. Each problem could be a land mine when you least expect it. And if you can get through all of them and still end up with some big dollars in the end, congratulations. You deserve it.

Let's talk about real examples of this. When PRTV, a California public infomercial company, ran their hair extension program, they thought they only had a 15% return rate until the post office called them and requested they pick up all those returns they had been holding for three months. When it was all over, Mike Levey, their president, and PRTV were "scalped" (if you'll excuse the pun) and actually lost on the hair extension program. Mike's bottom line plummeted and his stock price soon followed.

Large Settlements Were Made

The ab wars—those companies each knocking the other off selling exercise devices that strengthened your abdomen—were confronted by an inventor who came out of the woodwork to sue them. Large settlements were made to get rid of the guy.

When I look at the lawsuits I attracted as a result of my BluBlocker commercial, they amaze me. First, I was threatened by a music publisher claiming we had infringed on the music that was playing in the background while we were shooting. Then I was sued by a company who received four patents over eight years ago on what was supposedly embodied in our lens. We did not infringe on their invention but had to fight this in court.

And then there are a lot of companies who jump the gun and start advertising their products before they even have them— often getting into trouble due to defects or late shipments. When National Media came out with their Juice Tiger juicer, the product had such a weak motor that the unit broke down after a few weeks of use. The company got thousands back in returns before the defect was discovered and corrected. And then when the juicer was sold at retail, the retail market was so saturated with other similar products that the product died on the shelves.

Or how about a product called Rio Hair—a hair straightener for blacks. It was a great product. It sold well and it worked. But it had a small side effect. It also caused your hair to fall out. Thousands of balding customers sued the company.

One company even went bankrupt it was so successful. SLM, a former public company that specialized in fitness and toys, created a product called "The Gravity Edge." Their early tests showed great promise. Their spokesperson was Fernando Lamas pitching in his very persuasive style. Everything was in place. The product was being manufactured. The testing was completed and the test results were in and were quite positive. They even knew their customer dissatisfaction return rate, which was reasonable. It was the stuff infomercial producers can only dream of.

But Somebody Was About to Sink the Ship

But somebody in charge of marketing and media planning was drafting a big plan that was about to put the company out of business. The plan was simple. Saturate the market in the fourth quarter of the year taking every available infomercial slot regardless of price and then roll the product out at retail as the infomercial reaches its peak. Then cream the retail market. Great plan. Wonderful idea. Stupid mistake. First, you don't pay excessive prices for media simply for the chance of being on the air. That's not very bright as you already know. It makes it very difficult for you to make any money and it drives everybody's media costs higher too. Second, they just assumed that the product would sell at retail. It didn't. Matter of fact, it bombed. So did their infomercial. The media rates they were gladly paying were so high that the product didn't have a chance to earn a profit. It was a great opportunity but one that just didn't work.

And let us say you have already had a huge success. You've managed to walk past all the land mines and you're sitting on top of the world. You've uncovered a formula that works for a certain class of product and all you have to do is to take the product, come up with a new version of it and run it again using your same formula. Hell, who needs to test? You've already proven the concept works. Big mistake.

The company that did that had created a very successful cosmetic line and a continuity program to sell it. They lost money on each show they ran, but they more than made up for it when customers bought, on average, five shipments before canceling. They had a gold mine. So they created a new product, ran it under the same assumptions only to discover that customers did not buy five times but rather much less and they experienced a very high return rate. The loss: close to $13 million and still counting. Ouch. So even after you've had a truly successful show and try to repeat your success, there is always a chance it won't work like before.

With today's business morality, how can you successfully market a product? Knocking off a product is now a game. Rolling out a commercial before product is even in the warehouse is common. And frivolous lawsuits are the norm. It's all part of the terrain and the terrain is dangerous indeed.

Difficult to Gauge Return Rates

And how can the companies that defy ethics truly know what their real profits are from their tests when there is no way to judge their return rates?

I got out of the infomercial business in 1993 for several reasons. First, I was taking my number one lead product, the BluBlocker sunglasses, into retail stores. My focus was on the brand name that I had created and not on the advertising medium. In short, I was looking at what it took to bring BluBlocker sunglasses to the next level and not what it took to keep the sunglasses in another infomercial.

Second, I saw infomercial rates triple. Major corporations were getting into the business and paying excessive media rates, thus driving up the cost of advertising. Companies like SLM were buying media at outrageous prices. I also saw the economy going up and up and up. Whenever that happens, media rates follow.

Although I've followed the industry closely thanks to Steve Dworman's newsletter, *The Infomercial Marketing Report*, I haven't had any need to get back into the business. Until now, that is. After working on this book for the past few months and watching the new computer video editing technology grow, I'm feeling the bug again.

But with all the headaches and problems, the joys and the frustrations, my infomercial experiences were a time that I'll remember fondly. The thrill of several hit shows, the thrill of selling out on QVC, the thrill of appearing on German television and selling BluBlockers in the German language—it has all added to my life's experience and given me memories that I will always cherish.

This is the last book of a three-book series that I have written on the lessons I taught at my exclusive marketing seminar during the '70s and '80s. At the end of these seminars, I always concluded with my philosophies about business and life in general. Since the next chapter will be the last and final chapter of my course (if you've been studying all three books), I will cover these philosophies there. It is my theory that everything you have learned from my books is useless unless you have those "forces" working on your side. And that's the guidance I'd like to share with you in the next chapter.

Chapter 40 | The Power to Succeed and Win

All the issues discussed in my three marketing books were presented at my seminar and all within one week. And to add to what you have read in this book were many videos, slides, stories and experiences that I presented to the class. I've included the most significant ones in this course.

On the last day, at the end of the course, I explained my business philosophies and the principles with which I have run my company. I have been lucky. I have worked very hard and there have been a lot of coincidences and serendipitous events in my life that guided me into a world of success I never imagined I could achieve. And through all these experiences, I was determined to find a higher meaning to what I experienced without getting into the New Age mumbo jumbo that so many preach.

It was through observations that I developed a philosophy—a belief system that I shared with my students. Being in business and knowing the rules was only part of the path to success. The actions that you took in running your business and personal affairs were even more important and truly impacted your chances of success.

At the End of Our Experience Together

In 1980 I wrote a book called *Success Forces* in which I outlined many of my principles. I shared these principles with my seminar participants in a very serious and somber way towards the end of our long journey together. We had all been through a lot and examined ourselves, our abilities and our work ethics from many angles. My students wanted to learn what it really took to be successful. Some of my students were already quite successful. Others were just starting out. But it was this part of the course that had a tremendous impact on all who attended.

In my course and in my book I explained that there are certain forces in life that seem to power you towards success when you act a certain way, and then there are those same forces that power you towards failure if you act in the wrong way. And it seems that these dynamics worked flawlessly almost every time. The following are what I call my seven "success forces" and what they mean.

1. Honesty: This is a very important trait to have in all your dealings. Honesty means no white lies, no fudging. It means the strict and candid expression of the truth. If you don't know the truth or can't be honest, chances are you're not successful. Be honest in all your dealings and you'll start noticing the change. Sure you can slip. Every once in a while we all do. But you'll experience the consequences in some subtle form of retribution. Always be honest. It's great advice.

2. Focus: If you focus, you concentrate all your energy into something very powerful. And whatever you focus on expands. Focus on your business and it will expand. Focus on writing great copy and it will get better. But focus on money and you're making a big mistake. Why? Money is a mere symbol representing your work and toil. So when you focus on the money, you are actually focusing on work and toil so the work and toil expand and not necessarily the money. Instead focus on what you do best, what you enjoy and what you are trying to achieve—not on the money.

3. Failure: As hard to believe as this may seem, failure is one of the greatest of the success forces. Each time you fail, you develop a force that pushes you closer and closer to success. Fail enough times and your chances of success multiply. And each time you succeed, you create a force that is driving you closer to failure. Obviously there's a balance here. But the most incredible fact in the dynamics of this success force is that we all fail so many more times than we succeed. So if we accept failure for what it really is—a powerful success force—we will be less likely to give up.

4. Problems: Each problem you encounter has hidden in it an opportunity so powerful that it literally dwarfs the problem. The greatest success stories were created by people who recognized a problem and turned it into an opportunity. Failure and problems appear to be negative forces, but in reality problems have hidden within them the seeds to create great success. In the future, if a problem confronts you, pause and say, "Where is the opportunity in this?" You'll be amazed at the powerful success force that will follow the solution.

5. Innovate: The key here is, don't copy. If you copy, you create a negative force. If you innovate, you create a success force. There's a point in time and space where all the elements for success are present and something very positive happens for someone. And the problem with trying to copy that person is that you are not in the same space and time as that person was and you don't know the real reason for that success. You might see seven reasons for the success, but hidden below the surface there may be a million other reasons that converge in perfect synchronicity—a pattern that would be impossible to duplicate. Don't copy! Always innovate.

6. Cleanliness: At the end of the day, clear off your desk so when you arrive in the morning a clean desk is staring you in the face. In order to accomplish this, you'll have to have the proper file system to store everything. You'll have to have a place to put things that you can't file. And if you don't have organizers, get them. Then when you step into your office, you should start on the first project of the day and work on it until you finish it. When you operate from this type of clean environment, you create a positive force that is driving you towards success. When you don't follow it, you create a negative force. Clean your desk!

7. Humility: The Chinese say that a big tree catches more wind and that a big roof holds more snow. Be humble. After all, our life on this planet is so infinitesimally short and we are such a tiny insignificant part of it that we really don't need to take ourselves too seriously. For some of us humility might be tough. We've got big egos. We are striving valiantly towards success, but in the long run, the more humble you are, the more positive the success force. The less humble you are, the more you will catch the wind—or feel the effects of a negative force. This means don't try and show how much more significant you are than somebody else. You're not.

More Thoughts

In addition to the success forces mentioned above, I have two stories I'd like to share that I also shared with my students.

They are powerful philosophies that can act as great guideposts for your thinking in the future.

The first one involves my cousin, Dr. Arnold Mandell, who now lives in Florida and teaches at one of the universities there. Arnold was a very smart young man who went on to become a psychiatrist in San Diego. While practicing there, he got a very unusual assignment. His job was to study the players on the San Diego Chargers football team and other players on other teams to determine what it takes to become a football superstar.

Arnold studied the players and found out a lot more than the management of the team and the National Football League cared to hear about, but that's another story. The final conclusions he shared with me one day over lunch.

"I have found that the difference between a superstar as opposed to a great player," remarked Arnold, "is that a superstar falls into one of two very distinct personality profiles. The superstar either is deeply religious or has a tremendously big ego."

After I left Arnold, I thought about what he had said and realized that the two types of football personalities had one thing in common. Belief. Each believed very strongly in something. One believed in God and the other believed in himself. And so the conclusion I came to is that belief is one of the most powerful motivational forces we have going for us. If you believe that you can be great, you will be. If you believe that you will become one of the nation's best copywriters or marketers or even infomercial producers, you will.

I Had a Very Strong Belief I Would Succeed

After I wrote my *Success Forces* book in 1980, a number of people wrote me and asked me how I managed to continue after experiencing so many failures in my life. My answer was simply that I totally believed that I would eventually be a success and that it was simply a matter of time. In short, I believed. Remember, it is not whether you win or lose, it matters only that you play the game.

This brings me to my last story. At the end of my seminar—I'm talking the very end—I told a story that I had heard from a former seminar participant about persistence. Throughout my life, the one overriding principle has been my resiliency after total failure—my ability to pick up the pieces and start again. And it always seemed to amaze my seminar participants how many times I failed yet managed to get back on my feet and start over again.

My last story is a tale about Winston Churchill, the legendary English prime minister. Churchill has had many myths told about him and the story I gave my students was probably nothing more than one of those myths. But it was not only the perfect way to end the seminar, it was the one point I wanted to make that capsulized everything I had taught them.

The story starts out in a small college town. The president of the college wanted to have a very strong speaker address their audience during graduation commencement exercises.

When the commencement committee examined the list of strong potential speakers, each one was so costly that the committee realized that such a speaker was beyond their budget. Finally after everybody was totally puzzled over whom to invite, one of the bright young professors on the committee raised his hand and said, "Why not invite Winston Churchill?"

Churchill Very Old

By this time, Winston Churchill was well into his 80s—a feeble old man in the waning years of his life. And when the young professor made his suggestion, everybody looked at him, smirked, and voted to suspend a decision until the next time they met. Of course having Winston Churchill come all the way from England to address the graduating class of this small college seemed ridiculous. But the young professor decided on his own to write to the great statesman anyway.

Within ten days he received an answer. Winston Churchill had agreed to accept the invitation of the young professor and speak at the college. At the next meeting of the commencement board a day later, the young professor presented the letter to the rest of the committee, who couldn't believe what this young man had done. To imagine that anybody could pull this off for a small college took everybody by total surprise.

Since Churchill was to arrive in a few weeks, all the townspeople spruced up their homes, and the main street looked better than it ever had before. The college scrambled to get a complete facelift and the spirit of the town could be felt as you drove through.

When Churchill finally arrived, the mayor of the town and the school president met him at the airport. There was a special parade through the town as a salute to the elder statesman. This was the biggest event ever to hit this town and it was going to be a moment people would remember for the rest of their lives.

When it came time for Churchill's speech, the mayor of the town appeared before the brightly scrubbed faces of the students and told them how lucky they were to hear such a distinguished person as Winston Churchill. He then went into Churchill's achievements and the stature that he commanded throughout the world. His 15-minute introduction ended and then the school president gave a 10-minute speech about the school and its struggle to get a good speaker and how Churchill so graciously accepted. Then it came time for him to introduce the elder statesman to the eager young graduating students and their parents. What words of wisdom would this great man impart to these young students?

A Long Pause

Churchill was guided to the podium by the young professor. He stood behind it for a few moments as he gained his composure and looked into the faces of the young graduates in the audience. The pause seemed like an awfully long time and you could literally hear a pin drop. Then he spoke.

"Never give up," he said. "Never give up." And then raising his voice even louder, "Never give up. Never give up." And then even louder, "Never give up. Never give up." And with just those remarks, Churchill ended his speech and sat down.

These were my very last comments in my seminar. And although I had many stories to share during the course, the final one was always my Churchill story. Remember, it's not whether you win or lose, it matters only that you play the game.

So never give up. Never.

Epilogue | Some Final Thoughts

Television should be the ultimate goal of any direct marketer who wants to capitalize on the most powerful marketing medium available, establish a famous brand name and eventually have a successful retail product.

When I was selling about 500 pairs of BluBlocker sunglasses per day through print advertising, I thought I was doing pretty good. But it was from selling on TV that my perception of "pretty good" got reevaluated.

On TV, at the peak of our sunglass advertising campaign, I was averaging over 10,000 pairs per day—more than 20 times what I did in print. On QVC, I could point to a time when I sold 135,000 pairs in one day.

If you've been a direct marketer specializing exclusively in print and you haven't taken a stab at TV, you're missing one of the most exciting and powerful mediums available. But a word of warning.

Even though the rewards of television are huge, and fortunes can be made overnight, so are the risks. But with a direct marketing background, and simply by having read this book, you have the opportunity to minimize those risks. And that brings me to another point.

Your success in this medium may be different than mine. In this book I have given you my experiences. There are books listed in Appendix D that relate other personal experiences and they too will give you a good perspective.

If you were to ask me for advice on what path you need to take to become successful on TV, I'd first recommend that you read every book you can get your hands on. If you haven't read my two previous direct marketing books, *Advertising Secrets of the Written Word* and *Marketing Secrets of a Mail Order Maverick*, do so. And if you have, read them again. The more knowledgeable you become on direct marketing and the art of selling, the greater the opportunity that awaits you.

I've always said that "luck is where opportunity meets preparation." You've just started on your preparation. The opportunities will swamp you when you're ready.

If you're in marketing and advertising, you've probably sensed that the Internet, cable TV, even the computer—all electronic media forms—represent the future. There are enormous opportunities in these areas, and those who stake a claim in this emerging new technology will prosper.

That will be the subject of my next book, *Computer Secrets of a Marketing Guru*. Although many people are focused on the Internet, there are other marketing innovations that will revolutionize the way we do business in the next century. In fact, all forms of marketing are changing. What worked in the '70s, '80s and even the '90s may not work in the future. But there is one thing for sure. All the same basic principles, axioms and theories that I've presented in my three marketing books will still apply, and your knowledge of them will put you in the best possible position to exploit your next marketing or selling challenge.

The future is indeed exciting and the challenges that await us offer more opportunities than ever before. Go for it.

Afterword | History Repeats Itself

Sometimes the study of the history of a subject gives you a unique perspective. From a knowledge of history and the realization that often history repeats itself, you can get quite a good insight into where we are, how we got here and where we are going.

That's the purpose of this "Afterword." Thanks to Alvin Eicoff, a true pioneer in this industry, much of the information of the past will be preserved and the many lessons of the past will help us reflect on where we might be going in the future. Let me cite an example.

Direct response advertising has for a long time been the stepchild of advertising in general. Why? All too often it was the more sleazy people in the business world who first used direct marketing in a particular new medium to promote their scams or at best their somewhat shady propositions. Add to this the ease with which almost anybody can sometimes enter a new medium and it is only natural that you'll see both the good and bad operators entering the field.

If you examine the recent history of infomercials (from 1985 forward), many of the early pioneers were not large corporations or very stable individuals, but rather one-shot entrepreneurs who saw infomercials as a way to get rich. On one hand we owe them a debt of gratitude, but on the other, in the beginning they hurt the image and reputation of the legitimate infomercial companies.

So let's start this little journey by examining the origins of electronic direct response and see how many parallels there are to our current industry.

Selling a Century Ago

I first need to explain what happened in the 1800s in direct marketing. In the late 1800s men selling patent medicines would go from town to town and sell their wares from their horse-drawn carts in almost a carnival-style atmosphere combining showman-ship and entertainment while incorporating the best of salesman-ship. (Sounds a lot like our current infomercials, doesn't it?)

Then in the early 1900s they discovered print advertising and started promoting their wares in newspapers and on flyers. Finally in the late '20s they discovered radio, and the medium became a direct response cesspool selling cures for backaches, headaches, bloody noses, arthritis, rheumatism, sexual impotency and a vague disease known in the South as "the miseries."

During this period, the most famous of all direct response commercials was conducted by Dr. Brinkley, the impeached gov-ernor of Kansas who sold sexual rejuvenation through a monkey-gland operation that cost his gullible customers $700.

Direct Marketing on Radio in the Early '40s

The more modern use of radio for direct marketing began in December of 1941. An agency in Chicago called Robert Kahn and Associates was in the mail order business running ads in magazines and newspapers. Kahn had earlier tested what was called a Weather House—something that predicted the weather and looked like a cuckoo clock. When the weather was good, a pretty princess popped out and when the weather was turning bad an ugly witch popped out. It was so unsuccessful in Kahn's mail order ads that the client, having invested all available capital in the manufacture of the product, went broke. Kahn ended up with thousands of Weather Houses in lieu of payment.

Then on December 6, 1941 after Japan bombed Pearl Har-bor, the publication and broadcast of all weather reports ceased as a defense measure. Stuck with the Weather House, Kahn thought he'd test his product on radio. He reasoned that people were with-out the customary weather information they normally got on radio and this medium might be the way to reach them. He was right, and not only did he get rich selling this single product but he became one of the early successful pioneers in the newly emerging modern era of electronic media.

Now let's stop to reflect on how often history repeats itself. Think for a moment on the origins of the Home Shopping Net-work—the pioneer in the home shopping revolution. A client couldn't pay his bill for radio time on a local Tampa station. In lieu of payment the client gave Bud Paxson, the station manager, can openers to sell on radio. The rest is history, as you already read in Chapter 7.

At the start of World War II, a St. Louis advertising agency, Schaeffer, Brennan and Margulies, had a major account called Blacks, which was a leading producer of chickens. During the war, food was rationed and chicken was the only unrationed meat you could buy. Blacks's custom was to destroy the male baby chicks as they needed the more prolific female chicks to propagate the species and produce the eggs and meat needed by the rationing public. The St. Louis agency saw this waste and destruction and convinced Blacks not to destroy the male chicks but to offer 100 of them for $2.98 in a radio campaign. The offer was so successful that the male chicks soon were in greater demand than the females. It not only solved the male chick problem but became such an instant success that Railway Express depots were soon filled with thousands of boxes of baby chicks. It was a bonus to the express company whose business was depressed due to the scarcity of consumer goods and certainly a great opportunity for radio stations who were suffering from a lack of customers for their radio time.

Reflecting on History Repeating Itself

Now let's reflect once more on how history repeats itself. It was the lack of advertising that made radio very interested in direct response offers at this time. The war effort and the scarcity of products also meant fewer advertisers. Why advertise when you couldn't sell more of your product than was allowed by the rationing effort? So radio rates dropped and it was the direct response offers that filled the airways. It was during the short recession in the early 1990s that the infomercial industry really took root. TV advertising rates were dropping and networks were scrambling to fill those time slots. It is during this time when the infomercial grew from just the cable channels to the respected networks such as ABC, CBS, NBC and the Fox network. The number of successful infomercials also increased due to the low media rates. But let's go back in history to the direct response radio era.

In 1947, a number of agencies began using radio, the largest of which were O'Neil, Larson & McMahon; E. H. Brown; Ruthrauff & Ryan; and Muriel Wagman—all from Chicago, which seemed to be the hub of this new activity. Only Maxwell Sackheim was using radio mail order out of New York.

Radio Infomercials in the Postwar Era

It was during this time that several highly effective radio infomercials were running. Al Eicoff, for example, had several winning products such as Dean Ross Piano Lessons, Lonnie Glossen's How to Play the Harmonica and a client called The Quilt Lady that used a 15-minute testimonial show selling quilt pieces that were sewn together to form blankets.

During this time of radio direct marketing, many brand names were stamped into the consciousness of Americans—Toni home permanents, Rulo reducing pills, Imdrin for arthritis, Milton Reynolds ballpoint pens and d-Con rat and mouse killer. Toni, in fact, started on a radio infomercial but quickly went retail.

It was during this period that Al Eicoff introduced about 50 products on radio including a pocket adding machine, gold tableware, several record offers, quilt pieces, Helbros watches, a fly spray, and a number of religious items including a tablecloth featuring a Last Supper picture that glowed in the dark. He also sold bibles and crucifixes that had soil from the catacombs where Christ walked. Religious products, record offers, adding machines (the predecessor to calculators and computers where I made my mark), kitchen or houseware products, watches (memories of the digital watch), and pest control products—all are similar to the products that continue to sell even today. Once again, history continues to repeat itself.

The First TV Infomercials

Meanwhile, all the TV commercials from 1949 through 1962 were infomercials. They ranged in length from 10 minutes to one hour. The first TV infomercial that Al Eicoff remembers was from Bill Barnard, who took his Vita-Mix commercial right off the popular fair midways of the time and filmed it for TV. It was an unbelievable winner.

About the same time, Roto Broil had a 15-minute cooking show on NBC starring Lester Morris. He pitched a rotisserie oven for $29.95 on the show, which ran daily for over a year. Again, the many kitchen products in infomercials on home shopping shows today had their origins during this time.

The most famous of all the infomercials of that period was released by the Rosen Brothers of Baltimore, Maryland, for a product called Charles Antell Lanolin Plus. Their sales pitch was captured live from a storefront on Broadway in New York City and played on TV. It featured a model washing her hair about 12 times a day—something nobody in their right mind would do. It was dramatic but it proved a point. Sheep produce natural lanolin and therefore the great positioning statement, "You never saw a bald-headed sheep," became well recognized at the time. And think of it. What a great way to position an anti-balding product without really saying so. Growing up in the '50s, I personally remember hearing Charles Antell Formula Number 9 (a derivative of the earlier product) being broadcast on radio and even bought some back then.

O'Neil, Larson & McMahon had an effective infomercial for a product called Weight On—a product for skinny kids who got sand kicked in their faces. I don't think this product would work today with our overfed population and everybody's desire to be thin or lose weight, but back then it was a big hit.

The TV Pioneering of Al Eicoff

During this period, Al Eicoff made about 400 infomercials. Reflect on this for a moment. Today, anybody in our business who makes 10 infomercials would be considered quite experienced in this venue. And who among us even heard of infomercials before 1985? But from 1949 until around 1962, or a period of 13 years, there was a major infomercial industry in the United States. There was no *Infomercial Marketing Report* to cover the industry, no *Adweek Source Book* to list the many services available to the infomercial producer or TV spot producer and certainly no controversy surrounding the medium. Infomercials were part of the TV landscape.

Al Eicoff remembers those original infomercials well. At first they were made on film. Al did the Salad Maker, the Auto Rocket, M-O-Lene, the Kitchen Magician, the Glass Cutter and several others in that format. The infomercials ran from 12 minutes to 30 minutes. If the actual presentation was 22 minutes, he would buy

25 minutes and use a 3-minute tag line. That was necessary as many of the orders were phoned in and shipped COD, so the longer the tag, the more time the viewers had to copy the number down and respond. In New York they used seven different phone services and in Los Angeles they used six to handle all the response.

In those early years of Eicoff's experience his most effective infomercials included Donatelli Honey and Egg Cream Facial, Turtle Oil, the Handy Screen, the Hair Wiz, Roll-O-Matic Mops, Tarn-X and dozens of others. All of these commercials were program length, or half-hour shows, but some ran in 10-minute and 15-minute formats.

But what is really surprising is how they were listed in TV programming. Every commercial was given a title just like a show and the commercials were listed in newspapers and in *TV Guide*. As a result, commercials were given names like *The Shining Night* for Tarn-X and *A Touch of Beauty* for Donatelli.

Commercials were also checked for ratings along with regular programming. The Nielsen organization, which did and still does the research for estimating how many people watch a specific show, helps determine how rates are established for advertisers. In fact, Al Eicoff recalls how CBS wrote a letter to Nielsen asking them to double-check their ratings when one night his infomercial for the Salad Maker rated higher than the *$64,000 Question* and the *Lawrence Welk Show*—both popular programs at the time. I had a similar experience when my last BluBlocker show was getting higher ratings than many of the popular local programs in many cities.

Two Decades of No Infomercials

Electronic direct response took a crushing blow in 1961 when Newton Minow, Chairman of the Federal Communications Commission (FCC)—the agency responsible for licensing all the radio and TV stations—gave his infamous "Vast Wasteland" speech and warned all stations against running both mail order commercials and any commercial over two minutes long. This two-minute limit lasted with most stations until advertising time was deregulated in the mid '80s. But for two decades the infomercial on radio and TV had disappeared.

This brief look at history and how it repeats itself stands as a testament to how important it is to study the roots of electronic media and the parallels between those early times and our own. This is also a special tribute to Alvin Eicoff, who was indeed one of the early pioneers of this significant phase of advertising history and who was very responsible for adding much of the dignity and the integrity that electronic direct marketing enjoys today.

Appendix A | Home Shopping Information

If you call the Vendor Relations Department at QVC at (610) 701-8282 and request a Vendor packet, they will send you a Product Information form and Product Data sheet along with a Commonly Asked Questions and Answers page.

I have included a similar list of questions and answers in this appendix as it may help you decide whether you have a potential product to put on QVC. Remember, if you have a product and would like to have it featured on QVC, call the Vendor Relations Department or write them at: QVC Vendor Relations Department, Department 0846R, 1200 Wilson Drive, West Chester, PA 19380.

1. How do I get my product on QVC?

A merchandise buyer will review a Product Data sheet that you will be asked to fill out. If your product is appropriate for QVC, a sample will be requested. This sample must pass rigorous Quality Assurance requirements, but once a sample has been approved, a plan is developed to work with your product. After your product is accepted, when you ship an order to QVC your product must be individually packaged, labeled and shipped directly to QVC's warehouse in accordance with their instructions. This ensures QVC's 7-10 day delivery guarantee to its customers. Once your product has been processed through the Quality Assurance stage and assigned a warehouse location, it is ready to be scheduled into QVC programming.

2. What type of product does QVC look for?

QVC looks for a wide variety of quality goods that can be demonstrated on-air. Exclusive product launches and unique products offered for the first time are always of interest. QVC programming is thematic and shows feature products that are appropriate to specific themes. Product selections are considered based upon how they will segment within those broadcast themes.

3. Is there a minimum quantity of product that QVC buys?

Yes. Although purchase quantities are negotiated on an individual basis, first-time orders usually range between $10,000 and $15,000 at their wholesale cost.

4. What is the lowest retail price QVC accepts?

It is unusual for QVC to retail products that sell for less than $15.00.

5. Is there a fee?

No. QVC does not sell airtime. As an electronic retailer, QVC selects and purchases manufactured products for its own programming.

6. What are QVC's demographics?

The demographic profile of QVC's customer base spans all socioeconomic groups and varies significantly depending on product appeal. For instance, a cooking program such as "In the Kitchen with Bob" attracts both men and women, an apparel hour draws a mostly female viewership, while "The NFL™ Team Shop," airing immediately prior to Monday Night Football, draws a primarily male audience. QVC continually strives to expand its appeal to an ever-broadening customer base by increasing the variety of products available to its audience of 52 million homes.

7. Are there product categories QVC does not program?

Yes. At this time QVC has elected not to sell products in the following categories: junior apparel, furs and fur-related products, guns and gun-related products, subscriptions, personalized items, 900 phone programs, service-related products, and novelty shirts and sweatshirts.

8. When will I know if my product has been accepted?

Upon receipt of your information, QVC will notify you in writing within three weeks.

9. How long does it take until my product is aired?

From the point of a purchase order, it takes approximately three months to air a product on QVC.

If you have any further questions, please contact the Vendor Relations Department of QVC at (610) 701-8282.

New Day Marketing
Cost Analysis Worksheet

For a $39.95 Sample "Widget"

Cost Analysis for "widget" NOT including value of upsells:

Revenue		**Expense**	
$39.95 unit		$ 7.82 cost of goods	
5.95 shipping and handling		3.43 actual cost of shipping	
$45.90		3.10 telemarketing	
		1.26 credit card processing	2.75%
		2.00 general and administrative	
		2.75 returns and declines	6.00%
		0.40 royalties	
Profit on single unit = **$25.14**		**$20.76**	

Cost Analysis for "widget" for each upsell:

Revenue		**Expense**	
$19.95 unit		$ 7.82 cost of goods	
5.95 shipping and handling		3.65 actual cost of shipping	
$25.90		0.00 telemarketing	
		0.71 credit card processing	2.75%
		0.00 general and administrative	
		1.55 returns and declines	6.00%
		0.40 royalties	
Profit on upsell = **$11.77**		**$14.13**	

Average % upsells = 35.00%

Gross allowable = *Revenue* minus *expense* $25.14

Gross allowable including
 average 35% upsells $29.26
 (35% of $11.77 = $4.12)

Theory 1: An infomercial is simply a three-act screenplay whose purpose is to cause your prospects to exchange their hard-earned money for your product or service. (page 139)

Theory 2: The main purpose of every element in an infomercial is to get your prospects to take one action—namely, to put down their remote control channel changer. (page 143)

Theory 3: The "glue factor" is a powerful attention-getting element at the beginning of an infomercial that causes viewers to watch the entire show in hopes of encountering a similar experience later in the infomercial. (page 145)

Theory 4: People expect to be entertained on TV and if you want to do well in the medium, you've got to entertain them. (page 147)

Theory 5: If you have a number of segments to present in an infomercial, present the humorous portions early in the show. (page 150)

Theory 6: Plant seeds of curiosity throughout your show to cause the viewer to be curious enough to keep on viewing. (page 151)

Theory 7: A satisfaction conviction is more than a trial period. It basically conveys a message from you that says, "Hey, I'm so convinced that you will like this product that I'm going to do something significant for your benefit to prove just how incredible my offer really is." (page 156)

Theory 8: The ideal satisfaction conviction should raise an objection and resolve it, going beyond what people expect. (page 157)

Theory 9: The desire to belong and identify with a group of people who own a specific product is one of the most powerful factors in why people buy. (page 159)

Theory 10: When the product is right for the market, it is priced right, it appeals to the broad audience for which it is intended and it is in a form that harmonizes with the needs of your audience. (page 180)

Theory 11: The closer you get to matching the demographics of those who are watching TV to the demographics of your product, the greater your chances for success because the larger your potential market the more efficiently you can reach this market. (page 181)

Theory 12: When you pick the show format, you also pick the demographics of your audience. (page 187)

Theory 13: In editing, you want to get the full emotional impact out of the time you've been allotted to sell your product or service. (page 196)

Theory 14: The most important part of the editing process is your ability to retain and enhance the emotional appeal of your product and your characters. You edit for emotion. (page 197)

Theory 15: TV media is one of the most negotiable of all the forms of advertising. (page 200)

Theory 16: Each time your infomercial runs, consider it a test. (page 204)

Theory 17: Every time you run your direct response commercial you are conducting a test. You are testing that commercial in a specific market at a specific time during specific financial conditions and during specific news events or political conditions at a specific place in time and space. (page 209)

Theory 18: One of the goals in testing is to make a profit. (page 209)

Theory 19: Money is made at the back end of your business from selling more of your product to those who respond to your infomercial. (page 215)

Theory 20: There is no better way to reach the emotional center of your prospects than by the personal appeal of the president of a company selling his or her product or service. (page 226)

Theory 21: TV and print are totally different media whose similar attributes, when understood, reveal powerful concepts about ways to market your product or service. (page 231)

Reading a number of books on a variety of subjects prepares you to become a good TV marketer and helps you avoid many of the mistakes others have made. That's one of the benefits you have realized from reading *Television Secrets for Marketing Success*. Many other people in the TV direct marketing industry have also written books that might be helpful to you. By reading other perspectives on selling through the medium of television, you can further your education and avoid costly errors that many before you have made. I wish I had read many of them earlier in my career.

Eicoff on Broadcast Direct Marketing, Al Eicoff. As the pioneer of broadcast direct marketing, Al Eicoff gives you the nuts and bolts and concepts you need in this field. He gives you first the history of each of the broadcast media and then covers the tools you'll need for operations as well as the creative end. He has been producing direct response commercials since the early days of television and his philosophies are simply, "A commercial is only creative when it sells," and "Good media buys are not measured in rating points, cpm's or cume's but only by the ring of the cash register." A good book to own. ISBN 0-8442-3144-4. NTC Business Books. 200 pages.

Sales Magic, Steve Bryant. Bryant is one of QVC's top show hosts and a master at selling. Here he talks about his proven techniques for selling that will give you new insights on what works and why. Here's your chance to increase your sales dramatically through many of the techniques this popular and effective salesman shares with you. I've personally seen him use many examples of good selling approaches on QVC in the sale of BluBlocker sunglasses. ISBN 0-936262-24-9. Amherst Media. 152 pages.

It's Better to Laugh, Kathy Levine. Probably one of the most successful hosts on QVC, Kathy gives you a firsthand view of what it is like to be a host on the popular home shopping channel. She relates her marketing philosophies and some of her experiences. She'll make you laugh with her failures as well as her successes. She speaks candidly about herself in an irreverent way that captures her true TV persona. I really enjoyed reading about her background and how she grew to become one of the nation's top TV shopping personalities. As *Entertainment Weekly* said, "Kathy Levine rivals Roseanne as the most amusing woman on the tube." ISBN 0-671-51107-6. Simon & Schuster Pocket Books. 290 pages.

Or Your Money Back, Alvin Eicoff. This is one of my favorite books on TV marketing. It's Al Eicoff's autobiography—how he started his Chicago-based advertising agency and his experiences on radio and later on TV. You'll learn how he used the jargon and the personalities of the fast-talking pitchmen of carnival days for some of his promotions. There's a wealth of direct selling techniques and examples of how to sell on TV that could apply to any direct response campaign. But what blew me away about Al is the prediction he made about cable television in this 1982 book—predicting cable home shopping shows and infomercials before anybody else. Al's a good guy. Read his book. ISBN 0-517-547392. Crown Publishers. 160 pages.

The Salesman of the Century, Ron Popeil. This is Ron's life story. It's a story about his family background and his entry into the direct selling business as a department store peddler back in the '50s. Starting out as a poor child, raised by his grandparents and left pretty much on his own, he managed to use direct selling as a step into television, eventually selling a myriad of products and concepts with the deft ability of a magician. If anybody could sell a product it was Ron. Popeil is such a significant factor in direct response selling that any TV direct response student should make this book a must-read. ISBN 0-385-31378-0. Delacorte Press. 310 pages.

This Business Has Legs, Peter Bieler. The story of the ThighMaster exercise device and how it became one of the hottest direct response exercise devices in history. I found it an interesting book as it talked about a product that I was nearly involved in marketing myself, as you might recall from reading this book. Any success is worth studying and the ThighMaster indeed was a big success. Over $100 million worth. And it was done without the big budgets you find with many consumer products. Read about how this product was born, recognized, named and then launched, and how direct response TV built up such demand for the product that when it hit the retail stores, it was a blowout success. ISBN 0-471-14749-4. John Wiley & Sons. 210 pages.

Marketing Channels, Craig R. Evans. This is a book on the history of TV from the early days of program sponsorship to the current infomercial phenomena and beyond to the interactive future. TV evolved from totally sponsored shows to the current multi-spot 30-second television commercials with no single sponsor. It describes how the infomercial got its start and the way TV has evolved throughout the years. If you're going to get into a new business like TV direct response, it's often a good idea to become an expert and know the history of the field you are about to enter. This book will help you a lot. ISBN 0-13-075151-0. Prentice Hall. 300 pages.

Screenplay, Syd Field. This is the book I referred to in Chapter 19 that turned my failure into a big success. Easy to read and understand, this commonsense book helped guide me to understand the basic structure of a screenplay, which is also the basis of an infomercial. The book is a step-by-step guide from concept to a finished script—a rare combination of a personable and lively book that seems to care about the writer. If you are responsible for writing a script for your infomercial, this is a good book to learn from. ISBN 0-440-57647-4. Dell Publishing. 250 pages.

The Complete Guide to Infomercial Marketing, Timothy R. Hawthorne. The first truly complete guide to the infomercial industry written from an advertising agency's perspective. There's good information in this book about the early history of infomercials and Tim Hawthorne is indeed one of the early pioneers. It covers the financial as well as the creative side of the business, the nuts and bolts and the media with a skew towards working with agencies rather than independent producers. If you want to know a great deal about the business, this is a good book to read. ISBN 0-8442-3445-1. NTC Books. 310 pages.

Advertising Secrets of the Written Word, Joseph Sugarman. A comprehensive textbook that teaches you the step-by-step approach to writing advertising copy. The well-illustrated book provides insights into the skills it takes to be a great copy-writer and what you can do to develop them. It then takes you into the thought process of ad creation, providing a very disciplined procedure that anybody can follow. A major chapter discusses the "psychological triggers" and how effectively they can be used to "cause prospects to exchange their hard-earned money for your product or service." The book also presents many personal stories, advertising examples and many of my own ads along with the reasons for their success or failure. ISBN 1-891686-00-3. DelStar Books. 320 pages.

Marketing Secrets of a Mail Order Maverick, Joseph Sugarman. A good complement to this book in that it takes you into the next phase of becoming a direct marketer. A compilation of many of the techniques I've created and the results I've experienced while selling thousands of different products to millions of people. Each lesson is preceded by a story that reveals a new technique or teaches a valid marketing lesson. Included in the book are chapters on how to find a winning product, successful layout secrets, how to avoid typefaces that actually hurt response, how to buy media for a lot less than anybody else, testing a product's potential and hundreds of insights that will guide the reader into understanding what works and what doesn't. ISBN 1-891686-06-2. DelStar Books. 400 pages.

The Seven Forces of Success, Joseph Sugarman. A book published in 1980 about those forces that drive you closer to success and those that draw you towards failure. Knowing the forces and controlling them is the goal of any successful person and this book describes how to do it. The first part of the book is autobiographical and the last half contains the basis of the Success Forces concept. This is a completely revised edition and will be available in the fall of 1998. Originally published as *Success Forces* in 1980 under ISBN 0-8092-7061-7. Contemporary Books. 215 pages. Soon to be published by DelStar Books under ISBN 1-891686-12-7. 240 pages.

Other Book Resources

Out of Print: Some of the books listed here might be out of print and no longer available. If you can't obtain a copy and all else fails, try reaching Carl Galletti and his Hard To Get Books and Tapes club. He can be reached at (609) 896-0245 or fax him for his latest catalog at (609) 896-2653. You might even check him out on the web at: www.magic7/htg.

Hoke Communications: This is another resource for a number of good direct marketing books. Call them at (800) 229-6700 for their comprehensive catalog.

Adweek Source Book

The Infomercial and Direct Response TV Source Book. We could publish lists of names and addresses of infomercial sources, but often within a year they become out of date. So rather than do that, *Adweek* magazine keeps a current listing of practically every source or service in the TV direct response industry. A really good resource for the names of infomercial companies, directors, producers, writers, law firms, manufacturers and product owners, media buyers, production and post-production facilities, stations and cable networks, telemarketing services, audio and video duplication sources, credit card processing and direct marketing consultants and dozens of other categories and valuable information. Just call *Adweek* at (800) 722-6658 to order this valuable resource.

Periodicals

The Infomercial Marketing Report, Steve Dworman. This well-written and lively newsletter is considered the bible in the industry and is quoted by over 3,000 press sources. It is also distributed throughout the U.S. and in 20 countries. Steve is an excellent writer and not afraid of controversy. He'll feature inside information about companies and personalities, commentaries on new shows and interesting editorials on the industry. He focuses strictly on infomercials and is probably the most knowledgeable person in that field. His newsletters range in length from 12 to 16 pages and give you a very good view of the industry on a monthly basis. Call (310) 472-5253 or fax (310) 472-6004 and mention you read about the newsletter in this book and Steve will send you a free copy.

The JW Greensheet, John and Clare Kogler of Jordan Whitney, Inc. This in-depth report prepared by the Koglers and their staff provides complete coverage of the entire direct response TV industry with reviews, spot TV and infomercial rankings, TV products being sold at retail and a host of other details about the TV direct marketing scene. There are also comprehensive reports on the home shopping area as well as a special tape service that will locate and ship to your company most any infomercial you request. Each monthly issue has approximately 180 pages and is printed with black ink on green paper (to prevent illegal copying), thus the *Greensheet* name. If you call (714) 832-2432 or fax (714) 832-3053 and mention that you read about their publication in this book, they'll send you a free sample issue.

Appendix E | A Tribute to Seminar Participants

As a special tribute to all my former seminar participants I would like to list, in alphabetical order, as many of their names as possible in this appendix. These are the men and women who over a period of eleven years went through my full five-day course—many taking it twice, three times and in one case four times. Courses were held in Minocqua, Wisconsin, Maui, Hawaii and even one in the Alps of Switzerland. It was a remarkable experience for each participant and for myself as well.

I've listed their company, location and title as given on their seminar application form. Much of this information has changed. Participants have moved to new locations, changed employers or have gone on to create their own businesses. Some have since passed away. One even built a large business and then went bankrupt. Some have had their companies acquired by other companies. Some changed careers and some totally disappeared. But I would venture to say that each one found the seminar a life-altering experience.

Each participant was unique. Each had their own interesting life story. I made it a point to spend enough time on a personal basis with each one to get to know them and then I would share their story with the rest of the group. If you are one of my former seminar participants or know of one on this list, please let me hear from you so we can update our records and make some plans for a future reunion. And for those of you interested in attending one of my seminars, simply fill out the Comments form at the back of this book and mail it to me personally. I read each and every comment submitted.

David Ahl
Creative Computing
Morristown, New Jersey

James R. Airaghi
Sundown Vitamins
Hollywood, Florida

Paul Allen
Cincinnati Microwave
Cincinnati, Ohio

Michael P. Alley
Los Angeles, California

Axel Anderson
Hamburg, Germany

Gene Anderson
A & A Fiberglass
Atlanta, Georgia

R. Anderson
Irvin & Stern Limited
Otahuhu, New Zealand

Norman J. Andrekus
The Tool Works, Inc.
Chicago, Illinois

Al Angelacos
Morton Grove, Illinois

Ed Axel
Energy Group
Roseland, New Jersey

John Balousek, Jr.
Foote, Cone & Belding
San Francisco, California

Gordon T. Beaham, III
Faultless Starch/Bon Ami Company
Kansas City, Missouri

Jan Beese
Wangels Forlag
Copenhagen, Denmark

Andrzej Bereza
Bandive Ltd.
New Barnet, England

Richard J. Bernard
Stereo Center
Flint, Michigan

Larry Blank
Shopsmith, Inc.
Vandalia, Ohio

Tony Blauvelt
Art Leather Manufacturing Company, Inc.
Arlington, Texas

Rudolf Boner
Jelmoli-Versand
Otelfingen, Switzerland

Irvin J. Borowsky
North American Publishing Company
Philadelphia, Pennsylvania

Beat Bosshard
Jelmoli-Versand
Otelfingen, Switzerland

Ken Boudrie
Barley Collection
Prairie View, Illinois

John Boulton
Electronic Logic Corporation
Newtown, Pennsylvania

Wallace Bradley
Digital Equipment Corporation
Nashua, New Hampshire

Mark Bragg
Public Affairs Broadcasting Group
Los Angeles, California

Kevin Brine
Sanford C. Bernstein & Co., Inc.
New York, New York

Bob Brown
Coast Catamaran Corporation
Oceanside, California

Lewis S. Brucker
The Lewis Brucker Company
Edina, Minnesota

Jerry Buchanan
Towers Club USA
Vancouver, Washington

John G. Bull
National Bancard Corporation
Fort Lauderdale, Florida

Stanley Burg
GTI Corporation
San Diego, California

Terry Butler
Broadlands Finance Ltd.
Auckland, New Zealand

James Calano
Execulists, Inc.
Boulder, Colorado

Hans R. Camenzind
Teldesign
Sunnyvale, California

Phil Campaigne
Digital Equipment Corporation
Nashua, New Hampshire

Jerry W. Carter
Fresno Trading Company
Fresno, California

Frank Cawood
Frank W. Cawood & Associates, Inc.
Peachtree City, Georgia

A. Harvey Cinamon
Cinamon Associates, Inc.
Brookline, Massachusetts

Jess F. Clarke
Garden Way
Norwalk, Connecticut

Kenneth E. Clolery
National Liberty Marketing
Valley Forge, Pennsylvania

Lee Coburn
Autsy
Boulder, Colorado

George Cohan
Cohan & Paul
Chicago, Illinois

Al Colbert
Rural Tours International
Kansas City, Missouri

James Colosimo
Adventure Outlook
Bradford, Pennsylvania

Thomas K. Connellan
The Management Group
Ann Arbor, Michigan

Norman Cooke
Abbey Tape Duplicators
Chatsworth, California

Alan Cottee
Pacific Film Laboratories Pty. Ltd.
Hurstville, N.S.W., Australia

Elizabeth Crouse
Epsilon Data Management, Inc.
Burlington, Massachusetts

Bill Cyrulik
The Mother Earth News
Hendersonville, North Carolina

Ken Dahlke
Dahlke Specialty Advertising, Inc.
Milwaukee, Wisconsin

Mark Dawes
Cincinnati Microwave
Cincinnati, Ohio

Diana Dawson
National Merchandising Corporation
Natick, Massachusetts

Jack H. Dean
Jack Dean Enterprises
Wimberley, Texas

Marcia DeHart
Victoria's Secret
San Francisco, California

Richard A. Delgaudio
Richard A. Delgaudio & Associates, Inc.
Chantilly, Virginia

Paul Dentone
Philips Business Systems
Woodbury, New York

Don M. Dible
Dible Company
Fairfield, California

George Douglass
Comtel Broadcasting Corporation
Noblesville, Indiana

Robert Drummond
Epsilon Data Management, Inc.
Burlington, Massachusetts

Barbara Dunlap
Victoria's Secret
San Francisco, California

Marilyn Eller
Warren B. Eller Agency
Farmington Hills, Michigan

Warren B. Eller
Warren B. Eller Agency
Farmington Hills, Michigan

Win H. Emert
Solfan Systems, Inc.
Mountain View, California

Joseph W. England
The Historic Providence Mint
Providence, Rhode Island

Bob d'Esterre
Horizon House Advertising Ltd.
Vancouver, B.C., Canada

Bob Evans
Ski West
Dallas, Texas

Don Feltner
Don Feltner Photography, Inc.
Wheat Ridge, Colorado

Frank E. Ferguson
Curriculum Associates, Inc.
Wellesley, Massachusetts

Lowell Fisher
Wenger Corporation
Owatonna, Minnesota

R. B. Fitch
Fitch Creations, Inc.
Carrboro, North Carolina

John Flynn
Kirkland, Washington

Jon Ford
First Travel Club
Schaumburg, Illinois

Avram Freeberg
Maximum Exposure Advertising, Inc.
New York, New York

Sallijo A. Freeman
Smith Advertising Specialties Inc.
Long Beach, New York

Dan Fryda
Spa Health Consultants, Inc.
Cranford, New Jersey

Stanley Fulwiler
Voxcom, Division of Tapecon, Inc.
Peachtree City, Georgia

Bill Gaible
Cincinnati Microwave
Cincinnati, Ohio

Allan Gardner
Brooksmith Associates
Ocean, New Jersey

Christine Gardner
Brooksmith Associates
Ocean, New Jersey

Pat Garrard
Free Enterprise
New York, New York

Jan Geddes
Newman Computer Exchange, Inc.
Ann Arbor, Michigan

Charles Gervais
Cockfield Brown & Company
Winnipeg, Manitoba, Canada

Edward Gillies
Edward Gillies Marketing
Lake Bluff, Illinois

Donald Ginn
The School of Better Eyesight
Santa Monica, California

Miki Giunta
Spa Health Consultants, Inc.
Cranford, New Jersey

Dana Glasgow
Cincinnati Microwave
Cincinnati, Ohio

Barry Goldberg
Citicorp
New York, New York

Joanne Goldstein
BMT Publications, Inc.
New York, New York

Stan Golumb
The Golumb Group
Hinsdale, Illinois

Peter Gordon
Microcomputer Laboratories
Watertown, Massachusetts

Joseph Graziano, Sr.
Ace Pecan Company, Inc.
Elk Grove Village, Illinois

John Groman
Epsilon Data Management, Inc.
Burlington, Massachusetts

Peter Gross
Eins Euro Industrie Service
Bad Schwartau, Germany

Raymond L. Gross
R. L. Gross & Associates, Inc.
Spokane, Washington

Richard J. Guilfoyle
Limited Editions Collectors Society
Hingham, Massachusetts

Chris Hahn
Spa Health Consultants, Inc.
Cranford, New Jersey

Keith Halford
Commonwealth Mint, Ltd.
Montpelier, Vermont

Renate Hammelmann
Idee & System
Munich, Germany

Paul M. Harmon
DRI Industries
Eden Prairie, Minnesota

Mark O. Haroldsen
National Institute of Financial Planning
Salt Lake City, Utah

John W. Harper
House of Ceramics, Inc.
Memphis, Tennessee

Bradley K. Haynes
B. K. Haynes Corporation
Front Royal, Virginia

Arthur L. Hecht
Hecht, Higgins, Petterson Advertising
New York, New York

Ben Hembree
Frieda's Finest
Los Angeles, California

Ernie Hemple
Brite Ideas
Wheeling, Illinois

Kim Henrie
Modern Farm
Cody, Wyoming

Lee Herrington
Kirtland, Ohio

William M. Highsmith
Rolamech Company, Inc.
Scottsdale, Arizona

Conrad Holzgang
Cable Software Corporation
Burbank, California

Fred Howard
Howard International Corporation
New York, New York

Lawton W. Howell
CommuniGroup USA
Laguna Hills, California

Roy M. Hutchins
Rochester, New York

John Iams
Poway, California

Joyce Igou
Signature Financial Planning
Chicago, Illinois

Tony Ingleton
The Presidential Card
Middle Brighton, Victoria, Australia

Arlen Issette
Lombard, Illinois

James L. Jaeger
Cincinnati Microwave
Cincinnati, Ohio

Richard J. Jean
Inventive Concepts
Manchester, New Hampshire

Frank D. Johnson
McKay Dymek Company
Pomona, California

K. C. Johnson
Trans National Sales
Newport Beach, California

Bruce C. Joslyn
Madison, Connecticut

Joe Karbo
Financial Publishers, Inc.
Huntington Beach, California

Michael J. Kelly
Mi-Bryn, Inc.
Cincinnati, Ohio

Michael Kerrison
Pacific Film Laboratories Pty. Ltd.
Hurstville, Australia

David A. Kessler
Dave Kessler Auctioneer
New Paris, Ohio

Martin A. Klest
K & G Enterprises
Oak Park, Illinois

John R. Klug
Continental Communications Group
Denver, Colorado

Steve Kurtin
Lane Research
Sherman Oaks, California

James K. La Fleur
GTI Corporation
San Diego, California

Hal Lashlee
Software Plus
Culver City, California

James Lavin
Euronova H.
Viglino, Italy

Audrey Leavitt
Devon, Pennsylvania

Robert Leavitt
Devon, Pennsylvania

Tom Liguorie
National Pen Corporation
San Diego, California

Stuart Linder
Piccadilly International
Trenton, New Jersey

Richard Lobel
Lobel's
London, England

Michael Love
Quadric, Inc.
New York, New York

Richard A. Lundquist
Communicators' Group
Carmel Valley, California

Ford MacElvain
Deep Rock Manufacturing
Opelika, Alabama

Joseph R. Mancuso
Center for Entrepreneurial Management
New York, New York

Gert Mandelartz
Allzeilt-Vertreib
Dusseldorf, West Germany

James D. Mantice
Jim Mantice Advertising
Chicago, Illinois

Albert Marty
Jelmoli-Versand
Otelfingen, Switzerland

Les Marzahl
Lanair Industries
Janesville, Wisconsin

Nancy Marzahl
Lanair Industries
Janesville, Wisconsin

Archie Mason
Monarch Trading Pty., Ltd.
Auckland, New Zealand

John Mauldin
Communications Management
Arlington, Texas

Fergus McCann
International Golf
Montreal, Quebec, Canada

LeeAnn McCarthy
Maui, Hawaii

Ronald McConnell
Ronald C. McConnell & Associates
Richardson, Texas

Bob McDonagh
Idea, Inc.
Caldwell, Idaho

Gayle McLean
Response Marketing Company, Ltd.
Toronto, Ontario, Canada

Thomas J. Minthorn
Omaha Steaks International
Omaha, Nebraska

Alex Mitchell
Parkell Products, Inc.
Farmingdale, New York

Don R. Monteith
Monteith-Keen Enterprises, Inc.
Charlotte, North Carolina

Jim Moore
Oral Roberts Evangelists Assoc.
Tulsa, Oklahoma

Hugh Moreland
Wintergreen Communications, Ltd.
Concord, Ontario, Canada

Scott Moskovitz
B. A. Pargh Company
Nashville, Tennessee

Robert Mumford
San Rafael, California

Steve Nevard
Garden Way Associates, Inc.
Norwalk, Connecticut

Jeffrey S. Nickles
Investors Thrift
Hanford, California

Vanessa Norbeth
Lobel's
London, England

Nancy Nordenhok
Nordenhok Design, Inc.
Newport Beach, California

Bob O'Brien
CJRN
Niagara Falls, Ontario, Canada

Ove Olsen
Firkloveren
Oslo, Norway

Phillip O'Malley
Broadlands Finance Ltd.
Auckland, New Zealand

Bernie Pargh
B. A. Pargh Company
Nashville, Tennessee

Ted Nicholas Peterson
Enterprise Publishing Company
Wilmington, Delaware

Robert Pettet
ADirections, Inc.
Shingle Springs, California

Harvey Plotnick
Contemporary Books, Inc.
Chicago, Illinois

Jack W. Plunkett
Dallas, Texas

Dan Presser
Blackburn, Victoria, Australia

George K. Price
ATVB Abrasive Steel Company
Chicago, Illinois

Lisa Price
American List Counsel
Princeton, New Jersey

Nancy Price-Fennell
B. A. Pargh Company
Nashville, Tennessee

Fred Pryor
Resource Associates
Mission, Kansas

Donn Rappaport
Market Builders, Inc.
Princeton, New Jersey

Roger Reed
St. Petersburg, Florida

John E. Reichard
Des Moines, Iowa

Tom Rigoli
Associated Ad Ventures, Inc.
Los Altos, California

Patricia Riley
MDR Fitness Corporation
Miami, Florida

Tom Risch
August West Systems
Westport, Connecticut

J. M. Robinson
Atlantic Richfield Company
Los Angeles, California

Jeffry Rochlis
Mattel Corporation
Santa Monica, California

Jerome Ruzicka
Wayland, Massachusetts

William Samuels
William Samuels, Inc.
Atlanta, Georgia

Frederick Sandven
Sandven Advertising & Marketing
Kansas City, Missouri

Jorgen Sannung
Bing & Groendahl
Copenhagen, Denmark

Jim J. Sarver
Shawnee Mission, Kansas

John R. Sauer
International Business & Finance
Dallas, Texas

Kent V. Savage
Fawn Vending Sales of Ohio
Cincinnati, Ohio

Michael J. Schaffer
Trans National Funding
Newport Beach, California

Chuck Schaldenbrand
Newman Computer Exchange, Inc.
Ann Arbor, Michigan

Robert F. Schultheis
Kock Supplies, Inc.
Kansas City, Missouri

Frank Schultz
Crest Fruit Company
Alamo, Texas

Mike Schultz
Rural Tours International
Kansas City, Missouri

John L. Schwartz, MD
Continuing Medical Education, Inc.
Santa Ana, California

Philip Schwarz
Photocolor Kreuzlingen
Kreuzlingen, Switzerland

Ed Scofield
Garden Way Manufacturing
Troy, New York

R. T. Scott
Scotcade Limited
Bridgnorth, Shropshire, England

Don Shifris
Skipper Marine Electronics
Chicago, Illinois

Eugene Shklar
Software House
Cambridge, Massachusetts

David Sibly
Auckland, New Zealand

Hermann Sieber
Diessenhofen, Switzerland

Barry Silverstein
Directech
Stow, Massachusetts

Frederick J. Simon
Omaha Steaks International
Omaha, Nebraska

Leonard Sklar
Medicon Corporation
San Francisco, California

Randy Smith
Marko Enterprises
Salt Lake City, Utah

Sanford Smith
Sanford Dental Labs., Inc.
Milwaukee, Wisconsin

Wes Smith
W. Glen Smith & Company
San Diego, California

William Sousa
Sousa & Lefkovits
Tustin, California

Jon Spoelstra
Portland Trail Blazers
Portland, Oregon

Susan A. Stap
Ball Hopper Products, Inc.
Northbrook, Illinois

Betsy Staples
Creative Computing
Morris Plains, New Jersey

Julie Steele
Sydney, Australia

James Steffen
Steffen, Steffen & Associates, Inc.
Westport, Connecticut

William Steinhardt
Steinhardt Direct
Shawnee Mission, Kansas

George A. Stephan
Interdesign, Inc.
Sunnyvale, California

Gene Stewart
Stewart & Coe, Inc.
New York, New York

Rick Stewart
Rick Stewart & Assoc. Pty. Ltd.
Artarmon, N.S.W., Australia

W. Stanley Stuart, Jr.
Schonfeld & Associates, Inc.
Chicago, Illinois

Randy Sueda
Torrance, California

Thomas Summer
Sales Achievement Limited
Reading, Berkshire, England

Phil Syrdal
Active Market Services, Inc.
Bellevue, Washington

Hal Taub
Beacon Photo Service, Inc.
New York, New York

Graeme A. Teague
Santa Ana, California

P. M. Thakker
LaGrange, Georgia

Richard G. Thau
General Parametrics Corporation
Berkeley, California

Michael Valentine
Cincinnati Microwave
Cincinnati, Ohio

Pierre Van De Vannet
Concordia Mail
Antwerp, Belgium

Hermann Van Hove
ICB
Antwerp, Belgium

Michael Vanwinkle
Newport, Inc.
New York, New York

Ned Van Woert
Garden Way Manufacturing Company
Troy, New York

Michael C. Vaughan
Deep Rock Manufacturing
Opelika, Alabama

Leo Verkoelen
C. V. Romar-Voss
Roggel, Holland

Richard A. Viguerie
Richard A. Viguerie Company, Inc.
Falls Church, Virginia

Bob Viner
Bob Viner Sales
Chicago, Illinois

Peter P. Vizel
Westwood, California

Laurie Wagman
North American Publishing Company
Philadelphia, Pennsylvania

Lawrence M. Waterhouse
Waterhouse Securities, Inc.
New York, New York

Bill Watts
Balmain, N.S.W., Australia

Alex Weiss
Megasonics, Inc.
Long Beach, California

Bern Wheeler
Wheeler Communications
London, Ontario, Canada

Anthony J. White
A. J. White Management Company, Ltd.
Edmonton, Alberta, Canada

Marvin Williams
Barefoot Grass Lawn Service
Worthington, Ohio

Robert Williams
Westlake Village, California

Bernard E. Withrich
Weinmann GMBH & Company
Germany

James Yates
Direct Marketing Magazine
Garden City, New York

Henri Yauck
The Executive Suite
Edmonton, Alberta, Canada

M. Yendell
Irvin & Stern Limited
Otahuhu, New Zealand

A. Zgorelec
London, England

Index

Your Guide to Relevant Topics

Your comments are important

    I am always interested in your comments, feedback and suggestions on the book you've just read and I may also want to use them for advertising purposes. Please feel free to copy or tear out this form and mail it with your comments to: Joseph Sugarman, JS&A Group, Inc., 3350 Palms Center Drive, Las Vegas, NV 89103. Thank you.

I herewith freely allow and give right and title to Joseph Sugarman and/or DelStar Publishing, or their assigns, to use the following comments, feedback and suggestions either to improve this or any of Mr. Sugarman's books or as a testimonial in the promotion of this book in any advertising medium solely determined by Mr. Sugarman or DelStar Publishing. I also agree to allow the use of part or all of a testimonial as determined by Mr. Sugarman.

_____

Your signature   Date

Would you agree to appear on a TV testimonial? _____

Continue on back of page.

Product Evaluation Criteria

Is your product a potential TV product?
Take this test.

If you have a product that you feel might be perfect either for QVC or for an infomercial, then first see if it passes some or most of the following criteria:

- ❏ Does the product have mass appeal?

- ❏ Will it solve a problem or make life easier?

- ❏ Will it stand out from comparative products?

- ❏ Will it demonstrate well on TV?

- ❏ Does it create that "I gotta have it" appeal?

- ❏ Is it patented or new?

- ❏ Does it appeal to women?

- ❏ Can you sell your product's benefits and features in 5 minutes or less?

- ❏ Do you have proper margins based on the information you've read in this book?

- ❏ Do you have capital and financing available?

- ❏ Is there a good "price-to-value" relationship?

If, after going through the above checklist, you indeed have a product that you feel would qualify for presentation on TV, then let me see if I can help you get this product to the right person or company. Simply fill out the form located on the back of this page and send it to me at the address indicated with a brochure or information on your product. If I feel you have a potential product, I will send you a list of the people who might be able to help you and you can contact them directly. There is no charge for this service if you are an actual purchaser of this book.

Free Product Evaluation Form

Please print or type legibly.

Product name:_____ Model #/Style #: _____ Date:_____

Manufacturer (Vendor):_____

Contact:_____ President: _____

Address:_____

Phone #:_____ Fax #:_____

Third-party rep: _____

Full product description: _____

_____

_____

What makes product unique for direct response?_____

_____

Country of origin: _____

Wholesale price ($/unit):_____Sugg. retail price: _____

Product demonstration video available? Yes _____ No _____

Has product ever appeared on TV? _____ (If yes, explain.) _____

_____

Is product currently available in stores or catalogs? _____ (If yes, where?) _____

_____

What price is it offered at? _____ Sales volume: _____

Do you have a product spokesperson? (Yes/No/Comments) _____

Is product patented? (Yes/No) _____ Patent #: _____

Safety approval required (indicate FDA, MSDS, UL, etc.): _____

_____

Any previous liability problems? _____

Do you carry liability coverage? (Yes/No) How much? _____

Carrier Name:_____

Production lead time for $50,000 in retail volume: _____

Additional comments: _____

Please send this form to: Product Evaluations, JS&A Group, Inc., 3350 Palms Center Drive, Las Vegas, NV 89103. Do not send your product as no samples will be returned. Submit only brochures or written information.

Advertising Secrets of the Written Word
The Ultimate Resource on How to Write Powerful Advertising Copy
From One of America's Top Copywriters and Mail Order Entrepreneurs

A comprehensive textbook that teaches you step-by-step how to write powerful advertising copy that sells. The illustrated book provides insights on what it takes to be a great copywriter and how to develop those skills. The book also takes you into the thought process of ad creation and provides a disciplined procedure that anybody can follow. A major chapter reveals the "psychological triggers" and how they can be used effectively to "cause prospects to exchange their hard-earned money for your product or service." ISBN 1-891686-00-3 (hardcover). 310 pages. $39.95

Marketing Secrets of a Mail Order Maverick
Stories and Lessons on the Power of Direct Marketing to Start a Successful Business, Create a Famous Brand Name and Sell Any Product or Service

The story of the techniques Joseph Sugarman created and the results he experienced while selling thousands of different products to millions of people. Chapters include how to find a winning product, secrets for a successful ad layout, how to avoid typefaces that hurt response, how to buy media for less, testing a product's potential and hundreds of other insights that guide the reader to an understanding of what works and what doesn't. The lessons are alternated with entertaining and enlightening marketing stories from Sugarman's personal experience. ISBN 1-891686-06-2 (hardcover). 390 pages. $39.95

The Sugarman Seminar Secrets Slipcase
A handsome slipcase designed to hold Joseph Sugarman's three books based on his exclusive marketing course is **yours free.**

If you've already purchased this book or any one of the hardcover versions of the three Sugarman marketing books, you may receive, free of charge (other than the minimal per order postage and handling), a slipcase (a $10 value) to hold all three books in the series. Buy all three of the Sugarman marketing books and keep them in this handsome display case. Refer to them often. And start to build your library of Sugarman marketing books. Offer available only in the United States.

The Sugarman Seminar Secrets Boxed Set
Joseph Sugarman's three books based on his exclusive advertising and marketing course in a special paperback edition complete with slipcase and at a special price.

Buy all three of the Sugarman marketing books in paperback and receive, free of charge, a handsome slipcase (a $10 value) as well as a $20 savings off the cost of the hardcover version. Available in paperback only as a complete set. $99.95

Order Form (See page 311 for details.)

❏ I wish to order the following books:

Advertising Secrets of the Written Word .... $39.95 _____
Marketing Secrets of a Mail Order Maverick ..... 39.95 _____
Television Secrets for Marketing Success........ 39.95 _____
The Sugarman Seminar Course Slipcase......... FREE _____
The Sugarman Seminar Course Boxed Set .... 99.95 _____

Postage & Handling **Per Order** .... <u>5.00</u>

Total: _____

❏ Please put me on the Sugarman mailing list for announcements of books, seminars and marketing courses.

Name_____

Address _____

City, State, Zip _____

Daytime Phone:_____

❏ I wish to charge my credit card:
_____ Exp_____
Visa, MasterCard and American Express Cards accepted.

❏ I am enclosing $ _____

Make all checks payable to **JS&A Group, Inc.**, and mail all orders to JS&A Group, Inc., 3350 Palms Center Drive, Las Vegas, NV 89103. Offer available only in the United States. Call (702) 798-9000 or fax (702) 597-2002 for prices in foreign countries.

Phone in your order: (800) 323-6400
Fax in your order: (702) 597-2002

Photocopy or cut out this page to mail or fax in your order.

Advertising Secrets of the Written Word
The Ultimate Resource on How to Write Powerful Advertising Copy
From One of America's Top Copywriters and Mail Order Entrepreneurs

A comprehensive textbook that teaches you step-by-step how to write powerful advertising copy that sells. The illustrated book provides insights on what it takes to be a great copywriter and how to develop those skills. The book also takes you into the thought process of ad creation and provides a disciplined procedure that anybody can follow. A major chapter reveals the "psychological triggers" and how they can be used effectively to "cause prospects to exchange their hard-earned money for your product or service." ISBN 1-891686-00-3 (hardcover). 310 pages. $39.95

Marketing Secrets of a Mail Order Maverick
Stories and Lessons on the Power of Direct Marketing to Start a Successful Business, Create a Famous Brand Name and Sell Any Product or Service

The story of the techniques Joseph Sugarman created and the results he experienced while selling thousands of different products to millions of people. Chapters include how to find a winning product, secrets for a successful ad layout, how to avoid type-faces that hurt response, how to buy media for less, testing a product's potential and hundreds of other insights that guide the reader to an understanding of what works and what doesn't. The lessons are alternated with entertaining and enlightening marketing stories from Sugarman's personal experience. ISBN 1-891686-06-2 (hardcover). 390 pages. $39.95

The Sugarman Seminar Secrets Slipcase
A handsome slipcase designed to hold Joseph Sugarman's three books based on his exclusive marketing course is **yours free.**

If you've already purchased this book or any one of the hardcover versions of the three Sugarman marketing books, you may receive, free of charge (other than the minimal per order postage and handling), a slipcase (a $10 value) to hold all three books in the series. Buy all three of the Sugarman marketing books and keep them in this handsome display case. Refer to them often. And start to build your library of Sugarman marketing books. Offer available only in the United States.

The Sugarman Seminar Secrets Boxed Set
Joseph Sugarman's three books based on his exclusive advertising and marketing course in a special paperback edition complete with slipcase and at a special price.

Buy all three of the Sugarman marketing books in paperback and receive, free of charge, a handsome slipcase (a $10 value) as well as a $20 savings off the cost of the hardcover version. Available in paperback only as a complete set. $99.95

Order Form (See page 313 for details.)

❏ I wish to order the following books:

Advertising Secrets of the Written Word	$39.95	_____
Marketing Secrets of a Mail Order Maverick	39.95	_____
Television Secrets for Marketing Success	39.95	_____
The Sugarman Seminar Course Slipcase.	FREE	_____
The Sugarman Seminar Course Boxed Set	99.95	_____

Postage & Handling **Per Order** 5.00

Total: _____

❏ Please put me on the Sugarman mailing list for announcements of books, seminars and marketing courses.

Name _____

Address _____

City, State, Zip _____

Daytime Phone: _____

❏ I wish to charge my credit card:

_____ Exp_____

Visa, MasterCard and American Express Cards accepted.

❏ I am enclosing $ _____

Make all checks payable to **JS&A Group, Inc.**, and mail all orders to JS&A Group, Inc., 3350 Palms Center Drive, Las Vegas, NV 89103. Offer available only in the United States. Call (702) 798-9000 or fax (702) 597-2002 for prices in foreign countries.

Phone in your order: (800) 323-6400
Fax in your order: (702) 597-2002

Photocopy or cut out this page to mail or fax in your order.

314